The End of Czechoslovakia

The End of Czechoslovakia

EDITED BY JIŘÍ MUSIL

CENTRAL EUROPEAN UNIVERSITY PRESS

Budapest   London   New York

First published in 1995 by
Central European University Press
1051 Budapest
Nádor utca 9

Distributed by
Oxford University Press, Walton Street, Oxford OX2 6DP
Oxford New York Athens Auckland Bangkok Bombay Toronto
Calcutta Cape Town Dar es Salaam Delhi Florence Hong Kong
Istanbul Karachi Kuala Lumpur Madras Madrid Melbourne
Mexico City Nairobi Paris Singapore Taipei Tokyo Toronto
and associated companies in Berlin Ibadan
Distributed in the United States
by Oxford University Press Inc., New York

© Jiří Musil 1995

British Library Cataloguing in Publication Data
A CIP catalogue record for this book is available from the British Library

ISBN 1-85866-019-X Hardback
ISBN 1-85866-020-3 Paperback

Library of Congress Cataloging in Publication Data
A CIP catalog record for this book is available from the Library of Congress

Typeset in Times by Koinonia, Manchester
Designed and produced by John Saunders
Printed and bound in Great Britain by Biddles of Guildford

For Ernest Gellner

Contents

Preface   ix
Note on Contributors   xi

1   Introduction
    Jiří Musil   1

I   Structural Aspects of the Break-Up
2   Czech and Slovak Demography
    Milan Kučera and Zdeněk Pavlík   15

3   Economic Development and Relations, 1918–89
    Václav Průcha   40

4   Czech and Slovak Society
    Jiří Musil   77

II   National Consciousness
5   National Consciousness and the Common State
    (A Historical-Ethnological Analysis)
    Jan Rychlík   97

6   Slovakia in Czech National Consciousness
    Zdeněk Suda   106

7   Mutual Perceptions in Czech-Slovak Relationships
    Petr Příhoda   128

8   Slovak Exceptionalism
    Miroslav Kusý   139

III   History of Czech-Slovak Relations
9   Political Power-Sharing in the Interwar Period
    Alena Bartlová   159

10 From Autonomy to Federation, 1938–68
    Jan Rychlík   180

11 Towards a Shared Freedom, 1968–89
    Petr Pithart   201

IV   The Process of Disintegration
12 The Politics of Transition and the Break-Up of
    Czechoslovakia
    Sharon L. Wolchik   225

13 The Velvet Divorce — Institutional Foundations
    Václav Žák   245

V   The International Aspects
14 The International Context
    Jacques Rupnik   271

Index   279

Preface

This book is the result of three workshops organized by the Central European University in the years 1992–3. The participants in these workshops, after extensive discussion, arrived at a consensus on the style of the studies to be written, and on the structure of the book. We agreed that we wanted to present a scholarly book which would also have a wider appeal to an educated public. We aimed to provide the interested reader with a balanced account of the history of Czech-Slovak relations, as well as with an analysis of the social, economic and cultural forces which in the seventy-year-long history of Czechoslovakia worked either for its integration or for its disintegration. Careful attention was paid to providing an objective analysis of the political contexts of the split as well as a description of the concrete steps leading to the end of Czechoslovakia.

Many people have helped us at various stages of writing and rewriting our texts. We are grateful to the Centre for the Study of Nationalism at the CEU in Prague, which not only gave financial assistance, but through its seminars provided the intellectual stimuli for the preparation of this book.

We should particularly like to thank Gordon Wightman of the University of Liverpool for his immensely valuable comments on the draft texts. We would also like to express our thanks to Pauline Wickham of the CEU Press for her patient encouragement and constant support for our project, and to Liz Lowther of the CEU Press for her tactful assistance in the preparation of the volume, in helping to discover mistakes and in helping to answer many queries. The first English version of many of the papers was considerably improved by April Retter of the CEU Prague Language Centre. Special thanks go to Dave Matley, without whose editing the papers would have definitely remained less English than they are now. The editor and all the authors are grateful to Hana Borčevská of the CEU, Prague, for the miraculously patient and cheerful way in which she organized the workshops and the contact between the authors, and typed various versions of the scripts.

For permission to use copyright material or to include data previously published, the authors and the publishers wish to thank the Acta Universitatis Carolinae (publishers of *Geographica*); the Institute of Sociology, Prague (publishers of the *Czech Sociological Review*); J. Friedrichs; and *East European Politics and Societies*.

Contributors*

Alena Bartlová, Senior Research Historian at the Institute of History of the Slovak Academy of Sciences

Milan Kučera, Senior Research Demographer at the Institute of Sociology of the Czech Academy of Sciences

Miroslav Kusý, Professor of Political Science at Comenius University, Bratislava

Jiří Musil, Professor of Sociology at the Central European University, Prague

Zdeněk Pavlík, Professor of Demography at Charles University, Prague

Petr Pithart, Fellow of the Central European University, Prague

Václav Průcha, Professor of Economic History at the Economics University, Prague

Petr Příhoda, Freelance columnist, Prague

Jacques Rupnik, Professor at the Centre for International Studies and Research (CERI), Paris

Jan Rychlík, Senior Research Historian at the Tomáš G. Masaryk Institute, Prague

Zdeněk Suda, Professor Emeritus, University of Pittsburgh

Sharon L. Wolchik, Professor of Political Science and International Affairs at the George Washington University, Washington, DC

Václav Žák, Member of the Presidium of Free Democrats, Prague

*Affiliations correct at the time of writing.

1 Introduction

JIŘÍ MUSIL

After 1989, Czechoslovakia was regarded by many observers as a stabilizing element in Central Europe, and many people hoped that it would become a model for the democratic transformation of multinational post-communist states. This hope, held by the Czechs and Slovaks themselves, as well as by foreign observers, was based on the country's democratic traditions, on its habitual political moderation and on the fact that no bloody ethnic conflict had arisen between Czechs and Slovaks in the past. On the contrary, the two nations had unusually similar languages and had cultivated friendly cultural contacts even before becoming part of the common state. Nevertheless – to the surprise and sorrow of many of its citizens as well as of sympathizers living abroad – this state has disintegrated.

The present volume, written by Czechs, Slovaks, and experts from the United States and France, tries to describe and to explain why, after the collapse of the communist regime, Czechoslovakia split up into two separate states. Besides this main goal, stressing the documentation and interpretation of a concrete historical process, the collection has some important ancillary objectives – both theoretical and practical. On the one hand, the Czechoslovak experience is used to explore the concepts and instruments of European integration as a whole, and the theory of contemporary forms of nationalism; on the other, it could well have some practical policy implications. The failure of the Czechoslovak Federation will perhaps become an impulse for a more sophisticated approach to European integration and may also serve as a reminder to countries facing similar problems – i.e. Belgium, Canada, the United Kingdom, Italy and Spain.

The book is the result of three workshops organized by the Centre for the Study of Nationalism at the Central European University in Prague in the years 1992 and 1993. The Centre, directed by Ernest Gellner, studies the theory of nationalism as well as concrete historical developments directly or indirectly linked to nationalism. Obviously an academic

institution located in Prague, whose function it is to study the transformation of Central European societies, will seek to find the deeper, underlying
causes of such an event as the division of one of the Central European states.

The authors have adopted an analytical, non-evaluative approach in
trying to understand the process of a modern state's peaceful disintegration.
The current trend in social and political science in the West is to concen-
trate on conditions conducive to integration; our point, by contrast, was to
inform the wider public how failed projects, too, can serve as a lesson.

The workshops showed that in the history of Czechoslovakia's disintegration the key role was played by the differences in conceptions and
opinions concerning the division of powers between Czech and Slovak
political institutions. Behind this explicit group of divergences, however,
were hidden other, less obvious, phenomena without which the constitutional crises could not have arisen. Foremost among these is the fact that,
in spite of extensive efforts by politicians and intellectuals in the interwar
period and partly also after the Second World War, the idea of a common
Czechoslovak state did not put down deep roots in Slovak soil. There are
many reasons why this did not happen – some structural, others cultural
and psychological.

The studies in this volume try to present the most relevant of these:
differences in economic, social and cultural developments in the Czech
Lands and in Slovakia; differences in value orientations in both ethnic
communities; mutual misperceptions of Czechs and Slovaks; and, last but
by no means least, different attitudes to the common state. The Czechs
regarded it too much as their own, and the Slovaks found it difficult to
identify with it. Both positions were understandable: when the state was
founded, the Czech element was considerably stronger and more active,
and this often led to paternalistic attitudes which continued to exist even
in times when the junior partner was expecting – with regard to the
economic and cultural progress which he had achieved – a relationship of
'an equal to an equal'. From the Slovak point of view, the Slovaks were
underestimated, discriminated against and underused in state administration and generally handicapped by the Czechs. Some Slovaks also held the
view that Slovakia was economically exploited by its more developed
partner, whereas the Czechs, especially during the socialist period, felt that
the economic growth of the Czech Republic was obstructed by an excessive
transfer of resources to Slovakia. Naturally, such attitudes of mutual
distrust steadily eroded the already fragile concept of a unitary Czechoslovakia. It should be stressed, however, that hardly any aggressive hostility
existed between the two communities – the relationship was more one of
misunderstanding, mistrust and disappointment. In the years 1990–92 there
also existed a feeling that the partners' concepts of the post-communist

future differed so much that, if one accepted the transformation philosophy of the other, he would lose his own future. This was mainly the feeling of the Czechs, who were afraid that the price of retaining the common state with Slovakia would be the distortion or considerable postponement of a radical economic transformation leading to a standard market economy.

Moreover, the above-mentioned structural, psychological and ideological factors leading to the break-up of the state were compounded by the inability to find a working compromise, by a lack of patience and by the effort of new political élites on both sides to gain popularity by playing the 'national card' and by the existing constitutional framework, i.e. the old socialist federative constitution.

Assuming that the split of Czechoslovakia was caused by long-term differences in economic, social and cultural structures between the Czech Lands and Slovakia on the one hand, by differences in value orientations and political ideologies on the other, and finally by the new political conflicts starting after the collapse of the communist regime, we considered it useful to arrange the studies in five parts. The structure of the book aims to show the plurality and historicity of the causes of the break-up. The authors agreed that the events of 1992 could not be understood without analysing the history of Czechoslovakia since its founding in 1918.

The first part of the book deals with the structure of Czech and Slovak societies in a comparative perspective. Milan Kučera and Zdeněk Pavlík compare demographic processes in the Czech Lands and Slovakia, Václav Průcha examines economic development and Jiří Musil describes and evaluates the different patterns of modernization in the Czech and Slovak societies.

The second part of the volume consists of analytical studies on national consciousness. Jan Rychlík concentrates on the formation of Czech and Slovak national consciousness, aiming to show parallels as well as contrasts. Zdeněk Suda studies the role of the relationship to Slovakia in Czech thinking and gives a historical perspective of recent Czech-Slovak conflicts. An important part in the steps leading to the definitive break-up was played by mutual misperceptions and misinterpretations of 'national character'. Petr Příhoda and Miroslav Kusý – Czech and Slovak authors respectively – try to make this delicate topic more transparent.

The third part concentrates on the political aspects of the relationship between Czechs and Slovaks from the foundation of the common state in 1918 to the velvet revolution of 1989. During the whole period, phases of successful moves towards integration alternated with phases of tension and disruption. Interpretations of Czechoslovak history differ as to whether, in the given period, integrative tendencies mostly prevailed, or whether these years can be described as a gradual retreat from the idea of a unitarian state.

In our view the chance to maintain the common state of Czechs and Slovaks existed all the time. What is remarkable in Czechoslovakia's short history is the fact that this state, although it had once split in 1939 – owing to external factors – reunited in 1945. This does not happen often.

The interwar period was a formative one and therefore had special importance. The decisions made during the first phase of building a new state are bound to have long-lasting effects. Agreements and contracts define future forms of cooperation, while any ambiguities left at this stage sow the seeds of future conflicts. This was certainly the case with the formation of the common Czech-Slovak state. Therefore we asked one of our authors to analyse the early formative agreements on which Czecho-slovakia was based.

Alena Bartlová points out that the first steps in arranging the constitu-tional relationship between Czechs and Slovaks were indeed full of ambiguities which later became the seeds of the break-up. Slovakia's dissatisfaction with Czech centralism appeared as soon as the state was founded and repeatedly reappeared in the interwar years as well as after the Second World War. The historical account by Jan Rychlík, which covers the period of great changes between 1938 and 1968, confirms that even in the socialist period the definition of Slovakia's position within the Czechoslovak Republic was a permanent source of political tension. There existed many larger or smaller crises, beginning with the year 1945. Others followed in 1948, 1956, 1960, 1968–9. The postwar quasi-federative system was gradually transformed into a more centralist one, but finally, after 1968, it was changed into a federative one, which then evolved again into a model with strong centralist elements. Petr Pithart's contribution concludes the historical studies and shows how, after the suppression of the Prague Spring in 1968, Czech and Slovak societies began drifting apart. This political alienation is all the more interesting for taking place in a period when the homogenization of economic and social structures in both parts of the country had already reached a high level. It shows a different perception and interpretation of the political situation. Slovakia understood the federalization of the state in 1969 as the fulfilment of its long-term goals and as a condition of its economic growth. For the Czechs federal-ization was merely a part of Gustáv Husák's normalization policies – introduced after the Soviet invasion in 1968 – and was in fact one of the instruments for stopping democratization, which was the Soviets' priority. The mutual alienation of both societies which took place after 1969 was an important factor in the crises which broke out in 1990.

The fourth part of the book, dealing with the final crisis itself, consists of two chapters. The political scientist Sharon Wolchik, who has been studying Czechoslovakia for many years, describes the political background which opened the way to the destruction of the state. She stresses the immense extent of changes in the life of the country after the velvet revolution in 1989 and the resulting global volatility of the political situation, the insufficient crystallization of political preferences and parties, the greater impact of political élites than in stabilized democracies, and the social uncertainties connected with the economic transformation. Wolchik also points out the paradoxical aspect of Czechoslovakia's split: according to the results of public opinion polls neither the majority of Czechs nor the majority of Slovaks wished the split to take place. A considerable part of the population asked for a referendum. The decision on the split, however, was made by a coalition of political parties which were the winners in the last Czechoslovak parliamentary elections in 1992 but which failed to get a substantial majority of votes in either republic.

In the chapter on the 'velvet divorce', Václav Žák carefully reconstructs the events between 1989 and the end of 1992 when Czechoslovakia split into two states. The study shows that after 1989 most Czech politicians underestimated the significance of the Slovak question. The Slovak political élites were more active in the fight to change the constitutional arrangements in the new situation, while the Czech representation was predominantly defensive in this respect. They concentrated their energy more on the concept of economic transformation and on forming a legal basis for democracy. As Václav Žák stresses, the Czechs did not offer the Slovaks a new type of marriage and did not understand that keeping the inherited concept of federation was not an attractive prospect for Slovakia. On the other hand, the Slovaks did not understand that they could not ask the Czechs to abandon radical democratization and economic transformation in order to maintain the common state. Both parties lacked the ability to make compromises and to share power. Both parts of the country lacked strong, highly qualified and imaginative élites capable of preserving the common republic. Žák's account shows that, for the decision-makers on both sides, preserving the republic was of less importance than their other political goals.

The fifth and last part of the book, written by the French political scientist Jacques Rupnik, throws light upon the international aspects of Czechoslovakia's demise. In Rupnik's view the break-up was caused by internal factors and the examples of the disintegration of the Soviet Union and of Yugoslavia had no significant influence. The international aspects are more the consequences of the event. Most importantly, the geopolitical situation of the separated parts has weakened compared with that of former Czechoslovakia, and, consequently, the same has happened to the so-called Visegrad group. This is undoubtedly a setback for the idea of Central Europe. Czechoslovakia's break-up may also contribute to a general destabilization of Europe, since it signals the end of the Versailles system and thus casts doubts upon the legitimacy of the frontiers established after 1918.

The seventy-five-year history of Czechoslovakia can be regarded as a kind of natural social and political experiment testing the effectiveness of two integration models for multinational communities. The two models can be described in short as liberal and socialist respectively. As for the third, fascist, model, which was also used in Europe, Czechoslovakia was more a passive and involuntary object of its application.

In the interwar period, the community of Czechs and Slovaks was built on the concept of a centralist democracy which was based on a liberal economy, a centralized state administration and a plurality of political parties, with great stress laid on education and on political freedoms. Integration should have been achieved by building a larger internal market, by a gradual unification of the legal system, by a unitarian system of state administration, by intellectual and professional help for the weaker partner from the stronger one and by cultivating the idea of one Czechoslovak nation using two languages.

In the postwar period, mainly after 1948 when the Communist Party had completely seized power, the integration of the country was based on the concentration of political power, on a centrally planned economy, and on a state ideology which comprised the Marxist theory of nationalism. This second, socialist, model assumed that ethnic and economic conflicts between nationalities inside one state are fundamentally conflicts between classes, caused by economic disparities. In Ernest Gellner's view, Marxism likes to think of ethnic conflict as camouflaged class conflict. By eliminating economic disparities, the sources of conflicting nationalism are quashed. By levelling economic and social conditions in territories inhabited by different ethnic groups, tensions or conflicts can be transformed into cooperation. In socialist Czechoslovakia the rapid industrialization and urbanization of Slovakia were the instruments of this model.

In spite of their considerable differences, both models have common roots in the theory of industrial society and can also be considered two variants of the modernization theory. According to the liberal model, the social and political integration of different ethnic communities can be achieved mainly by an increased division of labour, and by a growing exchange of goods and services, i.e. by the growth of mutually advantageous inter-dependencies. According to the socialist model, this is achieved mainly by diminishing social differences, by unifying legal systems and social policies, and also by deliberately homogenizing lifestyles. In practice, European integration processes combine elements of both models.

The Czechoslovak experience has, however, shown that neither the increase of economic and technical interdependence resulting from the market economy, nor the removal of basic macroeconomic and macrosocial disparities, leads *per se* to a higher level of political integration. It seems that this conclusion is one of the important lessons of Czechoslovak history. Moreover, the effects of diminishing disparities and increasing the homogeneity of ethnic communities do not materialize automatically and quickly. They must also be perceived by people. However, such a homogenization can have paradoxical and even inverse effects to those intended. It can lead to the disappearance of the accustomed complementarity or accepted dependence between two unequal partners. As soon as a kind of equality between communities is achieved and basic differences are removed, the relationships between them can, strangely enough, become more strained. They probably become more difficult mainly for the originally stronger, richer and more developed partner. In such situations the decisive role is then played by his political flexibility, imagination and ability to redefine his own position. On the part of the originally weaker partner, such a situation, on the other hand, requires political moderation and patience. The mere change of attitudes and psychology is, however, not sufficient: new political institutions and mechanisms must be sought as well and it is necessary to redefine as clearly as possible what is common and what is separate.

The studies written for this volume implicitly suggest that the Czech and Slovak élites did not find sufficient creativity, tolerance and strength to master the new situation which emerged after the collapse of communism and at a time when both societies had become structurally rather similar. The stress on equality in interethnic relations and the acceptance of the philosophy of genuine federalism point to two phenomena: on the one hand, to the remnants of paternalistic relations and attitudes and, on the other, to the habit of expecting the stronger partner – even in the new situation – to continue to offer his help to the weaker partner. The slogan 'equal to equal' means that all inconsistencies infringing this principle are felt much more negatively than at the time when the partners were only moving towards a new type of equilibrium based on equality. Inconsistencies in applying this principle can have worse effects than explicit economic and social disparities at times of accustomed inequality. The analogy with social strain created by status inconsistencies is evident.

The split of Czechoslovakia also raised a number of general questions about the new wave of nationalism in Central and Eastern Europe. Among the most pressing are the following:

What explains the fact that, in Central and Eastern Europe, the concept of a political nation could not and still cannot function, whereas the ethnic, linguistic concept of a nation prevails? Why is the position of the nation-state so extraordinarily strong in this part of Europe? Why has the collapse of communism caused a wave of nationalism? Does nationalism arise in societies which were, in Raymond Aron's terminology, until recently ideocratic, the vacuum left after the breakdown of the ideology of socialism? Is Central Europe witnessing the rise of new, as yet unknown forms of nationalism? Were the arguments of a strong part of the Czech political élite which supported the split of the state an expression of the desire of the stronger and somewhat richer partner to get rid of the weaker partner who would make the radical economic transformation more complicated?

In our opinion the nature of these new types of nationalism can be better understood when classifying the countries inside multinational states according to two parameters: the power status inside the state and the level of socioeconomic development. This can be best illustrated by examples: Slovenia and the Baltic states belong to a group of countries which combines a higher level of socioeconomic development with a lower power status; the Czech Republic is an example of a country which combines a higher level of socioeconomic development with a strong power position; Slovakia – like Scotland, Wales and Quebec – is an example of a country which is economically less developed than other parts of the state, and has at the same time a lower power status; finally Russia and Serbia represent a category of countries with a leading power position combined with a level of economic development lower than those in other parts of the multinational state.

The political orientations and actions of these four categories of countries, although often summarily described as nationalistic, nevertheless differ quite considerably. Slovakia left the common state without expecting any economic benefits to result from the divorce; Slovenia stressed explicitly that its separation from Serbia would bring economic improvement. Serbia and Russia tried to keep 'their' multinational state, and in both countries there exist strong nationalist movements with old hegemonial aspirations. The Czechs preferred the economic benefits and their own political stability gained from the divorce from the Slovaks. And so we can distinguish four types of post-communist nationalism:

(1) Secessionist nationalism without aspirations to economic advantages ensuing from the separation.
(2) Secessionist nationalism motivated partly by the prospect of economic advantages.
(3) 'Ectomic' nationalism, which desires to get rid of the poorer or trouble-making part of the multinational state.
(4) Hegemonial and possibly expansionistic nationalism.

During the process of Czechoslovakia's disintegration two of these types merged: Slovak secessionist nationalism and Czech 'ectomic' nationalism, forces which the federation could not survive.

The decomposition of multinational states in Central and Eastern Europe raises some uncomfortable, but at the same time innovative, questions about contemporary changes in Europe in general, such as: Is the splitting up of a multinational state necessarily a destructive phenomenon? Cannot such decomposition be considered as a necessary and positive part of a restructuring process, mainly when the relationship between the individual parts of such a state are of an asymmetric nature? Can, under certain circumstances, the division of the state according to ethnic criteria become a means to alleviate tensions and to achieve greater stability? Under certain circumstances is the rise of new nation-states and some limitation of economic interaction and the resulting shrinking of markets not a necessary and temporary price for achieving political stability in the given region? If we admit that these questions can be answered positively, some other questions follow: Is such restructuration not in fact a necessary precondition for integrating new states into the expanding European Union? Is it not a necessary, even if transitory, phase for the forming of larger cooperating political units unburdened by internal conflicts?

The disintegration of two countries, namely of Czechoslovakia and Yugoslavia, raises questions which are of a historical nature but which are of relevance for an understanding of the recent events. The studies in this volume also try, explicitly or implicitly, to give answers to questions which examine the potential for the long-term stability and viability of Czechoslovakia as one of the new states formed after 1918. The various assessments of its historical potential to become a stable state can be summarized as follows:

(1) Czechoslovakia was an artificial construction, which without external support and under external pressure would tend to disintegrate.
(2) Czechoslovakia was internally a relatively stable state which was destroyed towards the end of the 1930s by external forces and which never fully recovered from this catastrophe, i.e. from Munich.
(3) Czechoslovakia, as a state founded primarily by Czechs and Slovaks, but also inhabited by Germans, Hungarians, Poles and Ukrainians, had the chance – given a wise internal policy and favourable external conditions – to become a viable and stable multinational political unit.

Those who take the first view of the seventy-five-year history of Czechoslovakia stress the following facts. The split of Czechoslovakia in 1992 was a necessary result of its genesis, i.e. of the artificial merger of two differing national communities which for centuries had been parts of separate political units. The break-up in 1992 was in fact only one of the events in a more general process of disintegration of the Versailles system formed after 1918. Or, in a more positive formulation: the formation of the Czech Republic in 1993 was a return to the traditional foundations of Czech statehood, whereas the establishment of the Slovak Republic in 1993 was the ultimate fulfilment of Slovak national emancipation, a belated formation of a nation-state which for many internal and external reasons could not have been established earlier.

Those who take the second and third views see Czechoslovak history in the following way. The disintegration of Czechoslovakia in 1992 was a result of an unfortunate coincidence of circumstances and was not a necessary event. In 1939 it was a direct effect of the Munich agreement and in 1992 it was the consequence of a lack of experience, imagination and abilities among the Czech and Slovak politicians. But it was also the consequence of skilful activities of political élites who used the national card for their group interests. The 1992 break-up was, according to this second perspective, also caused by insufficient patience on the part of leading politicians and by the pressure to make crucial decisions without the knowledge of their probable results. The time factor undoubtedly played a part as well. Politicians as well as intellectuals underestimated the priority of defining the constitutional identity of the new state emerging from the ruins of communism. The understanding of the urgent need after the velvet revolution in 1989 to redefine immediately the constitutional arrangements between the partners was absent. But all this need not necessarily have been the case.

The reader of the following studies will easily discover that most of the authors who have contributed to this volume accept the logic of the second and third views. In their opinion Czechoslovakia's break-up was not a fatal necessity, and there was a chance, probably a small one, to save this state. The failure of the project had not been genetically inscribed in its foundation. On the other hand, the project was probably much more precarious than its protagonists – especially on the Czech side – had imagined. Nevertheless, it should be stressed that the founders of the new state, above all T.G. Masaryk, were aware of the internal dangers facing the republic. He and other Czechoslovak politicians in the years 1918–38 were mainly concerned with trying to establish a harmonious *modus vivendi* of all ethnic groups living within the new state. The conviction that the fundamentally democratic character of the state, its alliance with the Western democracies and a relatively decent policy towards the German and Hungarian minorities would provide sufficient barriers against disintegration was a typical expression of liberal democratic optimism.

The contributions in our book which analyse the developments in the postwar socialist decades show how the relations between the two parts of the country remained a permanent source of tension which was, however, concealed and belittled as much as possible. The events after 1989, when political freedoms and a pluralistic political system had been re-established, show that this latent problem came to the fore again in its full urgency. And, once more, on the Slovak as well as on the Czech side, liberal and democratic forces were taken aback by an outburst of nationalism. Their lack of readiness and energy to look for new forms of coexistence also played a considerable role in the demise of Czechoslovakia.

I

Structural Aspects of the Break-Up

2 Czech and Slovak Demography

MILAN KUČERA and ZDENĚK PAVLÍK

The creation of Czechoslovakia in the year 1918 was marked by both the spirit of the era and the geopolitical situation after the defeat of the central powers in the First World War: the new country inherited similar ethnic problems to those which had existed previously in Austria-Hungary. It was also just as heterogeneous in its social make-up, economic development, education level, settlement structure and population development. Along the whole historical border of the Czech Lands with Germany and Austria, and often in the interior of the country and in some towns there lived, according to the 1921 census, over three million Germans, representing 31 per cent of the population. This was mainly the original German settlement dating back to the Middle Ages and strengthened by colonization after the Thirty Years War (1618–48), as well as the original Czech population which had succumbed to Germanization. In Slovakia there were only 146,000 Germans, who had been living there since the Middle Ages, mainly in Bratislava and its surroundings and in some mining towns. Altogether in 1921 there were 3,207,000 Germans living in Czechoslovakia – almost a quarter of the country's population. In Slovakia there were 651,000 Hungarians, who formed almost 22 per cent of Slovakia's population, mainly along its southern border with Hungary, created according to the Trianon agreements of 1919. It was the original Hungarian settlement which had been strengthened by Magyarization for a long time. Within the framework of the whole republic Hungarians formed only 5 per cent of the population. Moreover, on the territory of the new state there lived 110,000 Poles (mainly in Silesia) and 102,000 Ruthenians, Ukrainians and Russians (mainly in Slovakia), as well as 109,000 Jews (of which 74,000 in Slovakia) and 21,000 persons of other nationalities (including Romanies). In Ruthenia, which is not considered here, 62 per cent of the total number of 607,000 inhabitants in the 1921 census were Ruthenians, including Ukrainians and Russians, 17 per cent Hungarians, 13 per cent Jews and only a little over 3 per cent of the population considered themselves to be Czechoslovak.

16   *Milan Kučera and Zdeněk Pavlík*

Table 2.1 Development of the crude birth rate (CBR) and the crude death rate (CDR) on the territories of the Czech and Slovak republics in the eighteenth to twentieth centuries (per thousand)

	CR			SR	
Period[a]	*CBR*	*CDR*	*Period*	*CBR*	*CDR*
1785–1824	42–44	28–34	–	–	–
1825–1889	37–40	28–31	1851–1899	41–45	28–42
1890–1909	31–36	22–28	1900–1909	37–41	25–26
1910–1914	28	20	1910–1914	34	22
1920–1924	24	16	1920–1929	31–35	18–20
1925–1944	15–20	13–14	1930–1949	23–27	14–15
1945–1949	21	14	1950–1954	28	11
1950–1954	20	11	1955–1964	21–25	7–9
1955–1992	13–18	10–13	1965–1992	15–21	8–10

Note: [a] No figures available for 1915–19.
Source: *Demografická příručka* ('Demographic Handbook'), Prague: 1982; and *Pohyb obyvatelstva* ('The Movement of Population'), Prague: 1993.

In the whole of Czechoslovakia (including Ruthenia) about 65 per cent of the population considered themselves Czechoslovak. This makes the importance of the union of Czech and Slovak nationality clear. This was made possible by the great similarity of the languages, but differences of historical development were not taken into account.

Main Features of the Overall Development

In the period of great economic, social and political changes in Europe since the end of the eighteenth century, population development can serve as one of the important indicators of global changes. In connection with the split of Czechoslovakia on 1 January 1993, we can ask how these changes were reflected in population development and whether this development itself contributed to a *rapprochement* or moving apart of the two principal national populations, and so also to their final separation.

The Czech Lands were much more industrialized than Slovakia when Czechoslovakia was formed – they were among the most industrialized countries of Austria-Hungary. Thirty-three per cent of the population were employed in industry and only 31 per cent in the primary sector (agriculture, forestry and fishery). In Slovakia 60 per cent of the inhabitants were employed in the primary sector and only 16 per cent in industry and crafts. By 1870 on the territory of the Czech Republic only 56 per cent of economically

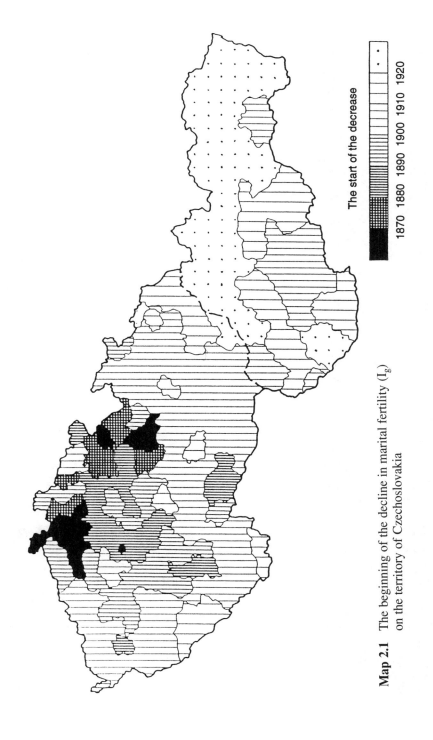

Map 2.1 The beginning of the decline in marital fertility (I_g) on the territory of Czechoslovakia

The start of the decrease

1870 1880 1890 1900 1910 1920

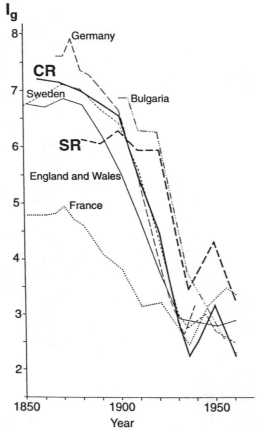

Fig. 2.1   Index of marital fertility (I_g), in Czechoslovakia and in selected countries of Europe, 1850–1960

active people were employed in the primary sector and by 1890 this had decreased further to 47 per cent. In Slovakia it was still 68 per cent in 1890. The level of urbanization was also much lower in Slovakia and significant urban centres were absent here. In 1921, 15.7 per cent of the population over six years of age in Slovakia were illiterate, compared with 2.4 per cent in Bohemia and 3.2 per cent in Moravia (in Ruthenia the figure was 65.7 per cent).

The differences in the overall development of society on the territory of the Czech Republic (CR) and the Slovak Republic (SR) are reflected by the course of demographic revolution on the territory of both republics, as is evident from the data presented in Table 2.1.

The decreases in the birth and death rates have some characteristic

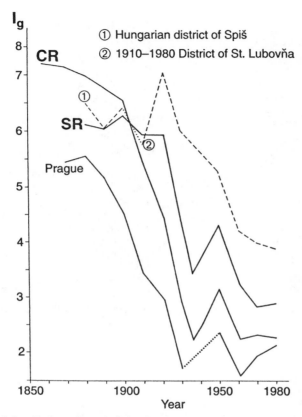

Fig. 2.2 Index of marital fertility (I_g), on the territory of Czecho-slovakia, 1857–1980

features in both republics. In comparable periods it is possible to note a greater variability of the death rate on the territory of the SR and an earlier decrease of its level on the territory of the CR. More striking differences can be seen in the decrease in the birth rate. As early as the first half of the nineteenth century a decrease in the birth rate under the limit of 40 per thousand was recorded on the territory of the CR. The population of the SR went under this limit for the first time at the beginning of the twentieth century. We should not overestimate this fact as it is most probably a reflection of a time lag in the process of modernization in Slovakia.

A rapid decrease of the level of fertility, especially marital fertility, which is the characteristic feature of the second phase of demographic revolution, did not begin at the same time in the whole population. There are significant differences

20   *Milan Kučera and Zdeněk Pavlík*

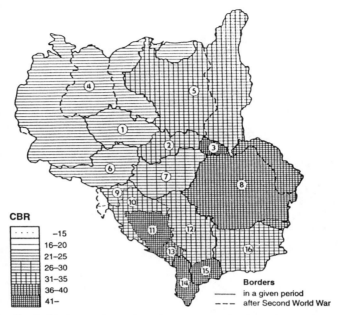

Map 2.2 Crude birth rate (CBR) in selected countries in Europe, 1920–29

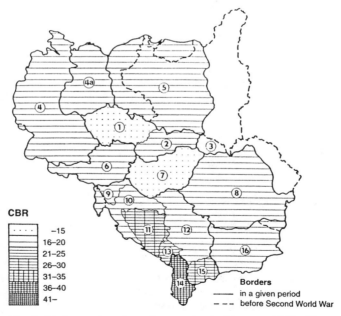

Map 2.3 Crude birth rate in selected countries in Europe, 1960–69

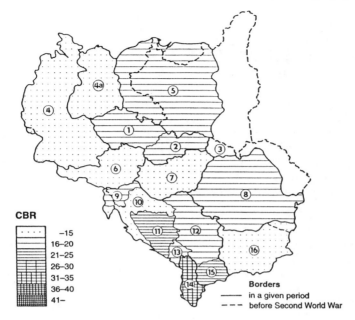

CBR

····	–15
	16–20
	21–25
	26–30
	31–35
	36–40
	41–

Borders
——— in a given period
– – – before Second World War

Map 2.4   Crude birth rate in selected countries in Europe, 1970–79

Key to countries in Maps 2.2, 2.3 and 2.4

1	The Czech Lands	7	Hungary	14	Albania
2	Slovakia	8	Romania	15	Macedonia
3	Ruthenia	9	Slovenia	16	Bulgaria
4	Germany	10	Croatia		
4a	Former GDR	11	Bosnia and Herzegovina		
5	Poland	12	Serbia		
6	Austria	13	Montenegro		

according to education, profession, social status, membership of a sector of the economy, religious affiliation etc., which are to a certain extent also reflected in regional differences. Map 2.1 shows how, in some regions of northern, eastern and central Bohemia, the initial phase of decrease of the level of marital fertility had already occurred before 1870, while in Slovakia it did not take place until the twentieth century. This regional view is complemented by Figures 2.1 and 2.2, where both populations are set in a wider European context, showing a country lagging behind the course of demographic revolution in Europe. Internal differentiation on the territory of former Czechoslovakia is then evident in the differences in the course of the decrease between Prague and the East Slovak region of Stara Lubovňa, presented in Figure 2.2.

It is also possible to document the end of the process of demographic revolution from a wider European view. On the territory of the CR this process ended in the 1930s, at the same time as in Germany and Austria, while in other countries of Eastern Europe it ended much later (Maps 2.2–2.4), and in Slovakia in the 1950s. It is interesting that in Albania the birth rate remained high for much longer – in the 1960s the crude birth rate here was, on average, 41 per thousand (Map 2.3). It seems that the later the process of demographic revolution comes, the faster is its course. A further equalization of the level of fertility between the CR and the SR came in the 1970s (Map 2.4), as a consequence of its rise in the CR, bringing the two populations closer as regards this important aspect of demographic behaviour. This increase in the CR was a consequence of a preceding low fertility level and a reaction to a series of 'favourable' circumstances. In some years there were even more second children born than first children. It was not possible to presume that this trend would continue, and this was confirmed in the 1980s when the fertility level increasingly approached that of countries of Western Europe, where its level reached notably low values at this time.

The time lag of the SR in comparison with the CR also exists objectively in the course of the urbanization revolution. The appropriate indicator of the territorial concentration of population appears to be the delimitation of the minimum extent of territory on which half of the population is concentrated (the indicator varies according to applied units). The percentage share of this area on the total surface of the country subtracted from 100 was denominated as H (relative territorial inequality – with possible values from 50 to 100) by M. Hampl. The evolution of this indicator since 1869 is in Table 2.2.

The data express the rapid course of population concentration from starting values of H around 60 (the beginning of the urbanization revolution) to values higher than 80 (when it is possible to observe a slowing-down of this process before it reaches its end). The level of population concentration in the CR is comparable with France, Belgium, the

Table 2.2   The evolution of relative territorial inequality (H) on the territory of the CR and the SR according to districts

Year	1869	1890	1910	1930	1950	1970
CR	63.7	66.9	72.0	75.1	78.9	81.3
SR	62.1	62.5	64.5	66.9	67.8	70.5

Source: M. Hampl et al., Regionální struktura a vývoj systému osídlení ČSR ('Regional Structure and Development of the Settlement System of the CSR'), Prague: UK, 1987, p. 28.

Netherlands and Switzerland. Higher values of *H* are reached in Great Britain, Sweden, the west of the USA, and Japan.

When the new state was founded, there was no network of larger and medium sized cities in Slovakia. Whereas in the Czech Lands in 1921 there were 65 towns with over 10,000 inhabitants, representing 22 per cent of the population, only 11 per cent of the population of Slovakia lived in the 15 towns of this size, i.e. one-half in relative terms. The population of Slovak towns was increasing more rapidly, but a complete equalization in the level of urbanization was never reached during the existence of the state. The capital of Slovakia had only 93,000 inhabitants in 1921 and Košice had 28,000 inhabitants, while no other town had more than 20,000 inhabitants; while in the Czech Lands, however, there were 21 such towns, in addition to Prague and Brno.

The Czech Lands belong to a group of countries where significant emigration had already started taking place before 1880. This year is sometimes considered to be a dividing line between the old European emigration of the nineteenth century, which took place mainly in Ireland, Great Britain, the Netherlands, Belgium, Scandinavia, France and Germany, and the 'young' emigration from southern and eastern Europe. In Slovakia, extensive emigration took place only after 1880. In the period 1900–1909 the Czech Lands lost 314,000 inhabitants due to emigration, while Slovakia lost 199,000, which was more in relative terms. In interwar Czechoslovakia an internal migration of varying character took place. Directly after the formation of the state, it was above all a migration of clerks and teachers to Slovakia. At the same time, however, the emigration of the population owing to economic reasons continued in the whole republic, and particularly in Slovakia. The differential method based on the 1921 and 1930 censuses gives an idea of the volume of this emigration. During this period Czechoslovakia lost almost 200,000 inhabitants, whereas Bohemia gained 31,000. Moravia and Silesia lost 93,000 and Slovakia lost 122,000. Ruthenia also lost 15,000 inhabitants. It is thus evident that some of the emigrants from Slovakia, as well as from Moravia and Silesia, moved to Bohemia. In the course of demographic revolution there is usually considerable population growth, which leads to greater emigration. This was also the case in Czechoslovakia, although with a certain time difference between the individual countries.

The Formation of Czechoslovakia and the Period 1918-38

The basic data about the state which came into existence after the First World War are shown in Table 2.3. In 1918 the joint development of considerably different wholes started, bringing with it a series of difficult problems inherited from the past. These were above all ethnic problems, which had already come to a head during the existence of Austria-Hungary. The right to self-determination was obtained only by the Czech partner, and only to a certain extent in the case of the Czechoslovak nation. The two largest minorities – Germans and Hungarians – were not provided for. On account of the existence of historical boundaries in the Czech Lands, a change in favour of the German minority – concentrated in the border regions – was unacceptable (disregarding the fact that such a solution would never be 'clean' and would create new minorities on the opposite side). The Hungarian minority was a consequence of the 'strategic' delimitation of new boundaries. A federal solution was excluded in the interests of preserving a unitary state and for fear of granting autonomy to the German minority (a fear so strong that there was no established regional organization in the Czech Lands) and so minorities were only granted extensive rights. These were not, however, regarded as sufficient by all, despite being relatively wide-ranging and strengthened by a democratic political system so rare in that part of Europe at that time. Proof of this was the participation of German parties, representing two-thirds of the German minority, in several Czechoslovak governments. The situation, however, changed after the victory of Nazism in Germany, when the majority of Germans in Czechoslovakia fell for the slogan 'Heim ins Reich' and thus contributed to the break-up of Czechoslovakia in 1938. As far as Czechoslovak nationality is concerned, from 68 per cent of the population claiming Czechoslovak nationality (excluding Ruthenia) 53 per cent were Czechs and 15 per cent were Slovaks according to native language. In 1921 there were 73,000 and in 1930 122,000 Czechs (2.5 per cent and 3.7 per cent of the population respectively) in Slovakia, compared with 16,000 and 44,000 Slovaks respectively (less than 0.5 per cent) living in the Czech Lands. The Czechs in Slovakia worked mainly in education, health services, transport and public administration, where they compensated for the initially considerable lack of a Slovak intelligentsia and technical workers. Slovaks in the Czech Lands worked mainly as agricultural workers. At the beginning the Czechs were favourably accepted in Slovakia, as aid in developing schools and other facilities. Later on, however, they were regarded as an obstacle to ambitions of the Slovak intelligentsia which had started to grow relatively quickly. Sometimes the

Table 2.3 Territory and population of Czechoslovakia

| Region | Area in in km² | Population in 1000s | Density per km² | Shares in % | |
				Area	Pop.
Bohemia	52.1	6,671	128	41	51
Moravia	22.3	2,663	119	18	21
Silesia	4.4	672	152	3	5
Czech Lands	78.8	10,006	127	62	77
Slovakia	48.9	3,001	61	38	23
Czechoslovakia	127.7	13,007	102	100	100

Note: The data for Ruthenia are as follows: Area: 12.7 km²; Population: 607,000; Density per km²: 48; Share of area: 10 per cent; Share of population: 5 per cent.
Source: Census of 15 February 1921.

Czechs were rejected in Catholic neighbourhoods for their liberal views. During the economic crisis of the 1930s, which affected the weaker Slovak economy very severely, they could not go back to their now occupied positions in the Czech Lands. In the years 1938–39, however, the majority of them had to leave Slovakia.

In contrast to the Czech Lands, Slovakia was an agricultural region when the new state was established. Ownership of agricultural land was spread throughout Czechoslovakia between a large number of small farms which were further divided among heirs whenever a farmer died. In Slovakia small farms were the only source of subsistence. In the Czech Lands, which had a more developed industrial sector, farms were often in the hands of peasants whose menfolk worked in agriculture only seasonally.

According to the 1921 census data 55 per cent of the population of the Czech Lands were classified as industrial workers against only 43 per cent in Slovakia, where the share of agricultural workers was higher. The different social structure and the level of economic development played an important role during the deep and prolonged economic crisis in the 1930s. This crisis was deepened by agrarian overpopulation in Slovakia. As far as the German and Hungarian minorities are concerned, the Germans lived mainly in industrialized regions, the Hungarians mainly in agricultural ones. The negative consequences of the economic crisis were joined with nationalist discord in ethnically mixed regions and thus contributed to the culmination of nationalist problems.

As is evident from Table 2.4, the initial differences in the educational level between the Czech Lands and Slovakia were only mitigated by 1940, but they were not eliminated. The data are based on the retrospective recalculation of the 1950 census data. The consequences of the retarded

Table 2.4 Population in the age group 25–29 years according to the level of school education in 1920 and 1940

Level of school education	Czech Lands				Slovakia			
	1920		1940		1920		1940	
	M	F	M	F	M	F	M	F
Without school education	0	0	0	0	2	3	1	1
Primary school (4–5 years)	63	74	36	48	85	88	74	83
Country school (7–9 years)	21	19	43	37	4	4	13	9
Vocational school (10–11 years)	8	4	12	10	3	1	5	4
Secondary school (12–13 years)	5	2	6	3	3	1	5	2
University (16–18 years)	2	0	2	1	1	0	1	0
Other schools	1	1	1	1	2	3	1	1
Total	100	100	100	100	100	100	100	100

Note: The number of years taken to complete the different levels of education are shown in parentheses. The data do not exclude the later acquisition of education; also the effect of migration in the period 1920–50 cannot be excluded. The generations of 25 to 29-year-olds in 1920 acquired education before the First World War, the corresponding generations in 1940 between the two World Wars.
Source: Based on the authors' recalculation of information from the 1950 census on education of the population in the Czech Lands and Slovakia .

development of the school system in Slovakia and the resulting lower educational level were still evident long after 1945.

The differences between the Czech Lands and Slovakia were very clearly visible in the religious spectrum of the population. They consisted mainly in a negligible percentage of atheists in Slovakia and in the existence of the Czechoslovak Church in the Czech Lands (more than 7 per cent of the population – this was a national Church, which was formed after 1920 by secession from the Roman Catholic Church). The dominant Roman Catholic Church was more widespread in the Czech Lands, while the Evangelical Churches together with the Orthodox and Greek Catholic Churches were stronger in Slovakia. In Slovakia membership of a Church was connected with a much more intensive religious life than in the Czech Lands, where the relationship to the Roman Catholic Church in particular was different. For many Czechs this Church was connected with the Habsburg monarchy and most recently so in the First World War (Czech military units were blessed before leaving to fight for Austria). This was the main impulse for the foundation of the Czechoslovak Church, although this had no impact whatsoever in Slovakia. The Czech intelligentsia demonstrated its liberalism, whereas in Slovakia the intelligentsia had hitherto closely been connected with the Church. In the years of awakening Slovak nationalism these differences, which had earlier seemed unimportant,

Table 2.5 Structure of population according to religious affiliation

Affiliation	Absolute data in 1000s			Structure in %		
	CSR	CR	SR	CSR	CR	SR
Roman Catholic	10,762	8,378	2,384	76.9	78.5	71.6
Orthodox/Greek Catholic	259	36	223	1.8	0.3	6.7
Evangelical total	1,056	500	556	7.5	4.7	16.7
of which: Czech brethren	297	291	1	2.1	2.7	0.2
Slovak Augsburg	406	6	400	2.9	0.1	12.0
Slovak reformist	148	2	146	1.1	0.0	4.0
Czechoslovak	791	780	11	5.7	7.3	0.3
Jewish	254	117	137	1.8	1.1	4.1
Other and unregistered	32	30	2	0.2	0.3	0.1
Atheist	350	833	17	6.1	7.8	0.5
Total	14,004	10,674	3,330	100.0	100.0	100.0

Source: 1930 census, after the founding of the Czechoslovak Church.

became evident and strengthened the anti-Czech attitudes represented especially by Hlinka's Slovak People's Party. The population composition according to religious affiliation in 1930 is shown in Table 2.5.

The detailed characteristics of population development of the Czech Lands and Slovakia in the interwar period as shown in Tables 2.6, 2.7 and 2.8, in a certain sense reflect the previous description of differences between the two parts of Czechoslovakia. In the Czech Lands the demographic revolution ended in the 1930s, in Slovakia it finished in the 1960s, even though the initial time lag at its beginning was approximately half a century. The differences were evident in all the demographic processes. At the time of the economic crisis, the previous differences had diminished, but the time lag of the demographic revolution in Slovakia had become more visible. The decrease of fertility under the level of simple reproduction was noted in the Czech Lands as early as 1925, in Slovakia not until 1935. Detailed comparative data describing the process of demographic reproduction show the more important role of traditions in the reproductive behaviour in Slovakia than in the Czech Lands and its slower reaction to external stimuli, as is typical for a predominantly agricultural population.

The level of mortality was much higher and life expectancy was much lower in Slovakia than in the Czech Lands immediately after the formation of Czechoslovakia. The reason for this was higher infant and child mortality

Table 2.6   Population development in the years 1920–37 (per thousand)

Period	Marriages	Divorces	Live births	Deaths	Natural increase	Infant mortality
			Czech Lands			
1920–24	11.1	0.46	24.1	15.6	8.5	154
1925–29	9.5	0.44	20.4	14.3	6.1	133
1930–34	8.8	0.50	17.5	13.2	4.3	144
1935–37	8.2	0.65	14.6	12.9	1.7	103
			Slovakia			
1920–24	9.7	0.18	35.4	19.5	15.9	173
1925–29	8.7	0.16	31.1	18.0	13.1	173
1930–34	8.0	0.20	26.7	15.4	11.3	159
1935–37	7.4	0.25	23.1	14.0	9.1	145

Source: Demografická příručka, 1982.

due to the lower level of medical care and hygiene. The network of medical facilities was only beginning to be built. The five-year difference in life expectancy was maintained until 1937, due mainly to the continuance of differences in child mortality. The differences after the age of 40 gradually equalled out.

The number of inhabitants increased in the period 1921-37 by 8.9 per cent (892,000) in the Czech Lands and by 18.7 per cent (559,000) in Slovakia; thus Slovakia's share increased from an initial 23.1 per cent to 24.6 per cent. Slovakia had 3,555,000 inhabitants and the Czech Lands 10,892,000 thousand inhabitants by the end of 1937. The data concerning the number and movement of inhabitants during the war period are more qualified estimates than a precise description of reality. During the period of the *Böhmen und Mähren* (Bohemia and Moravia) protectorate the fertility level temporarily increased. Certain traits of this tendency were already visible before the war; it was a consequence of child-timing as a reaction to a more favourable level of employment after the economic crisis had been overcome. During the war, efforts to escape the 'Totaleinsatz' in Germany had a similar effect. The increase in the fertility level in Slovakia during this period was relatively modest. The situation there differed from that in the Czech Lands, owing also to the fact that Slovakia was not occupied until the summer of 1944, but gained independence with the help of Germany, even though it lost its southern, predominantly Hungarian, territories. In the Czech Lands slow population growth continued during the war years, while in Slovakia there was a population decrease as a result of increased emigration.

Table 2.7 Fertility in the period 1920–37

Period	Czech Lands Fertility rate			Slovakia Fertility rate		
	Total	Gross	Net	Total	Gross	Net
1920–24	2.85	1.38	1.11	4.56	2.20	1.55
1925–29	2.29	1.11	0.90	3.82	1.85	1.30
1930–34	1.95	0.95	0.77	3.22	1.56	1.11
1935–37	1.68	0.81	0.66	2.81	1.36	0.96

Source: *Demografická příručka*, 1982.

Table 2.8 Life expectancy at selected exact ages

		Czech Lands				Slovakia[a]			
		0	10	40	60	0	10	40	60
Male	1920–22	47.0	51.8	28.0	13.7	43.4	51.1	27.7	13.3
	1929–32	53.7	54.2	28.9	14.4	48.9	53.6	29.1	14.7
	1937	56.5	55.6	29.7	14.8	51.8	55.2	31.4	15.0
Female	1920–22	50.8	53.1	29.3	14.3	45.1	50.8	28.1	13.4
	1929–32	57.5	56.8	31.4	15.6	50.9	54.1	30.1	15.0
	1937	60.5	58.4	32.2	16.1	54.7	56.7	31.8	15.7

Note: [a] Including Ruthenia in the period 1929–32.
Source: *Demografická příručka*, 1982.

Czechoslovakia after the Second World War

In accordance with the decision of the superpowers at the Potsdam conference, the majority of the German population was transferred out of the country (2,870,000 including those who had fled before the organized evacuation – leaving only about 200,000). In Slovakia a partial exchange of about 200,000 people took place with Hungary. Thousands of Slovaks moved into the depopulated Czech frontier regions and a portion of unutilized industrial capacity was moved from there to Slovakia. A small number of Slovaks linked with the regime of the Slovak state emigrated; some of them were later engaged in propaganda against a united Czechoslovakia. In the period 1945–7, about five million people were on the move on the territory of the whole state.

The war losses were not extremely high on the territory of Czechoslovakia in comparison with neighbouring countries: 55,000 were executed or died violently in the Czech Lands and 77,000 Jews died in concentration camps; in Slovakia, 20,000 people perished and 67,000 were taken to concentration camps. The displacement of Germans, the return of thousands of re-emigrants and the settlement of the Czech borderlands with a Slovak agricultural population created new populations in both parts of the state. Periodical censuses from 1950 to 1991 produced data about the results of this process. The short period of relatively free democratic development after the war ended in February 1948 with the communist putsch, which was followed by a bitter oppression of the regime's adversaries; they ended up in prison with disproportionate sentences, or they emigrated. About 200,000 people emigrated in the first wave. Other contributions here pay more attention to these questions.

After the displacement of Germans the Czech Lands became ethnically homogeneous. Ninety-four per cent of inhabitants claimed Czech nationality in the 1950 census; there were 258,000 (2.9 per cent) Slovaks, 160,000 (1.8 per cent) Germans and 71,000 who claimed Polish nationality. During the whole period up to 1991 the ethnic structure of the Czech Lands changed very little. Only the number of Slovaks increased by immigration. They came first looking for jobs and in 1980 there were 359,000 (3.5 per cent) of them; their number had decreased again by 1991 to 315,000 (3.1 per cent), mainly because a part of them claimed the newly recognized Romany nationality. Due to the usual national mixture by marriages between persons of different nationalities there was a certain assimilation of Slovaks, especially of children of mixed marriages. The number of Germans continuously decreased through emigration and through their higher crude mortality rate.

Slovakia stayed more heterogeneous from an ethnic point of view after the war. Eighty-seven per cent of its population were of Slovak nationality in 1950 and 10.3 per cent (355,000) of Hungarian nationality (some Hungarians were unwilling to admit their nationality); there were only 48,000 persons (1.4 per cent) of Ruthenian, Ukrainian and Russian nationality. In the period up to 1991 there occurred only minor changes in the nationality structure of Slovakia. In the 1961 census there were already 519,000 Hungarians and by 1991 their number had increased to 567,000 (10.8 per cent), and only 30,000 persons claimed to be of Russian or Ukrainian nationality, owing to the assimilation under way in Slovakia. In 1950 there were only 40,000 Czechs in Slovakia, and by the year 1991 their number had reached 59,000 (1.1 per cent). In both parts of the republic the percentage of Romanies had been increasing constantly. Before the war there were around 30,000 of them in Slovakia and only several hundred in the Czech Lands. A considerable proportion of them died in German concentration camps during the war. In 1947 there were 17,000 in the Czech Lands and 84,000 in Slovakia. They had come to the republic mostly as 're-emigrants' from Romania, Hungary, Yugoslavia and other countries. By 1980 their numbers had increased as a consequence of a substantially higher birth rate and internal migration, up to approximately 100,000 in the Czech republic and 200,000 in Slovakia (data from the registers of gypsies and censuses). In the 1991 census a much smaller number of Romanies was registered because only some of them declared that they belonged to this nationality (taking into account the growing immigration from Slovakia, the estimate for the Czech Republic was 160,000). The Czechs in Slovakia, as well as Slovaks in the Czech Republic, had completely equal rights. Because of considerable linguistic similarity and dispersed settlement there was no mutual interest in establishing elementary schools that would be divided according to nationality.

Industrialization in Slovakia and the creation of a sufficient number of jobs allowed a rapid increase in employment, especially that of women. The level of economic activity of men in the two republics equalized by the 1960s; in the case of women it was lower and began to equalize much later. The earlier and faster increase of employment among women in the Czech Republic was caused by a fictitious lack of labour source as early as the 1950s. The slower increase in Slovakia was affected by a higher number of children in families and by fewer employment opportunities. With the equalization of the economic situation in the two parts of the state, the migration of workers from Slovakia gradually decreased. The net migration at the beginning of the 1950s (the period of construction of heavy industry in the Ostrava region and the settlement of the Czech borderlands) amounted to 11,000 annually. It was almost 8,000 at the beginning of the 1960s, 3,000 yearly in the 1970s, and this level was maintained up to the end of the 1980s (2,000-3,000 yearly). The level of Romany migration, which has increased in recent years, is difficult to ascertain. Slovak local and economic authorities put the brakes on emigration from Slovakia to the Czech Lands from the 1960s. With the help of the government they founded industrial factories in districts with high population growth, irrespective of traditions, economic relations and effectiveness. This reduced the migration of the labour force and the Slovak economy became more closed to the outside world.

The lower level of education of the Slovak population ended after two postwar generations. The level of education in Slovakia has increased in such a way recently that there has been a higher proportion of people with secondary and university education (Table 2.9). This fact can be partially explained by the planned placement of the new generation of 15-year-olds. The labour force shortage in the Czech Lands meant that more jobs were available; more young people were 'left' for studies in Slovakia because of the larger young population. As early as the beginning of the 1960s relatively more young people studied in Slovakia than in the Czech Lands. A certain number of graduate students from Slovakia looked for jobs in the

Table 2.9   Inhabitants over 15 years of age with secondary and university education

Level of education	Czech Lands					Slovakia				
	1950	*1961*	*1970*	*1980*	*1991*	*1950*	*1961*	*1970*	*1980*	*1991*
Secondary										
in 1000s	331	643	1,044	1,348	1,867	74	198	420	644	964
in %	4.8	9.0	13.4	17.1	22.9	3.1	6.9	12.7	18.0	24.3
University										
in 1000s	62	156	263	394	583	13	46	100	190	307
in %	0.9	2.2	3.4	5.0	7.2	0.5	1.6	3.1	5.2	7.7

Sources: Data from the Czechoslovak censuses of 1950, 1961, 1970, 1980 and 1991.

Czech Lands (e.g. among Slovaks in the Czech Lands there were 17,000 graduates and 39,000 secondary school-leavers).

At the beginning of the 1950s the majority of the population belonged to some religious affiliation and only in the Czech Lands was there a substantial number of atheists (Table 2.10). The hostility of the communist regime towards religion accelerated the process of secularization. Religious orders were banned and dissolved, many priests were imprisoned or were refused state permission to fulfil their function (some of them ministered illegally). Religion was not taught in schools and activities with young people were limited.

The number of people belonging to Churches had decreased considerably by 1991. It was mainly elderly people who declared their religious confession in the Czech Lands in 1991 (up to the age of 40 less than 30 per cent, between 40 and 50 about one-half, and over 60 around 70 per cent). There were not, however, big differences according to age and profession in Slovakia. Attitudes towards the Church and religion remained unchanged in Slovakia much longer than in the Czech Lands, including participation in Church ceremonies. In some Czech border districts only 20-25 per cent of the population were Church members, in traditional districts 60-70 per cent. The minimum district percentage was around 60 per cent in industrial regions, the maximum between 85 and 90 per cent. Slovaks living in the Czech Lands were less frequently members of a Church than Slovaks living in Slovakia.

The intensive urbanization related to industrialization was the most important change in the postwar development of Slovakia. Urbanization in the Czech Lands was much less visible; it affected the network of historical but often stagnating towns and was less marked than in Slovakia. Slovakia had only 23 towns with more than 10,000 inhabitants in 1950

Table 2.10 Church membership (religious confessions)

Professed to Church	Czech Lands			Slovakia		
	1950	1991		1950	1991	
	in %	in 1000s	in %	in %	in 1000s	in %
Total	94.1	4,524	43.8	99.7	3,841	72.8
of which:						
Roman Catholic	76.3	4,021	39.0	76.2	3,182	60.4
Evangelical total	5.7	225	2.5	16.3	420	8.0
Czechoslovak-hussite	10.6	178	1.7	0.1	1	0.0
Greek Catholic	0.4	7	0.1	6.6	179	3.4
Atheists or unknown	5.9	5,778	56.1	0.3	1,433	27.2
Total	100.0	10,302	100.0	100.0	5,274	100.0

Note: Appurtenance to the Church was recorded in 1950, the declaration of religious confession in 1991; during the 40 years in between religious confession was not recorded.
Source: Censuses of 1950 and 1991.

(excluding the two biggest cities of Bratislava and Košice). There were 41 in 1979 and 70 by 1991. The number of towns with more than 20,000 inhabitants increased during the same period from 6 to 38 (in the Czech Lands from 27 to 61 – not counting the four biggest cities). The share of inhabitants living in towns with more than 10,000 people increased from 34 per cent in 1950 to 56 per cent in 1991 in the Czech Lands; it increased from 11 per cent to 50 per cent in Slovakia. Bratislava – the capital of Slovakia – reached 441,000 and Košice 235,000 by 1991; four other towns increased from 20-25,000 to 85-95,000 inhabitants.

Towns in the Czech Lands grew in the long term due to migration; these migrants were often former commuters to industrial factories or they followed the path from smaller to bigger cities. The urban population in Slovakia grew mainly through direct migration from agriculture to newly built industry. It was the first generation to live in large towns. It was usually younger, more educated and skilled, less secularized, but greatly affected by its rapid immersion in production without any tradition in urban life. The migrants brought with them their preference for living in houses, rather than flats, since houses represented a higher proportion of dwellings in Slovakia than in the Czech Lands.

General changes in economic, social and political developments were also reflected in demographic reproduction (Table 2.11). The similarity of these changes in the two parts of Czechoslovakia brought the patterns of reproduction of the Czech Lands and Slovakia closer together, although certain specific

Table 2.11   Population reproduction 1950–91 (per thousand)

Period	Marriages	Divorces	Live births	Deaths	Natural increase	Infant mortality
			Czech Lands			
1950–59	8.2	1.26	17.7	10.5	7.7	37
1960–69	8.4	1.64	14.4	10.8	3.6	21
1970–79	9.3	2.47	17.5	12.4	5.1	19
1980–84	7.7	2.76	13.8	12.9	0.9	15
1985–89	7.9	2.96	12.8	12.5	0.3	12
1990	8.8	3.09	12.6	12.5	0.1	11
1991	7.0	2.85	12.6	12.1	0.5	10
			Slovakia			
1950–59	8.8	0.50	26.4	9.6	16.8	60
1960–69	7.4	0.61	19.3	8.1	11.2	26
1970–79	8.8	1.1	19.9	9.5	10.4	23
1980–84	7.9	1.35	18.4	10.1	8.3	19
1985–89	7.3	1.58	16.3	10.1	6.2	14
1990	7.6	1.67	15.1	10.6	4.5	12
1991	6.2	1.50	14.9	10.4	4.5	13

Source: Demografická příručka, 1982; and Pohyb obyvatelstva, 1985, 1990, 1992.

characteristics remained, owing to the two parts' different historical development. Small differences exist in the number of marriages. More people remain single in middle- and old-age in Slovakia. More pronounced differences exist in the relative frequency of divorces: it is only one-third in young age groups and around one-half later. The family still has a higher value in Slovakia, perhaps due to the more traditional country population and the higher incidence of religious belief. In growing urban areas (e.g. Bratislava), the divorce rates are comparable with those of the Czech Lands.

Differences in the level of demographic reproduction between both republics are still noticeable. In Slovakia family planning and a rational approach to the number of children in a family and the period of their conception is still less common. Especially among rural people, there is still an acceptance of unwanted pregnancy, which is visible afterwards in a less frequent rejection of an unexpected pregnancy; the influence of religion is obviously one of the underlying reasons for this. In the postwar period Slovakia still had a high birthrate, and until 1960 the total fertility here was more than three children (in the Czech Lands it was less than 2.1 children at that time). Since then, however, the birthrate has steadily approached the model of a two-child family. In the Czech Lands, where the demographic revolution ended roughly 30 years earlier, this model had been accepted by the 1950s (Table 2.12).

Table 2.12   Population reproduction 1950–91 (fertility)

Period	Czech Lands		Slovakia	
	Total fertility	Net repro-duction rate	Total fertility	Net repro-duction rate
1950–54	2.71	1.24	3.55	1.52
1955–59	2.40	1.12	3.32	1.52
1960–64	2.19	1.04	2.94	1.37
1965–69	1.96	0.92	2.55	1.20
1970–74	2.16	1.02	2.50	1.18
1975–79	2.35	1.12	2.50	1.14
1980–84	2.01	0.95	2.29	1.09
1985–89	1.92	0.92	2.17	1.04
1990	1.89	0.91	2.09	0.99
1991	1.84	0.88	2.05	0.98

Source: Demografická příručka, 1982; and authors' calculations based on data from Pohyb obyvatel-stva, 1985, 1990, 1992.

Abortion was legalized in 1957, even though approval of a special board was required in the beginning. Especially in the early years and, to a certain extent, even today abortions are considered to be 'morning-after contraception' in some population groups. A more liberal approach towards abortion in the Czech Republic can be seen by a more frequent refusal of an additional child. Even in this field, however, differences between the two republics have been diminishing gradually (Table 2.13).

Where the two republics came the closest was the level of mortality, first of all in its decrease up to the year 1960 and then in its lack of change. Not until the 1980s did a new difference in the rate of mortality appear between the Czech and Slovak republics (Table 2.14). The Slovak population still has a somewhat higher level of infant mortality, as well as a higher level of mortality for children and persons below 30 years of age. It does, however, have a lower level for people over 60 years of age.

Population growth in Slovakia was higher than that of the Czech Lands because of a higher natural increase. The Czech Republic also lost more population by emigration for political reasons. Two emigration waves after 1948 and 1968 meant the loss of 450,000–500,000 people, around 340,000–370,000 from the Czech Lands and 110,000–130,000 from Slovakia. Among 74,000 people prosecuted for illegal desertion of the republic (according to paragraph 109 of the penal code) in the years 1975–89, 56,000 were from the Czech Lands and 18,000 (24 per cent) from Slovakia. The level of illegal emigration was twice as high in the Czech Lands as in Slovakia. The standard of living increased considerably in

Table 2.13 Induced abortions 1960–91

Indicator	Czech Lands				Slovakia			
	1960	*1970*	*1980*	*1990*	*1960*	*1970*	*1980*	*1990*
Number:								
in 1000s	67.6	71.9	68.9	111.3	20.7	27.9	31.2	48.4
per 1000								
births	51.9	48.3	44.6	84.9	23.2	34.3	32.6	60.3
Total								
abortion rate	1.05	1.03	0.91	1.55	0.72	0.89	0.84	1.23

Source: Demografická příručka, 1982; and Pohyb obyvatelstva, 1991.

Slovakia in the postwar period and this partly compensated for the lack of political and social freedom.

The number of inhabitants increased in the period 1950–91 by 1,400,000 in the Czech Lands (16 per cent) and by 1,800,000 in Slovakia (53 per cent). The overall economic and social stagnation lasting 40 years was felt more in the Czech Republic than in Slovakia. The differences could also be seen after 1989 (Table 2.15).

Conclusion

Czechoslovakia's more than 70-year-long history revealed a process of gradual equalization of social structure, educational level and standard of living. In spite of the intense process of urbanization in Slovakia, certain differences in the settlement system still remain for geographical reasons. Differences in ethnic and religious structures also remain. Population development shows similar tendencies, with a time lag as a consequence of dissimilar historical conditions. The two main demographic processes – fertility and mortality – became almost identical in the 1980s; in the history of Czechoslovakia they differed most at its beginning. Certain differences still exist in the rates of divorce and the frequency of abortion, but even here the tendency towards equalization has been clearly visible.

Internal migration and mixed-nationality marriages have a considerable importance for the existence of a common state. Internal migration was very intensive especially after the war, while subsequently a process of a certain closing and isolation of both populations is evident, as can be seen from Figure 2.3. It is not without interest that a similar process started

Table 2.14   Life expectancy in years

Period	Czech Lands				Slovakia			
	0	*10*	*40*	*60*	*0*	*10*	*40*	*60*
Male								
1949–51	62.2	57.7	30.6	15.0	59.0	58.2	31.8	16.2
1970	66.1	58.0	30.1	14.1	66.7	59.2	31.5	15.5
1990	67.5	58.6	30.2	14.5	66.6	57.8	29.6	15.0
Female								
1949–51	67.0	61.8	33.9	16.9	62.4	60.6	33.6	16.9
1970	73.0	64.6	35.6	18.0	72.9	65.0	36.0	18.4
1990	76.0	66.9	37.6	19.6	75.4	66.4	37.2	19.6

Source: Demografická příručka, 1982; and *Pohyb obyvatelstva*, 1991.

between Bohemia and Moravia. These preferences of internal migration are consequences of the unnatural planning of the labour source; the closing of regions and districts did not help the integration of the state. Only in border districts between Moravia and Slovakia did the numbers of the other nationalities steadily increase in comparison with more distant districts. Mixed-nationality marriages were frequent, and the number of mixed marriages grew both absolutely and relatively. On average, in 1970, 50 per cent of Slovak men living in the Czech Republic had a Czech wife. By 1991 this figure had increased to 66 per cent; whereas 72 per cent and 83 per cent of Czech men living in Slovakia had a Slovak wife in 1970 and 1991 respectively. Younger marriages were more often mixed than older ones.

The increasing similarity of the population processes and structures of the Czech and Slovak republics did not lead to the suppression of the national identity of either population. As before, the Czech Republic's

Table 2.15   Population of Czechoslovakia 1950–91 (in thousands)

Census year	Total	CR	SR	SR in %	Density per km²		
					Total	CR	SR
1950	12,338	8,896	3,442	27.9	97	113	70
1961	13,746	9,572	4,174	30.4	107	121	85
1970	14,345	9,808	4,537	31.6	112	124	93
1980	15,283	10,292	4,991	32.7	119	130	102
1991	15,576	10,302	5,274	33.9	122	131	108

Source: Demografická příručka, 1982; and the 1991 census.

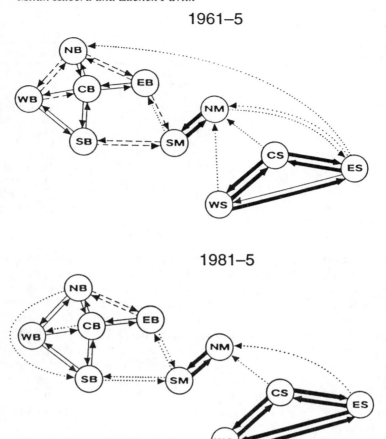

1961–5

1981–5

Indices of preference

▬▬▬ 200.0+
———— 150.0 – 199.9
– – – – 125.0 – 149.9
············ 100.0 – 124.9

Regions

Bohemia		*Moravia*		*Slovakia*	
CB	Central	SM	South	WS	West
SB	South	NM	North	CS	Central
WB	West			ES	East
NB	North				
EB	East				

Fig. 2.3   Migration flows in Czechoslovakia

Source: K. Kühnl, *Indice de préférence des mouvements migratoires entre les grandes régions de la République socialiste tchécoslovaque et ses changements dans les 25 dernières années.* Acta Universitatis Carolinae, *Geographica 23*, vol. 1, 1988, p. 45. The authors are grateful to the publishers for their kind permission to reproduce the figure in this volume.

population was more sensitive towards external impulses in its development, reacted faster and more rationally, was more pragmatic and adaptable. Slovakia's population developed at an accelerated pace while maintaining a traditional way of life, more stable behaviour, with a stronger orientation towards family relations, but also in greater seclusion.

It is therefore possible to affirm that population development was not a cause of the dissolution of the country, but rather that it documents the very similar basic living conditions of the people. From the analysis of population development it is further evident that the two populations are much closer to each other today than was the case at the foundation of Czecho-slovakia, and that, at the same time, they are mutually closer in their demographic behaviour than either is to any other population.

3 Economic Development and Relations, 1918–89

VÁCLAV PRŮCHA

The Interwar Period

The disintegration of Austria-Hungary and the rise of the successor states after the First World War brought about not only radical changes on the map of Europe and in the political alignment of the vast European region, but also the break-up of an extensive economic area which had been formed in central and south-eastern Europe over centuries of development of that part of the continent. After the fall of the Habsburg monarchy, Czechoslovakia inherited a territory with a considerable industrial and export potential, with a completely structured industry, relatively intensive agricultural production, a satisfactory infrastructure, and a large skilled labour force. From various sources, which are, however, far from consistent, it can be estimated that Czechoslovakia inherited about 60 per cent of the manufacturing industry of Austria-Hungary, approximately two-thirds of this from the Cisleithan regions and nearly one-fifth from the manufacturing industry of Hungary. The Czechoslovak share of the territory and the population of the old monarchy equalled only 21 per cent and 25 per cent respectively.

Interwar developments did not bear out the sceptical prognoses of Austrian, Hungarian and West European politicians and economists, whose forecasts were based on the assumption that the disintegration of Austria-Hungary into small states would lead to an economic collapse of these successor countries. Reality corrected these gloomy prognoses: despite the postwar feelings of hopelessness, even the greatly reduced territories of Austria and Hungary proved economically viable. For the neighbours of these two countries the breakdown of the clumsy and conservative system of a multinational monarchy, which involved pumping funds to Vienna and Budapest, and which was linked with the privileges of the Austro-German and Hungarian landed gentry, the nobility and the Catholic Church, dynamized the efforts of politicians and the population to prove their capability of building up and managing the new states. This psychological factor was particularly strong in the early stages of the development of the newly established countries.

The economic development of Czechoslovakia was more favourable than that of its neighbouring countries. The chaos caused by the war was quickly overcome and a deflationary policy prevented any hyperinflation of the German or Hungarian type. Foreign relations were established with numerous countries. The democratizing and social reforms that were embarked on represented a qualitative shift forward in comparison with the state of affairs in the Austro-Hungarian era. As early as 1921–2 Czechoslovakia was viewed as an island of stability in central Europe and its credit abroad was thus greatly enhanced. The business circles of the Entente started to make a distinction between the developments in Czechoslovakia and the developments in the countries surrounding it, and they began exporting capital to the new state and embarked on speculative buy-ups of quantities of Czechoslovak currency, in the hope of capitalizing on the appreciation of the Czechoslovak koruna.

According to B.R. Mitchell, the index of Czechoslovak gross national product in 1929 exceeded that of 1913 by 52 points, whereas in Austria gross national product went up by 5 points only over the same period; the averages for the years 1920–29 were 19 per cent higher and 11 per cent lower respectively than those of 1913. In 1929 the index for the Czechoslovak manufacturing industry was higher than the average for 18 European countries (excluding the USSR); a more favourable index was achieved only by Greece, Finland, the Netherlands and Italy. The Czechoslovak index, perhaps a little overstated, reached 172 points (with 1913 equal to 100), whereas in Austria and Hungary it did not exceed 118 and 114 points respectively. The Czechoslovak share of world manufacturing output in the years 1913–29 increased from 1.4 per cent to 1.6 per cent.[1]

The economic detachment from Vienna and Budapest had an effect on relations of ownership. In the period immediately following the breach of relations, the position of the capital-holding Germans living in Czechoslovakia remained strong and out of proportion to their share of the population of the country. The initial economic subordination to Austria and Hungary was quickly overcome, however, and the headquarters of joint stock companies started moving to Czechoslovakia. Through innumerable commercial transactions Austro-German and Hungarian capital was taken over by Czech and Slovak nationals, dependence upon Austrian and Hungarian banks was gradually weakened and the role of Vienna and Trieste in the re-export of Czechoslovak goods was reduced.

Intervention by the Czechoslovak government in land ownership must be viewed as one of the most far-reaching land reforms in postwar Europe. The breaking up of the latifundia owned by the nobility and by the Church had three main aims: to weaken the effects of Germanization, Magyarization, re-Catholicization and social oppression of the rural population in the past centuries; to create conditions for farming which were more effective than those practised on the post-feudal latifundia; and to assist the social enhancement of hundreds of thousands of Czechoslovak farmers and peasants. The importance of the land reform was reflected in President T.G. Masaryk's claim in 1927 that it had been the greatest act carried out by the new Czechoslovak Republic.

A chronic problem throughout the interwar years, which had negative national and political effects, was the economic and social heterogeneity of the Czechoslovak Republic. Inside the newly established boundaries, the old differences, namely those between the Cisleithan and the Hungarian level and structure of economy, continued with some variations, the Cisleithan regions and Hungary having been two administrative regions of the Habsburg monarchy, parts of which were taken to form the new Czechoslovak Republic. While the Czech Lands as a whole were industrially relatively advanced, the eastern parts of the republic were dominated by agriculture, the development of which, however, lagged behind the agriculture of the western parts by more than fifty years. The output of a ten-hectare Slovak farm equalled approximately the output of a four-hectare farm in the Czech Lands. The backwardness of Slovakia was also clearly observable in the other sectors of the economy and in the social sphere; in certain areas of the economy it was estimated to be thirty to seventy years behind.

The differences in the economic structure of the Czech Lands and of Slovakia are shown in Table 3.1, which relates to the whole population including the non-working members of families. In the Czech Lands trade and the manufacturing and building industries prevailed over farming and forestry as early as the beginning of the twentieth century, whereas in Slovakia more people were employed in the agricultural sector as late as the second half of the 1950s (and as far as the structure of labour was concerned even until several years later – see Table 3.8).

From its creation Czechoslovakia displayed both an industrial and an agrarian structure. The former structure was provided by the economic profile of the western part of the country, which was generally more developed and considerably larger with respect to area and population. Slovakia, on the other hand, was an agrarian country. In spite of the fact that industrialization had been encouraged and supported by Hungarian laws as early as the late nineteenth century, it had reached only the initial stage of

Table 3.1   Occupational distribution of the population, 1910–61 (in per cent)

Sector	Country	1910	1921	1930	1950	1961
Agriculture and	CR	34.4	31.5	25.5	18.4	15.9
forestry	SR	62.6	60.7	56.7	41.9	27.0
Manufacturing industry,	CR	39.6	39.7	39.5	37.8	45.0
building industry and crafts	SR	18.4	17.4	17.8	27.1	37.7
Transport and	CR	4.9	5.4	7.1	7.4	5.7
communications	SR	3.2	3.5	5.6	7.2	7.2
Trade and banking	CR	6.0	6.3	7.6	7.8	5.6
	SR	4.8	4.1	4.9	5.2	4.7
Public services and	CR	5.3	5.9	5.4	8.9	11.1
liberal professions	SR	4.4	5.0	4.8	7.3	9.7
Others and	CR	9.8	11.2	14.9	19.7	16.7
non-earners	SR	6.6	9.3	10.2	11.3	13.7

Sources: Statistická ročenka Republiky československé 1938 ('Statistical Yearbook of the Czechoslovak Republic 1938'), p. 15; *Statistická ročenka Protektorátu Čechy a Morava 1941* ('Statistical Yearbook of the Protectorate of Bohemia and Moravia 1941'), pp. 145–6; V. Srb, *Demografická příručka* ('Demographic Handbook'), Prague: 1967, p. 35.

industrial development. However, in view of the generally low level of industrial development in the Hungarian part of Austria-Hungary, this initial stage proved sufficient for Slovakia to rank second after the Budapest agglomeration as far as the industrial development of the Hungarian regions were concerned. The share of Slovakia in Hungarian industrial production declined gradually after 1900.

Some years later, the Slovak historian, Ľ. Lipták, characterized the economic level of the two parts of the future Czechoslovakia as follows: 'Slovakia ... considerably lagging behind the developed countries of western and central Europe did not, however, rank in any respect with the most backward regions of Europe either. While the Czech Lands were some kind of easternmost foreground of western capitalist industrial civilization, but standing a little lower than its peak, Slovakia represented an advance post of the poorer half of Europe.'[2]

Considerable differences between the Czech Lands and Slovakia could also be observed in the sphere of property ownership. In the Czech Lands the participation of Czech nationals in business and entrepreneurial activities began increasing in the early ninteenth century, and on the eve of the First World War the Czech share of total capital stock was estimated at one-third. Czech capital was spreading from agriculture and trade via the food processing industry, cooperatives and small banking companies into such spheres as the engineering industry and big banks. The positions held by Slovak nationals in the economic life of Slovakia, except agriculture, were, by contrast, next to negligible. In the manufacturing industry only three small enterprises were in Slovak hands and in the financial sphere only some banking companies of local importance were owned by Slovaks. After the foundation of the Czechoslovak Republic the position of the Slovak monied classes was strengthened in the course of the land reform and various capital transfers in the manufacturing industry and banking, but hegemony shifted from Hungarian and Austro-German hands primarily in favour of the Czech capital.

The linking of Slovakia with the Czech Lands brought the Slovak nation considerable benefits in the sphere of politics, national independence and culture; and demographic statistics also took a turn for the better. The pressure for Magyarization, which had been a real threat to the very existence of the Slovak nation for decades, was followed by a regeneration and flourishing of the nation's potential. This development was accompanied by gradual democratization of political and public life, which proved to be an undisputable step forward, despite a number of slips, in comparison with the aristocratic, clerical and bureaucratic Hungarian regime. There was a particularly marked improvement in social policy, education, enlightenment of the population, art, and in the overall education level of the young generation. However, the dynamism of the Slovak national movement gradually came into conflict with the prevailing state ideology which did not recognize the independent identity of the Slovak nation, viewing it as a mere branch of Czechoslovakia.

In the economic sphere, grave problems arose in Slovakia after 1918. The adjustment of the Slovak economy to the new situation was far from easy under the conditions of the competitive prevalence of Czech capital, and it is fully understandable that numerous economic and social disorders should have arisen. Until 1938, Slovakia – and the extremely underdeveloped Carpathian Ruthenia – was little more than an agrarian appendage of the Czech Lands, supplying it with raw materials. In trade with the Czech Lands, Slovakia exported items like cereals, flour, livestock, meat, textile raw materials, iron and manganese ores, magnesite, crude oil, timber, paper, and building materials. On the other hand, Slovakia depended on Czech exports of, among other things, coal, coke, metals, engineering products, chemicals, glass, porcelain and beer. Generally, as an outlet for Czech goods Slovakia ranked fourth or fifth, after Germany, Austria, Yugoslavia and perhaps Britain.

Czechoslovakia had a very mixed population from the point of view of individual nationalities, which were quite differently socially structured and participated differently in the various branches of social activity. (See Tables 3.2 and 3.3.) According to the 1930 census, Czechoslovakia's population was 14,730,000 (including 250,000 foreigners).

Table 3.2 Nationality and social structure of the population of Czechoslovakia, 1930 (in per cent)

Nationality	Total	Self-employed and tenants	White-collar workers	Manual workers[a]
Czechs[b]	49.9	35.2	19.8	45.0
Slovaks[b]	15.9	51.4	12.4	36.2
Ukrainians, Ruthenians and Russians	3.7	66.2	3.8	30.0
Germans	21.9	34.2	18.0	47.8
Hungarians	4.7	50.0	8.5	41.5
Poles	0.6	19.6	16.8	63.6
Jews	1.3	68.8	18.0	13.2

Notes: [a] Including day labourers and apprentices. [b] In the census the nationality was given as Czechoslovak. In the first line, Czechs and Slovaks in the Czech Lands and in Ruthenia; in the second line, Slovaks and Czechs in Slovakia. Foreigners and the nationalities not quoted in the table accounted for 2 per cent of the population.
Source: Československá statistika: Pramenné dílo ('Czechoslovak Statistics: A Source Book'), vol. 116, Prague: 1935, pp. 12–16.

Table 3.3 Occupational distribution of the nationalities of Czechoslovakia, 1930 (in per cent)

Nationality	Sector					
	A	B	C	D	E	F
Czechs[a]	26.9	39.1	7.0	7.6	5.7	13.7
Slovaks[a]	59.8	19.0	5.1	4.2	3.5	8.4
Ukrainians, Ruthenians and Russians	82.1	6.2	1.9	0.8	2.1	6.9
Germans	23.0	45.5	4.0	8.9	4.3	14.3
Hungarians	63.8	16.9	2.6	3.8	3.8	9.1
Poles	16.2	55.6	6.0	3.1	2.3	16.8
Jews	13.1	22.2	3.6	42.6	6.6	11.9

A Agriculture, forestry and fisheries.
B Mining, manufacturing industry, building industry and crafts.
C Transport and communications.
D Trade and banking.
E Public services and liberal professions.
F Other branches.

Note: [a] See Table 3.2, note b.
Source: See Table 3.2.

As far as the Czech population was concerned, the industrial component was the most numerous, and the majority were workers in the manufacturing industry or low-grade clerical workers. This was even more marked among those of German and Polish nationality. Among the Slovaks, Ukrainians, Ruthenians and Hungarians, the number of those engaged in farming was clearly the highest, and this was reflected in the high percentage of 'self-employed persons'. The proportion of agricultural labourers in the total workforce was larger in the eastern part of the republic than in the Czech Lands. Jews, or those who claimed to be of Jewish nationality (in the western part of the country, many of those who were of Jewish origins did not declare this), were mostly linked with trade, commerce and finance, and very few of them were workers, farmers or peasants. The rate of employment of women declined towards the east, regardless of nationality.

Large differences could be seen in the cultural level of the population of various nationalities, which, naturally, was reflected in both the structure of the skills of the workforce and the cultural standard of work. Considering the elementary indicator, literacy, in 1921 7.4 per cent of people were illiterate in the whole Czechoslovak Republic, less than 3 per cent among the Czechs and the Germans in the Czech Lands, and 6 per cent among the Poles, whereas among Slovaks and Czechs living in Slovakia (and also among Jews throughout the whole republic) this percentage was 16, and among Hungarians it was 11. An extreme 61 per cent of illiterate people was recorded among the Ukrainians and Ruthenians living mostly in the easternmost regions of the Czechoslovak Republic – in Carpathian Ruthenia. The differences were the effect of the unequal standards of the systems of education in the western and the eastern parts of Austria-Hungary, and were also caused by Magyarization which had hindered the non-Hungarian population in Slovakia and Carpathian Ruthenia in acquiring education.

The specific feature of the structure of the monied classes of the population in both the western and the eastern parts of the republic can be derived from tax statistics. In the 1928 boom, 11,000 people reported an annual taxable income of over 100,000 Czechoslovak koruna; Slovakia's share was considerably lower than its population would have suggested. As far as the kind of income is concerned, Slovakia had a particularly high share of income from landed property and, on the other hand, a very low share of income yielded by securities. A net annual income of over one million Czechoslovak koruna was reported by 327 inhabitants in Czechoslovakia; only nine of these (6 per cent) lived in Slovakia. (The rate of exchange between the Czechoslovak koruna and the US dollar was 29.60 koruna for one dollar in 1928.)

Table 3.4   Structure of banking in Czechoslovakia according to nationality, 1929 (in million Czechoslovak koruna)

Banks	Equity capital	Deposits	Total accounting balance	Net profit
Czech	927	4,277	13,929	114
Czech and German (mixed)	645	2,815	10,872	97
German in Czech Lands	290	1,897	6,277	42
Based in Slovakia	377	2,946	–	34

Source: Statistická příručka Republiky československé ('Statistical Handbook of the Czechoslovak Republic'), vol. 4, Prague: 1932, pp. 257–62.

Table 3.5   Structure of manufacturing trades by the number of the persons employed, 1930

Number of persons employed	Number of plants in Czechoslovakia	of which in Slovakia and Ruthenia	
		number	in %
1	180,606	29,818	16.5
2–5	153,363	22,623	14.8
6–20	27,952	3,417	12.2
21–100	10,039	889	8.9
101–500	2,475	248	10.0
501–1,000	325	36	11.1
1,001–2,500	108	7	6.5
2,501–5,000	10	–	–
5,001 and over	6	–	–

Source: Československá statistika: Pramenné dílo, vol. 114, 1935, p. 176.

In banking, capital of Czech provenance grew dynamically; soon after the foundation of the new state it took the leading position in the Czech Lands and also succeeded in penetrating into Slovakia. Despite a process of concentration, Slovak banking was far more atomized and the Hungarian and German banks surpassed those that were in Slovak hands as far as the volume of banking transactions and turnover were concerned (Table 3.4).

In the first decade of the existence of the Czechoslovak Republic the Czech manufacturing industry quickly adapted itself to the new situation and stepped up production and exports after 1923. Slovak industrial potential, however, was considerably weakened, firstly by the removal of part of the enterprises in Hungarian ownership to Hungary and then by a strong wave of de-industrialization which hit the eastern half of Slovakia with particular strength, sweeping away the non-competitive enterprises of the manufacturing industry. In view of the low density of the industrial plants, this process had particularly grave social consequences in a number of areas and fostered a radicalization of the working class. According to the statistics for 1921 and 1930, the number of employees in the manufacturing industry, trade and the building industry rose by 15 per cent in Slovakia, but, in fact, the whole increment was accounted for by three technologically less demanding branches of industry: the building industry, the building materials industry and the timber trade. On the other hand, the number of employees in the metal-working industry, ore mining, the industries of chemicals, glass, leather and ready-made clothing declined (Table 3.5).

The striking differences between the western and the eastern parts of the republic in both the level of industrialization and the rate of its advance were testified to by the number of workers employed in the manufacturing industry per 1,000 inhabitants. In the period between the censuses of 1921 and 1930, this number grew in the Czech Lands from 159 to 175, but in Slovakia only from 33 to 36, and in economically underdeveloped Carpathian Ruthenia, from 23 to 28. In 1930 the rate of employment of the workforce in manufacturing industry was three times higher in the Czech Lands than in Slovakia.[3]

Data about the concentration of production and labour are also an indicator of the different levels of the process of industrialization: in 1930 there were 117 manufacturing plants with more than 1,000 employees in the Czech Lands, while in Slovakia and Carpathian Ruthenia together there were only seven plants of this size. In the eastern parts of the republic a great majority of businesses had five or fewer employees.

In a market economy which is not regulated by the state, economic development invariably tends to deepen economic and social differences, since enterprise offers more advantages to economically more advanced areas. The policy of the state organs is thus of particular importance: they should be able to face unrestrained development by choosing and applying the right instruments. In 1918 Czechoslovakia was in great need of equalization, or at least of a lessening of the differences between the economic levels of the individual parts of the republic. This applied not only to Slovakia and the Czech Lands but also to regions inside these. The organs of the state did not, however, try to deal with this key problem systematically, nor did they draft any programme of economic equalization of Slovakia with the Czech Lands.

It was not until the late 1930s that signs began to appear of a more programme-based approach to the economic development of Slovakia. In April 1937 a programme for the economic development of Slovakia, based on the principle of industrialization, and drawn up by an advisory economic organ of the government's Regional Office in Bratislava, was submitted to President Edvard Beneš. A month later the oppositional Communist Party published their 'plan for the economic, social and cultural enhancement of Slovakia'.

The big differences between the two parts of the Czechoslovak Republic were also characteristic of the agricultural sector. Slovakia's conditions for agricultural production were, in general, less favourable, because Slovakia is a more mountainous country than the Czech Lands, its soil is of inferior quality and its climate is more continental. The southern fertile region of Slovakia, however, made it possible to grow thermophile crops such as maize, some kinds of vegetables and fruit, grapes and tobacco. The intensity of agricultural production and the productivity of labour were much lower in Slovakia than in the Czech Lands. In the years 1934–8 (and as far as livestock production was concerned, in 1936) the comparison between Slovakia and the Czech Lands in the productivity of farming was the following (with the Czech Lands equal to 100): yield of cereals per hectare 78; potatoes, 72; and sugar beet, 85; output per hectare of farmland: bread and cereals, 60; potatoes, 54; meat, 30; milk and eggs, 42–3; the number of pigs per comparable acreage of arable land, 62; cattle per comparable acreage of farmland, 59; and the average annual milk yield per cow, 67.

The Czech Lands were far ahead of Slovakia in market orientation and the level of specialization of production, in the development of the food-processing industry and warehousing capacity, in the number of agricultural schools, in the electrification of the country, the quality of the road network, the mechanization of farming and the application of chemicals, in the development of the cooperative system, in the integration of smaller strips of land into large units and in agricultural research.

As far as land ownership was concerned, Slovakia showed greater polarization between large estates and small homesteads farmed by peasants or petty farmers. The rural poor were numerous; they did not own any land and had to rent it, very often under semi-feudal conditions. In Slovakia's mountainous regions, land was partitioned to an unbelievable extent: according to 1931 statistics the average size of each individual plot of land held by a Slovak or Ruthenian peasant or farmer tilling between two and twenty hectares in total equalled 0.4 hectares, which was only slightly more than half the size of plots of land on equally large homesteads in the Czech Lands.

Rural overpopulation was the main cause of the mass emigration which afflicted both Slovakia and the poor rural regions in the Czech Lands. Over one-third of the Slovak nation left Slovakia in the course of several genera-

Table 3.6   The results of the land reform, 1937

Indicator	Agricultural land		Woodland and other land	
	Czech Lands	Slovakia	Czech Lands	Slovakia
Land subject to the reform (in thousand hectares)	758.6	507.2	1,649.0	900.2
Taken over by new acquirers	68.7	63.7	31.9	40.8
Released to original owners	30.2	35.1	60.5	42.6
Deferment of the reform till 1955–67	1.1	1.2	7.6	16.6

Sources: Statistická ročenka Protektorátu Čechy a Morava 1941, p. 165; Dvacet let čs. zemědělství 1918–38 ('Twenty Years of Czechoslovak Agriculture 1918–38'), Prague: 1938, p. 36.

tions. In addition, seasonal jobs, particularly in the Czech Lands, Austria and Germany, were extensively taken up by Slovaks. Emigration declined due to restrictions in the traditional immigration countries during the recession of the 1930s.

The land reform was applied to 29 per cent of the territory of the republic. The severity of this reform which was fully enforced in its first years, 1918–22, was later alleviated and the legal regulations were very often evaded. Although several hundred thousand peasants and farmers were allotted land under the reform, the whole drive nevertheless ended halfway along the road towards its original objectives. It brought great benefits to the 2,291 owners of the newly established farms of average acreage of 100 hectares. The owners of these farms were able to achieve better economic results than the owners of the latifundia surviving from the days of the Habsburg monarchy. Public ownership of forests was greatly extended. Aristocratic owners lost their titles, but a great deal of the land, particularly woodland, which was to have been expropriated in accordance with the regulations of the reform, was left to these owners, who thus continued farming it. The greatest land owner – the Catholic Church – remained virtually untouched by the land reform. The completion of the reform was delayed from the late 1930s until 1955–67. For the total balance of the reform the reader is referred to Table 3.6.

The Slovak share in the macroeconomic indicators did not rise more markedly in the interwar period. Slovakia's share of the total population of the Czechoslovak Republic (excluding Carpathian Ruthenia) was 25.5 per cent, but its share in the creation of national income was estimated at 15 per cent, manufacturing output at 8 per cent, gross agricultural output at 22 per cent (1936) and marketed agricultural output at 16 per cent. The network of railway lines and roads was only half as dense as the network in the Czech Lands and the number of motor vehicles stood at only one-third. The Slovak share of the equity capital of the Czechoslovak Republic amounted to 5 per cent, savings to 7 per cent, and direct tax revenue and turnover tax to 11.5 per cent.[4]

Some progress was recorded in Slovakia in the tertiary sector, thanks partly to investment by the government of the republic. Starting in the early postwar years, construction of public building complexes, telecommunications projects, schools, cultural and health service facilities, spas and the tourist industry infrastructure was increased. As far as transportation was concerned, a considerable number of government capital goods projects were started in Slovakia at that time. Therefore, the network of railway lines was gradually reconstructed, modernized and reoriented in an east-west direction; attention was also paid to the construction of new roads, Danubian harbours and airports. In competition with the Czech Lands, the Slovak economy was handicapped by the high costs of transportation caused by the distance from the Czech market and from the main foreign markets, as well as by the difference between the system of tariffs of the state-owned and the privately owned railways, the latter's share of the transportation services having been higher in Slovakia than in the Czech Lands.

Despite this progress, considerable differences continued to exist between the eastern and the western parts of the republic in the social sphere as well as in their general way of life. Urbanization was advancing very slowly and there were greater contrasts between the level of civilization in towns and the level of civilization in rural areas. Slovakia's rural districts were overpopulated and there were few employment opportunities in these areas and in their surrounding towns. In the Czech Lands both nominal and real wages were higher and the indicators of the consumption of food and manufactured goods, the size and furnishing of homes, and the development of electrification were more favourable. The Czech rural districts were also better served by public transport, medical care and secondary and vocational education. The levels of social security for the sick, the invalid and the aged also differed: in Slovakia the number of the employed entitled to assistance under the social security scheme was markedly lower.

The worldwide depression after 1929 interrupted the upward trend of the economy. The effects of the recession were exceptionally intense and protracted in the Czechoslovak Republic. The output of the manufacturing industry had declined by 40 per cent by the year 1933, the turnover of foreign trade in current prices by 71 per cent, and unemployment had reached about one million. A clear revival did not start until 1936.

The crisis exposed all the backwardness of the structure of industry, which practically dated from as far back as the nineteenth century. In the early 1930s Czechoslovakia not only experienced the effects of the world recession, but was also in need of a solution to the long-term catastrophic structural problems of its economy. Heavy industry was able to recuperate from its decline faster than light industry, and this cannot be attributed only to the new boom of the armaments industry. Light industry, however, particularly the typical exporting branches, was unable to deal with the crisis until 1938. In this forced transformation, accompanied by social and nationalistic turmoil fomented by the economic decline of whole regions of the republic, a new, more progressive structure of industry slowly started to crystallize. In harmony with global development, the centre of gravity of industry began shifting in the direction of heavy industry, particularly steel and iron, the manufacturing industry, the chemicals industry and the electric power industry. Naturally, this trend was mirrored in the changes of the structure of Czechoslovak exports. In the years 1929–37 the share of commodities of the light and the food-processing industries declined from 61 per cent to 43 per cent of total exports, whereas the share of the metallurgy and metal-working industries increased from 15 to 25 per cent.

The crisis hit the industrialized and export-oriented Czech Lands harder than agrarian Slovakia, where, in addition, agriculture was oriented towards consumption in kind. On the other hand, in Slovakia the depression raged in a social environment where living standards had been far from satisfactory before 1929, so that even though the living standard of the Slovak population fell relatively less than the living standard of the Czech population, it proved much more burdensome. This was demonstrated by the sudden increase of pauperism and the extraordinarily large number of evictions and forced sales, which deprived tens of thousands of people of their homes and shelter or farmland.

When the worst period of this depression had passed, signs started to appear of a positive turn in the development of the Slovak economy. The difficult and often painful adjustment to the political changes of 1918 came to an end and Slovakia entered a period of development which was more dynamic than that of the Czech economy. This process of raising the economic level of Slovakia to that of the Czech Lands was then pursued until the 1980s. When this process started in the late 1930s, it so happened that factors which had long been present merged with the specific circumstances of the time. In Slovakia population growth was more rapid than in the Czech Lands, its demographic structure was more favourable and the upcoming younger generation had already enjoyed education of a higher quality. Marked progress could be recorded in the formation of the Slovak middle classes and entrepreneurial circles. Higher investment was financed from both public and private funds. At this time Hitler's Germany was intensifying its aggressive stance and the construction of heavy-arms factories had started in north-western Slovakia, an area considered to be the least vulnerable part of the Czechoslovak Republic in the case of a military conflict. The construction of new railway lines, roads and belts of fortifications along the Hungarian border was accelerated. Intending to take advantage of the low wages paid in Slovakia, the Baťa conglomerate started building plants in the eastern part of the republic.

The overall economic situation, however, was determined by the economic development of the Czech Lands, which was far from favourable despite the existing armaments boom. This was also shown by the loss of position that the Czechoslovak Republic suffered on a worldwide scale. The index of world manufacturing production (excluding the USSR) was 4 per cent higher in 1937 than in 1929, but in the Czechoslovak Republic the index of manufacturing production was 4 per cent lower. The index of overall European exports (with 1928 equal to 100) stood at 76 points, while that of Czechoslovakia was only 67. In the years 1928–38 the Czechoslovak share of total world exports declined from 1.9 to 1.6 per cent and of European exports from 4.2 to 3.6 per cent. The position of the Czechoslovak Republic was also weakened as far as most of the indicators of agricultural production are concerned.

The economic problems of the 1930s led to much keener competition between various groups of capital (agrarian capital, export industry, armament) and to an escalation of social conflicts, which were very often intensified by nationalistic ideas. Decentralizing tendencies, externally encouraged, were growing. The adverse economic development thus contributed to the destabilization of the Czechoslovak Republic at a time when the republic was facing a grave external threat.

In spite of the fact that Czechoslovakia's position in the European economy was weakened in the 1930s, the country managed to retain its former place on the divide between rich western and northern Europe and the poorer eastern and southern parts of the European continent, thanks to its economic level and the real income of the population. It could even be claimed that the dividing line crossed the territory of the Czechoslovak Republic following the border between the Czech Lands and Slovakia. According to a retrospective statistical analysis published by the United Nations Organization, in 1938 Czechoslovakia ranked 14th among European countries in the volume of national income per capita.[5] Outside Europe there were at least four countries ahead of Czechoslovakia: the United States of America, Canada, Australia and New Zealand. In the countries of north-western Europe (the United Kingdom, Ireland, Sweden, Norway and Denmark) national income per capita was 106 per cent higher than in Czechoslovakia, and in western Europe (Germany, France, Switzerland, the Netherlands, Belgium and Luxembourg) it was 71 per cent higher.

Austria and Finland had only a negligible lead over Czechoslovakia, while in Italy this indicator was 28 per cent, in Hungary 36 per cent, in Poland 42 per cent, and in Bulgaria 61 per cent lower than in Czechoslovakia.

The Period 1938–45

Despite the economic decline of the 1930s, Czechoslovakia recorded clearly identifiable economic expansion and social and cultural development in the course of the twenty years of its independence. The 1937 indicators were considerably higher than those from the most prosperous prewar year, 1913. Judged on their legislative quality and the level of their actual effectiveness, the social security and the democratic rights of the population were of a higher standard than those in the neighbouring countries with fascist and authoritarian regimes. In the Czechoslovak Republic, however, there were still large differences in both the economic sphere and the standard of living. This situation incited growing discontent in Slovakia and criticism was directed against the recognition of the position of the Slovaks in the Czechoslovak Republic. One of the internal consequences of the Munich dictate forced on Czechoslovakia by the European powers was the legalization of the existing Slovak centrifugal tendencies by the establishment and recognition of an autonomous Slovak government with Hlinka's Slovak People's Party at its head. This was soon followed by the appointment of an autonomous government in Carpathian Ruthenia (which was renamed Carpathian Ukraine).

In autumn 1938 and mid-March 1939 Czechoslovakia twice fell victim to the aggressive policy of fascism and was divided up. After the borderlands had been annexed to Germany, Hungary and Poland, the German army occupied the inner territory of the Czech Lands, and the so-called Protectorate of Bohemia and Moravia was established there. In Slovakia a state with a puppet government was immediately founded, fully controlled by Germany, and Carpathian Ruthenia was annexed to Hungary.

The loss of the borderlands in autumn 1938 reduced the territory and population of the Czechoslovak Republic by 30 per cent and one-third respectively. Czechs, Slovaks and Ukrainians remained behind the new borders. The new frontiers were deliberately marked out so that they would sever the main arteries of transport and make any future military resistance ineffectual. The regions separated from the former Czechoslovak Republic contained more than two-fifths of the industrial capacity of the country, complexes of the Czech borderland forests and the agricultural lands of Slovakia in the south of the country. Germany gained a considerable part of Czechoslovak rolling stock and gold reserves. The new political situation of the states of central Europe also stimulated considerable capital transfers. West European capital started flowing out of the Czechoslovak Republic, as did a large amount of Jewish capital assets; Czech and Slovak capital was gradually forced out of the separated borderland regions.

The alignment of Czechoslovakia with Germany led to disintegrating tendencies in the economy of the country. This was particularly indicated by weakening economic relations between the Protectorate of Bohemia and Moravia and Slovakia, and between the newly established Slovak state and the territories occupied by Hungary. On the other hand, the individual parts of Czechoslovakia were being forcibly integrated into the Nazi 'great economic space' (*Grossraumwirtschaft*) by both economic means, and political and military pressure. The Czech Lands were viewed as part of the industrial core of the forcibly integrated European economy and they thus became one of the arsenals of the German Reich. The role of Slovakia as the agrarian rear, producing raw materials, is testified to by the protocol concerning economic and financial cooperation between Germany and Slovakia, signed in 1939.[6] Germany took possession of Slovakia's mineral resources, undertook extensive geological prospecting, won control of agricultural production, timber mining, the system of transportation and exports. The manufacturing industry was to develop in harmony with German needs and the Reichsbank in Berlin was to 'cooperate and partici-pate in any important decisions' taken by the National Bank of Slovakia.

The events of 1938–9 led to a discontinuity of Czechoslovak economic development, which was more marked in the Protectorate of Bohemia and Moravia and the Czech borderlands than in Slovakia. The system of a controlled war economy changed the whole operating mechanism of the economy and considerably strengthened the role of the state. In March 1939 the German mark was put into circulation in the protectorate as legal tender alongside the Czech koruna, and in 1940 customs duties were abolished on the frontiers between the Protectorate of Bohemia and Moravia and the German Reich. The militarization of the economy resulted in the imposi-tion of a restraint on civilian production and in an unusual expansion of any production essential for waging war. In 1945, 54 per cent of the popula-tion of the protectorate working in the manufacturing industry were employed in metallurgy and the metal-working industries, while only 25 per cent of the working population were engaged in light industry. In the aircraft industry alone there were 141,000 employees in 135 plants in the Czech Lands, including the borderlands, at the beginning of 1945. Despite the mobilization of hundreds of thousands of people, industrial production had risen only by 18 per cent by 1944 compared with 1939, with the produc-tivity of labour showing a marked decline.

The Germanization of the economy, part of which consisted in the so-called Aryanization (i.e. the liquidation) of the non-Aryan population and in privileges given to the so-called Nordic race, also caused discontinuity in the sphere of property ownership. However, the discontinuation of the long-term developmental tendencies manifested itself in other spheres too: in the application of a number of methods of exploitation of the Czech economy, the reorientation of external economic relations, the restructuralization of plant production and exports, the inflationary development of the Czech money supply and the one-sided orientation of and limitations on investment. Great changes affected the social sphere as well: for example, curtailment of democratic rights; forced labour; the extension of working hours; state-controlled deployment of labour, including the mobilization of young people for work in Germany and in the Czech armaments industry; the regulation of prices and wages; and the lowering and levelling of consumption through a system of rationing.

The Germanization of 'the whole region and population', which was to have destroyed the Czech nation by making it German, evacuating and partly also liquidating it physically, was an important feature of Nazi policy. The gravity of this menace is testified to by the annihilation of the Jewish and Romany populations in concentration camps and the terror that was unleashed against the Czechs during the German occupation.

Czech society at this time was characterized by a decline of social mobility. All Czech universities and tertiary colleges were closed in autumn 1939, and the network of secondary and vocational schools was greatly reduced, resulting in an interruption of the reproduction of skilled and qualified labour. Whole groups of the population were persecuted or forbidden to continue their occupations. This applied to the politicians active during the period of the pre-Munich Czechoslovak Republic, officers of the Czechoslovak army, diplomats, university lecturers and professors, workers in research and cultural institutes, etc. The Czech monied class of businessmen was weakened both in number and also as far as the disposability of their capital was concerned. Small tradesmen's businesses and carrier and training firms were forcibly closed in several waves. A large number of workers and technicians were hit by the loss of their qualifications. The patterns of factory teams changed radically because the original staff was replaced with people from outside the working classes, housewives and school-leavers. The Czech population was evicted from 293 villages and towns. One hundred thousand Czechs were assigned to manual work in Germany – at first in the building industry and on large farming estates, later mostly in the armaments industry and semi-military organizations such as the *Technische Nothilfe*, *Todt Organisation*, and *Luftschutz*.

In Slovakia the features of disruption of the development of the economy and of the structure of society were less pronounced. The Nazis formally recognized the sovereignty of the Slovak Republic and only decided to occupy Slovakia as late as 1944. At first, the regime of the new state was able to lean on a relatively wide social base, whereas in the Czech Lands there existed clear-cut antagonism between the Czech population and the occupiers from the moment the Nazis invaded the country. German capital, which controlled key positions in the Slovak economy, did not deny the Slovak entrepreneurial class the possibility of prospering economically. This fact was also greatly contributed to by Aryanization, which confiscated smaller Jewish businesses as well as Jewish-owned land into the hands of Aryanizers of Slovak nationality. (In the Protectorate of Bohemia and Moravia this property was placed in German hands.)

In Slovakia, the controlled war economy was introduced at a much slower pace and was not as complete as in the Czech Lands. Customs duties continued to be collected at the frontiers with Germany, and the German mark did not become legal tender in Slovakia. The development of agricultural production was unsatisfactory, but the manufacturing industry experienced a wartime boom. However, militarization led not to a decline in production in the civilian branches of industry, but to differentiated growth in all the important branches of industry. In 1943 the total output of the manufacturing industry was 63 per cent higher than in 1937, nearly 50 per cent of which could be attributed to Slovak industry in the period of the Slovak Republic. The main causes of the rise of industrial production may be seen to lie in the decline of Czech competition, growing German demand (even for minerals of inferior quality), the completion of the construction of Slovak plants started before the separation of Slovakia from the Czech Lands and the increase in demand caused by rising inflation. The supply of foodstuffs and agricultural produce was much more plentiful in agrarian Slovakia than in the Czech Lands, the rate of employment was rising and people were sent to work in Germany on a more or less voluntary basis.

Even though the economic problems of Slovakia slowly became more acute and the social situation of the population deteriorated, the main causes of the imminent crisis of the Slovak regime should nevertheless be sought in non-economic factors: in the fact that the country was being dragged into an extremely unpopular war on the side of Hitler's Germany; in the gradual curtailment of the democratic rights of the population and the clerical-fascist methods of the government; in the hostile attitude towards a growing number of groups of the population; in the government's failure to fulfil the pledges of a new land reform and other social measures; in the deepening social polarization caused by the rise of a monied class of upstarts and political timeservers; in the newly confirmed privileges of the Catholic Church; and in the moral decay of the ruling politicians.

In August 1944 the internal crisis of the Slovak state resulted in the Slovak National Uprising, in which the Slovaks demonstrated their desire to re-establish the joint state with the Czechs. In its demands the programme of the Slovak National Uprising anticipated the revolutionary transformation of 1945. Armed anti-fascist struggle flared up in large parts of the country, disrupted the logistical rear of the German eastern front and tied up considerable forces of the German army. The Slovak National Uprising paralysed German efforts to scale up armaments production in Slovakia and also managed to reduce German exploitation of the country in the final period of the war.

Due to their geographic position the Czech Lands were the last of the countries occupied by Germany to be liberated. The May 1945 uprising of the Czech population coincided with the last days of the Second World War on the European continent.

During its occupation by fascist Germany Czechoslovakia suffered a great loss of human lives and was also greatly damaged materially. The terror and the war claimed about 360,000 victims, and imprisonment and the hardships of war destroyed the health of further hundreds of thousands of people.

Czechoslovakia lost the greater part of its gold and foreign exchange reserves, huge debts were frozen in Germany, and the currency and savings of the population were devalued by inflation. After the war the total damage caused to Czechoslovakia by the Second World War was estimated at about 347.5 billion Czechoslovak koruna, which corresponded to Czechoslovak national income for the years 1932–7.

The Period 1945–8

After the defeat of Germany and the restoration of the joint state of Czechs and Slovaks in spring 1945, two trends of economic development of the country became clear. Firstly, there were efforts to deal with the pressing problems linked with the fateful division of the state, the war and fascist exploitation: ensuring the subsistence of the population, reconstructing transportation, speeding up coal mining, unifying the currency, overcoming inflation, and rebuilding factories, residential blocks and houses destroyed by the war. The currency reform, aimed at blocking superfluous currency in non-interest bearing accounts, was put into effect in November 1945. The transformation of the controlled war economy, which was intended to bring it into harmony with reality, and the conversion of the armaments industry were given full priority. Economic relations with other countries were re-established and extended within a surprisingly short period of time. Complex problems arose in the legislative sphere as well as in the application of the government's economic policy to the problem of the re-integration of the individual parts of the Czechoslovak Republic, which had been split up in 1938–9 and had then developed quite differently. Millions of people were affected by internal migration accompanied by radical changes in the sectoral and regional deployment of labour (namely the repatriation of prisoners and of the part of the population assigned to work in Germany; the re-emigration of Czechoslovak nationals from a number of countries; the transfer of the greater part of the German minority; the return of those affected by the events of 1938–9 to their original homes; an influx of new settlers into the Czech borderlands; the extensive fluctuation of the workforce after the abolition of forced labour; and the liberalization of state regulation of the labour market).

The other trend of economic policy reflected the revolutionary situation of the time. The population that had lived through a 15-year economic recession with all its pernicious social and political effects – the breakdown of Czechoslovak foreign policy at the time of the Munich agreement, the loss of independence, the horrors of war and the fascist oppression which had threatened the very existence of the Czech and Slovak nations – overwhelmingly rejected the idea of continuing with the prewar economic and political system and sought a solution either in far-reaching reform or a radical and revolutionary renewal of society. The revolutionary trend of economic policy can be briefly characterized by four revolutionary slogans: the confiscation of the property of the enemies of the country and their collaborators; the nationalization of capitalist big business, banking and insurance; land reform; and the transition to economic planning. The transfer of the German minority, which was effected in a similar way in Poland and in Hungary, in accordance with the resolution of the Allies at the Potsdam Conference, required additional steps as far as the economic policy of the country was concerned.

The transformation of ownership in the early postwar years was based on President Beneš's decrees; later on, the rules of this transformation were enacted by the National Assembly of the Czechoslovak Republic – the Czechoslovak parliament. The enforcement of these new acts of the National Assembly, however, reflected the specific characteristics of the two parts of the state. The nationalization of big business, large manufacturing enterprises, banking and insurance companies in October 1945 was more radical and comprehensive in the Czech Lands, where big business was traditionally more widespread and financial capital more concentrated. The result was that the public sector acquired a relatively stronger position in the Czech Lands than in Slovakia. The problems of confiscation of the property of the 'enemies of the state' and their collaborators were also more acute in the Czech Lands, and the same is true of the changes in the resettlement of the borderlands.

Land reform was launched in 1945. During the first stage the criterion for confiscation of land was not the size of the privately owned land but the owner's activity at the time of the occupation of the country by Nazi Germany. This applied primarily to the land owned by Germans along the Czech border, which was confiscated and allotted mostly to private individuals. Confiscation also applied to the land owned by Hungarians, but because the peace conference with Hungary had not adopted the motion that the Hungarian minority be transferred, most Hungarian peasants were given their land back (and their farming of that land should be regarded as continuous). In view of the fact that the acreage of the land confiscated from Czech and Slovak nationals was far less extensive, this stage of the land reform did not contribute to the reduction of rural overpopulation in Slovakia, while in the poorer foothill regions of the Czech borderlands there was an acute workforce shortage. Numerous settlers coming from Slovakia were thus able to find work in these parts of the Czech Lands, and not exclusively in farming.

The limited extent of the initial stage of the land reform fomented discontent in the Slovak rural regions and pressure was increasingly brought to bear to launch a reform that would substantially curb the ownership of large areas of land by individuals. The second stage of the land reform became part of the programme of the government put in office by the general election in May 1946; it was enacted in 1947 and enforced mainly in 1948. This stage was aimed at completing the prewar land reform by the strict and full enforcement of the acts of the Czechoslovak parliament of the years 1919–21. It concentrated particularly on the land owned by the one-time aristocracy and the Catholic Church, and it considerably raised the number of those farmers and the poor rural population who received land. Woodland was exempted from transfer to private ownership: it mostly remained publicly owned and it was cultivated by state farms, village authorities or cooperatives.

The great extent and application of the two stages of the land reform is fully testified to by the fact that a change of ownership was effected for approximately four million hectares of farmland and woodland, i.e. 31 per cent of the territory of the country. This acreage does not include the land given back to the original Hungarian peasants.

In the course of 1946, when the general election strengthened the position of the Communist Party, except in Slovakia where it brought a sweeping victory for the Democratic Party, the centre of gravity of economic policy shifted towards the preparation of a two-year plan of economic development, the implementation of which was to have brought the postwar economy to the 1937 level. This two-year plan was not, however, as directive and detailed as the later five-year and annual plans, and it did not encompass all branches of the economy. In the years 1947–8 the Czechoslovak government intervened in the economy of the country and it stimulated interest in the fulfilment of the plan by using prevailingly economic instruments.

One of the aims of the plan for 1947–8 was to embark upon the accelerated industrialization of Slovakia and the less developed Czech regions. This process began with a transfer of industrial plants from the over-industrialized regions of the Czech borderlands where there was a shortage of labour. Three hundred and thirty-seven plants were moved to Slovakia to provide it with 24,000 additional jobs. At the end of 1948 these plants accounted for 13 per cent of the total number of jobs in the Slovak manufacturing industry.

The policy of the industrialization of Slovakia began very soon after the re-establishment of the joint state of Czechs and Slovaks. It was supported – though the reasons for support may have been rather different – by all the political parties in Slovakia and in the Czech Lands, particularly by the Communist Party and the Social Democrat Party. The Communist Party of Slovakia declared industrialization the platform of its economic policy and the congress of the Communist Party of Czechoslovakia held in March 1946 emphasized the importance of the industrialization of Slovakia as a road leading to the equalization of the economic levels of the two parts of the republic and as a way of strengthening the unity of the state. The acceleration of the development of the Slovak economy was also high on the list of priorities of the long-term economic policy of the government which came to power in 1947. This is testified to by the documents issued by the government and the plans for the development of the national economy of the Czechoslovak Republic.

In view of the weakness of the Slovak economy and the absence of foreign capital, the success of the programme of industrialization depended to a great extent on whether the required part of the financial and material resources of Czech provenance would be transferred to Slovakia. This problem first became the subject of nationalist debate on the occasion of the transfer of a part of industrial capacity from the Czech borderlands to Slovakia. It may be interesting to note that the main clash of ideas occurred in the years 1945–6 between the National Socialist Party in the Czech Lands and the Democratic Party in Slovakia, i.e. between parties that later established close collaboration. The National Socialists did not agree that the economic potential of the Czech Lands should be weakened for the benefit of Slovakia, and instead of the transfer of industrial plants from the Czech Lands to Slovakia they proposed increasing the influx of labour from

Table 3.7   Basic indicators of the economic rise of Slovakia to the level of the Czech Lands, 1948–89

Indicator	1948	1960	1970	1980	1989
Share of Slovakia in the totals of Czechoslovakia (in per cent)					
Population	29.7	29.3	31.6	32.6	33.7
Workforce (excluding trainees)	27.5	25.9	28.4	30.8	31.6
National income created[a]	19.2	23.5	26.7	29.1	30.9
National income used	21.5	25.6	29.5	31.2	32.0
Capital construction[b]	30.3	30.7	32.7	33.8	34.4
Industrial output[c]	13.5	18.9	24.2	29.0	30.0
Agricultural output[d]	29.3	30.8	31.3	32.2	32.3
Retail trade turned	19.8[e]	24.0	27.8	30.5	31.1
Personal consumption by population	23.9	25.4	28.3	30.6	31.8
Material costs of non-material branches	18.6	22.7	26.5	28.5	30.2
The level of Slovakia correlated with the Czech Lands (Czech Lands = 100)					
National income created[a] per inhabitant	61.2	74.4	78.8	85.2	85.7
per active member of the workforce	58.9	87.2	91.2	92.1	95.1
National income used per inhabitant	70.9	83.1	90.7	94.1	92.4
Personal consumption per inhabitant	81.0	82.3	85.5	91.4	91.6
Fixed assets in the material sphere					
per worker	57.9	80.2	85.8	95.1	98.3
Fixed assets in the non-material sphere					
per inhabitant	53.3	64.3	70.8	80.8	82.6
Industrial output[c] per inhabitant	48.4	64.5	76.6	89.0	89.0
per worker in industry	95.4	107.3	106.1	108.3	109.8
Agricultural output					
per inhabitant	98.7	109.4	100.3	99.3	94.6
per worker in agriculture	59.4	65.5	74.8	77.8	79.5
per hectare of agricultural land	69.8	74.0	77.2	82.0	83.7
Average monthly wages	91.6	96.7	98.2	98.3	98.5
Share of workforce in the total number of population (in per cent)					
Czech Lands	44.8	46.1	50.7	49.8	52.1
Slovakia	43.9	38.9	43.2	45.7	47.3

Notes:
[a] Excluding foreign trade.
[b] Periods: 1948, averages 1951–60, 1961–70, 1971–80, 1985–9.
[c] Gross industrial output.
[d] Gross agricultural output. Periods: 1948, averages 1956–60, 1965–70, 1976–80, 1985–9.
[e] 1949.

Sources: Historická statistická ročenka ČSSR ('Historical Statistical Yearbook of the CSSR'), Prague: 1985; statistical yearbooks of the CSFR, 1991, 1992, on various pages. Mostly calculated from absolute data.

Slovakia to the Czech Lands. Naturally, the Slovak Democratic Party was opposed to this proposal; it stressed the idea of moving plants towards the pools of labour regardless of any economic logic and ignored the partial drawbacks that sometimes accompanied the territorial transfer of industrial plants.

The comparison of data from 1937 with those relative to the final year of the two-year plan (1948) reveals that the Czech Lands had more or less reached the prewar level of industrial output, whereas in Slovakia output had nearly doubled. This contrast cannot be accounted for only by the different rates of growth of the manufacturing industry in the period of the two-year plan, but also by the relatively higher initial state of the manufacturing industry in Slovakia – the result of the expansion of Slovak industrial capacity during the war. If these data are calculated per capita, the difference between the two parts of the country was less marked in 1948, because the population of the Czech Lands had declined by nearly one-fifth. The prewar level of agricultural production had not been reached by 1948, but Slovakia was closer to it than the Czech Lands were.

For the correlation between the various macroeconomic indicators relating to the Czech Lands and Slovakia during the period of the start of 'socialist industrialization', the reader is referred to Table 3.7.

It can be seen that Slovakia's share of the population and labour in the republic's totals was substantially higher than its share of the creation of national income, manufacturing production and fixed assets. Calculated per capita, in 1948 Slovakia reached 61 per cent of the level of the Czech Lands in the creation of national income, 48 per cent in manufacturing production, 105 per cent in agriculture and 109 per cent in capital goods construction. In the effectiveness of labour the figures were 95 per cent for the manufacturing industry and 59 per cent for agriculture; in the intensity of farming measured by the value of the output per hectare of farmland, Slovakia's level equalled approximately 70 per cent of that of the Czech Lands.

In the course of 1947 the internal political situation of the Czechoslovak Republic changed. Cooperation between the ruling political parties was slowly reaching an impasse and new conflicts arose continuously. Soviet pressure forced the Czechoslovak government to refuse the offer to participate in the Marshall Plan. In the autumn crisis the Slovak communists managed to gain most of the top positions in local government in defiance of the election results of 1946. The economic demands of the Communist Party of Czechoslovakia were stepped up. The communists were pushing for further stages of the land reform. They were able to enforce a limit on the legal private ownership of land of only 50 hectares, a one-off payment by the monied classes of the population and, at the beginning of 1948, further nationalization. The internal political scene reflected contemporary international development which was approaching the Cold War and the division of the world into two hostile blocs. The control of the Soviet Union over a number of the countries of central and south-eastern Europe was being reinforced and the real chance of an 'independent road to socialism' was dwindling.

The February 1948 solution to the problem of political hegemony was also a landmark in the economic policy of the country. In spring 1948 a new wave of ownership changeovers swept the country: large manorial estates and medium-sized private business were nationalized, and private enterprise was forbidden in a number of branches of the manufacturing industry, wholesale trade, foreign trade and public transport. By the end of 1948 there was only a negligible number of private businesses with more than 20 employees left in Czechoslovakia, although the constitution of the republic had fixed a limit of 50.

In social policy, an important reform was introduced in 1948: the introduction of 'national insurance', which extended health insurance, old-age insurance and disability insurance to peasants, farmers, tradesmen and other self-employed people. On account of different social patterns, this reform affected a substantially greater percentage of people in Slovakia than in the Czech Lands, where the large class of wage-earners had already enjoyed the benefits of a system of social insurance for longer.

The Period 1949–89

The changeover from a pluralistic system to the monopoly of power of the Communist Party had a marked effect on how economic and social policy was to be shaped, namely in accordance with the decisions of a narrow circle of the leading representatives of the Communist Party of Czecho-slovakia (who also held high government posts). With the declaration of the dictatorship of the proletariat certain classes of the working population (particularly those employed in heavy industry) were granted various privileges. Another effect of this policy was the transfer of a considerable number of workers into posts in public administration and the armed forces. Also, thousands of young workers began attending various courses at secondary and vocational schools, and at universities. In addition, central administration and top management were cleared of both 'bourgeois specialists' and those communists who were critical of some economic policy measures. The ensuing emigration of specialists and experts in economics and technology resulted in a considerable loss of expertise.

The change of Soviet policy towards Yugoslavia and the campaign directed against Yugoslav communism strengthened the tendency in the

Communist Party of Czechoslovakia which favoured mechanically copying the Soviet experience of the construction of socialism. The reorientation of economic policy and the whole conception of the construction of socialism in Czechoslovakia manifested itself in the suppressive measures inflicted upon small-scale enterprise and in a sudden change in the attitude towards the middle classes in 1948–9. The Communist Party of Czechoslovakia's earlier idea of the long-term coexistence of small-scale private production and other types of small business alongside the public sector was abolished by the declaration of the policy of the accelerated socialization of small-scale farming and small tradesmen's businesses. According to the Soviet doctrine which began to be applied, the aim of the period of transition from capitalism to socialism was to restructure the multi-sector economy into a single-sector economy with an exclusive socialist sector in a state or cooperative form. This theory advocated eliminating both the capitalist sector and any small-scale private enterprise; only the private ownership of personal property was permitted to continue, and, in agriculture, the ownership of a limited amount of private farmland by the members of agricultural cooperatives.

Over several years after February 1948 the Soviet method of industrialization was applied to the Czechoslovak economy and the Soviet system of planning was gradually introduced (in its full extent from 1 January 1953 onwards) with the absolute control of the national economy suppressing the market mechanism. The participation of the working collectives and the trade unions in the management of nationalized companies was considerably reduced. In the case of private enterprise, the Soviet method of cost accounting under the name *khozraschet* was copied slavishly, instead of any efforts being made to develop the existing Czechoslovak system of business management based on the progressive principles of organization of the foremost Czechoslovak enterprises of the past.

The process of the centralization of management involved limiting the powers of the Slovak national organs in favour of the Prague-based centre. This process also hit the Communist Party of Czechoslovakia itself, where the autonomous position of the Slovak communists was greatly weakened. Opponents of the drive aimed at curtailing the authority of the Slovak national organs of power as defined by the Košice Government Programme of April 1945 and by the 1948 constitution were accused of 'bourgeois nationalism', and a number of them were framed and convicted on fabricated charges in sham trials at the start of the 1950s.

The period of the first five-year plan (1949–53) was a turning point in the postwar development of the Czechoslovak Republic. The five-year plan was approved in October 1948 and in its original form it constituted a fairly realistic project of further economic development. The structural policy mirrored the then prevailing global trends while taking full account of the specific Czechoslovak conditions; it did not envisage any departure from a market economy or the policy concerning the peasants, farmers and tradesmen, or any abrupt and radical change in the orientation of foreign economic policy. From the beginning of the 1950s, however, its aims were drastically altered.

A curb on the large-scale ownership of private property was characteristic of the years 1945–8, and this trend was continued as the five-year plan was put into effect, resulting in the formation of a qualitatively different profile of the whole national economy. Its rise was linked with the adoption of the Soviet model and the era of Stalinism, but also with the period of the most acute tension between the East and the West. Czechoslovakia, situated in exposed central Europe on the divide between the two hostile blocs, was particularly severely hit by the Cold War. The profile of the economy which had been formed in the period of the intensifying Cold War was later altered to suit the changing conditions and continued in this form until the late 1980s. Its principal features can be characterized as follows:

- State control of the economy and the absolute exclusion of private enterprise.
- Centralization of control; directive and detailed planning of all the sectors of the national economy; suppression of the market mechanism; prioritization of the speed of results at the expense of quality and effectiveness.
- Long-term internal economic disequilibrium.
- Prioritization of heavy industry and a slow rate of growth of the tertiary sector.
- A structure of industry making excessive demands as far as raw materials, energy, investment, transportation and imports were concerned.
- Mitigation of regional differences in both the economic level and the standard of living of the population as well as those concerning the branch, social and occupational structure of the population.
- One-sided orientation of external economic relations towards the Soviet Union and the other member-states of the Council for Mutual Economic Assistance.
- In social policy, progressive legislative measures exceeding the economic possibilities of the country.
- Solving the problems of unemployment and agrarian overpopulation; a high rate of employment of both male and female labour.
- The levelling of wages and salaries, thus removing any material incentives and interest of the workers in upgrading and extending their qualifications.

With management highly centralized and directive, the organs of state administration were easily able to push through the aims of their economic policy formulated in the period of the heightening Cold War. The concentration of resources and their cross-allocation in accordance with certain priorities served as an instrument for financing large capital goods projects, restructuring the manufacturing industry, increasing the output of the armaments industry, furthering regional development and alleviating the effect of the economic blockade practised by the West in a situation where, in 1946–7, foreign trade turnover with the future member-countries of the Council for Mutual Economic Assistance (COMECON) had accounted for less than 20 per cent. (By 1953 this share had already been reversed, with foreign trade turnover with the countries of the Soviet bloc rising to 80 per cent.)

With Europe politically divided between two blocs, the Czechoslovak Republic was aligned with a bloc whose average economic level and standard of living were considerably lower. As the industrially most advanced COMECON member (with the German Democratic Republic busy completing its postwar reconstruction), the Czechoslovak Republic won extensive stable outlets for its products and as a reliable rear supplying it with foodstuffs, and gradually also imported raw materials. On the other hand, under Stalinism the logic of development resulted in a complete disregard for the specific characteristics of Czechoslovak society and of the economy, in an ineffective utilization of resources, an underrating of the qualitative aspects of economic development and an increasing technological gap between Czechoslovakia and the economically advanced countries of the world.

As far as the position of the Czechoslovak Republic and the implementation of its economic policy were concerned, partial differences appeared between the Czech and the Slovak parts of the country. For instance, the agricultural output of the prewar period was exceeded in Slovakia as early as 1949, whereas in the Czech Lands this was achieved as late as the 1960s. In Slovakia collectivization of agriculture was effected at a slower pace than in the Czech Lands. In 1960, when the process of mass collectivization of agriculture had nearly been completed in the western part of the republic, in the Czech Lands the private sector still accounted for 7 per cent of farmland and 12 per cent of those employed in agriculture, whereas in Slovakia these figures were 19 per cent and one-third respectively. In Slovakia, collectivization was completed as late as the 1970s.

These differences can be attributed to the fact that Slovak agriculture was to a great extent of the foothill type, thus not so suitable to large-scale production. A more intensive resistance of the peasants to forced collectivization in some parts of Slovakia may also have had an effect. This is testified to by the fact that in the period of the partial liberalization of agricultural policy after 1953 most of the agricultural cooperatives in north-eastern Slovakia broke up. In Slovakia, farming on private plots allotted to and tilled by cooperative farmers was relatively more extensive than in the Czech Lands. Its share, however, was much lower than in the Soviet Union. One of the driving motives behind the accelerated collectivization of agriculture was the recruitment of labour for the industrialization process. This resulted in a considerable alleviation of the burden of rural overpopulation in Slovakia. The drain of labour from agriculture reached its climax in the 1950s – in two waves, interrupted in the years 1954–5 by a short-term shift of the country's economic priorities in favour of agriculture after Stalin's death. In the years 1949–60 Czechoslovak agriculture lost 770,000 labourers; in the Czech Lands the agricultural workforce declined by 32 per cent, in Slovakia by 39 per cent.

From the mid-1960s onward agricultural production was on a long-term rise and agriculture changed from an economic bottleneck into a stabilizing factor of the Czechoslovak economy. Agricultural enterprises were able to achieve good economic results; the adverse development of the age structure of agricultural labour was stopped and a large part of skilled and fully qualified labour took up jobs in both farming and the management of the cooperative or state farms. In the 1980s domestic production was able to cover 95–100 per cent of the relatively high consumption of agricultural produce grown in the climatic conditions of central Europe, even with a relatively low acreage of land per capita. Czechoslovakia ranked among the countries with the smallest differences between urban and rural districts in some indicators; for example, in the case of the level of income in agriculture compared with the level of income in the manufacturing industry, or the extent of individual housing construction and the average floorage of homes, the rural districts were able to catch up with the urban districts. Considerable differences between the individual agricultural enterprises still survived, however, as far as the organizational level and effectiveness of production were concerned. In the 1970s and 1980s, cooperative farms achieved better aggregate results than state farms.

The long-range priorities of economic policy also included the industrialization of Slovakia as a basis for a gradual raising of its economic level to the level of the Czech Lands and the mutual approximation of the economic structures and the standards of living in the two parts of the republic. At its beginnings industrialization principally involved the construction of new plants rather than the modernization of existing enterprises. Branches of heavy industry were given high priority, particularly the engineering industry, the armaments industry, the chemicals industry and the hydroelectricity generating industry. The orientation was mostly towards medium-sized enterprises and very often also towards so-called 'social investment', i.e. investment that contributed to the acceleration of the development of the most backward regions but which did not take account of the criteria of effectiveness, not to mention the problems of skilled and qualified labour and transportation. In the early 1960s Slovak economists began to protest about the orientation of the industrialization which had resulted in the atomization of the manufacturing industry rather than in the construction of big centres of industry. The manufacturing industry was overly oriented towards final production and it was mostly discharging the function of a cooperative hinterland for Czech enterprises.

The decisive part of investment was at first directed to central and western Slovakia. After 1957, when work on the conception of the long-term development of the Slovak economy was completed, eastern Slovakia, the economically most backward part of Slovakia, began to receive ever increasing attention. A large metallurgical combine was built near Košice and a number of new engineering plants followed. At that time a considerable amount of Czechoslovak investment went into the Slovak chemicals industry, and the first nuclear power station in Czechoslovakia was also located in Slovakia. From the late 1960s onward, new construction started receding into the background and the development of the manufacturing industry aimed at continually raising the existing potential.

Slovakia thus had a more complete structure of industry than in the interwar period. Some of the traditional structural characteristics of the two parts of the Czechoslovak Republic still survived, but new ones also appeared. In the 1950s, Slovakia accounted for a relatively large share of the republic's non-ferrous metallurgy, the output of the building materials and chemicals industries, the electrotechnical industry, the armaments industry, and the wood-working, paper, pulp and ready-made clothing industries.

The industrialization of Slovakia and the development of some other branches were supported by a transfer of funds from the Czech Lands. This was made possible by centralized decision-making and the directive system of planning. From Table 3.7 it can be seen that Slovakia's share in the creation of national income at no period matched its expenditure in both personal consumption and in investment. The noteworthy mutual reduction of differences between the economic levels and structures of the two parts of the Czechoslovak Republic can be made even more impressive by a comparison with the surviving deep economic differences between the individual republics of the then Soviet Union and Yugoslavia. (For instance, in Yugoslavia in the late 1980s national income per capita was seven times higher in Slovenia than in Kosovo.)

A more precise quantification of the cross-allocation of funds between regions is a very difficult (if not absolutely impossible) task in a centrally planned economy. It has become the subject of well-intended analyses, but also of nationalistic polemic. If we consider the differences between the creation and the use of national income in the two parts of the republic, use prevailed permanently over creation in Slovakia, whereas in the Czech Lands it was quite the reverse, except for the period when the country had accrued foreign debts. By using the differences between these two indicators as a basis we can estimate that 2.5–5 per cent of the national income created in the Czech Lands was allocated to Slovakia in various periods. The Czech economist, A. Bálek, arrived at this conclusion, stating that in the years 1950–90 Slovak national income used was nearly 11 per cent higher than the national income created in Slovakia, which must have slowed the economic development of the Czech Lands.[7]

Some Slovak economists consider that the creation of Slovak national income has been rather understated statistically because the output of a number of the republic's enterprises, the majority of which had their headquarters in the Czech Lands, were included in the statistics for the Czech Lands, where the finalization of the process of production and the ensuing export operations were effected. The same argument applies to the prices of agricultural produce and the output of raw materials, branches of industry where Slovakia's share was relatively large, as well as to the deliveries of subcontracted products for Czech enterprises effected by Slovak enterprises, towards which the Slovak manufacturing industry was primarily oriented. The creation of income in the Czech Lands was contributed to by a substantially greater number of Slovaks permanently domiciled there or commuting from Slovakia than the number of Czech workers resident in or commuting to Slovakia. On the other hand, Slovakia was able to rely on Czech assistance in launching new plants equipped with modern technology and in training new employees.[8]

In 1960, as a response to the problem of nationalism, the Communist Party of Czechoslovakia tightened its grip by recentralizing control of the republic. This move fomented discontent among the population throughout Slovakia and also dissatisfaction in the leadership of the Communist Party of Slovakia. The Slovak historian, M. Barnovský, characterizes the measures of 1960 as follows: 'The reduction of the Slovak question to the problem of the industrialization of Slovakia, or of economic equalization, was virtually the expression of a peculiar kind of vulgar economism. The fact that the decision to curtail the authority of the Slovak national institutions was made roughly at the very time that the slogan of the achievement of economic equality between Slovakia and the Czech Lands was being coined is thus only an apparent paradox. The publicity campaign of the time even claimed that the Slovak national institutions would be restructured so as to contribute towards the acceleration of the process of equalization by enhancing the efficiency of the central administration. Social practice did not, however, bear out these predictions.'⁹

The stagnation of the economy in the first half of the 1960s and the growing criticism of the public directed against the existing forms of control and management gave rise to another attempt at reforming the economy, which was announced in January 1965 and launched in 1966. At the time of the Prague Spring stormy social developments brought new aspects to economic policy. The programme of reform was aimed at a changeover from the centrally planned command economy to a market economy, but it did not include any mass privatization of state enterprises. Planning was to be based on long-term scientific prognoses, and targets were to be achieved with the help of purely economic instruments, not simply on the command of the government.

One of the key principles of the reform movement was the federalization of the republic, which proved to be a complex problem, particularly as far as the economic sphere was concerned. The division of responsibilities in the newly restructured state had to be defined in a situation where the forces of integration were gaining ground worldwide, and where the Czechoslovak economy had for long decades been built up as an integrated system. It was no wonder that a wide range of points of view, including extremes threatening the country with destabilization, should have appeared when a compromise was being sought between meeting Slovak demands and ensuring the continuation of the process of integration.

Negotiations concerning the model of the Czechoslovak federation were started in April 1968 and they continued even after 21 August, when the military intervention waged by five countries of the Warsaw Pact put a stop to the process of democratization. The new federal arrangement was enacted by a constitutional act of parliament on 27 October 1968, effective from 1 January 1969. As of this date new legislative bodies, governments and other organs of the Czech and the Slovak Socialist Republics came into existence. Some of the articles of that constitutional act, however, were soon amended (in 1970); some of the responsibilities of the republics were transferred to the federation, the reason given being 'reinforcement of the integrating function of the federation'.

According to these amendments, in the economic sphere the federal organs were charged with the control of the fuel and energy-generating industries, metallurgy, the engineering industry, the electrotechnical industry, foreign trade, communications, and most branches of transportation; they also dealt with issues relating to the two republics in the sphere of planning, research and technology, capital goods projects, foreign economic relations, and agricultural, monetary, financial, pricing and social policies.

The formalization of many of the responsibilities of the republics, as well as of the lower organs of state administration and enterprise management, was contributed to by the restoration of the central system of directive planning and management of the national economy effected in the course of the years 1969–70. The ideological campaign launched against the reformers active in the period of the Prague Spring and the opponents of the military intervention by the countries of the Warsaw Pact was accompanied by persecution which was more oppressive and more extensively applied in the Czech part of the Federal Republic than in Slovakia. In the period of 'normalization' any free exchange of views and opinion in the humanities was precluded and this also applied to discussions of possible variants of economic policy. The reforms of the 1960s oriented towards a gradual transition to a market economy were stalled, not only in Czechoslovakia but also in Hungary and in other countries, including the Soviet Union itself. In this anti-reform climate the long-term programme of economic integration of the COMECON countries adopted in July 1971 naturally had no chance of succeeding.

A continuing raising of the economic level of Slovakia to that of the Czech Lands remained one of the objectives of the plan for the national economy in the 1970s. Considerable funds were released to finance the development of the Slovak capital, Bratislava, the industrialization of the least developed north-eastern part of the country, the modernization of the expanding Slovak armaments industry, the first Czechoslovak nuclear power plant located in western Slovakia, and considerable improvements in the eastern lowlands of the country afflicted by frequent floods or droughts. In the mountainous part of northern Slovakia, collectivization was again begun and was completed within a short period of time. In the 1980s the joint Gabčíkovo-Nagymáros hydroelectric project on the river Danube, based on a treaty with Hungary, was already under construction. Towards the end of the decade this project became a highly controversial issue between the two countries involved.

From the mid-1970s onwards a gradual shift in policy could be observed in official documents and in plans and prognoses of the national economy, attenuating the emphasis placed on the economic equalization of Slovakia with the Czech Lands in favour of a demand for some substantial contributions by the two republics towards higher economic effectiveness. This resulted in stronger pressure to deal with long-neglected problems such as the gloomy state of the tertiary sector and the environment. Although after 1975 the economic growth of the country went into a long-lasting decline in both parts of the federation, the planned rate of growth of Slovakia continued to be higher than that of the Czech Lands. Higher effectiveness was to be achieved with the help of better utilization of the specific

ニング

demographic, natural and economic conditions of Slovakia: a higher birth rate and a more favourable demographic pattern, an increasing amount of skilled labour, geographic proximity of the main outlets for Czechoslovak goods in the COMECON member-countries, and relatively more modern technological equipment in factories compared with the situation in the Czech manufacturing industry. Particular emphasis was placed on the need for more effective utilization of Slovak raw materials for upgrading the quality of products and the export of commodities, and for raising the intensity of agricultural output, whose lower level compared with that of the Czech Lands was only partly attributable to objective factors.

In the postwar period Slovakia recorded a high mobility of labour between the different sectors of the industrial economy, which was mostly in harmony with worldwide trends. The more differentiated rise of the rate of employment in the individual branches of social activity as compared with the Czech Lands resulted in a very uniform branch structure of labour in the whole Federal Republic in the 1980s. The share of female labour in the total workforce was also nearly equal. In the younger and middle-aged populations the earlier differences of skill and qualifications between the Czech and the Slovak working populations were quickly wiped out. As Table 3.8 shows, in the years 1948–89 the working population increased by 65 per cent in Slovakia, but, for instance, in trade the rise was 236 per cent, in education and culture the rate of employment rose nine-fold, in medical and social services eleven-fold and in science and research around nineteen-fold. In the 1980s Slovakia could boast of more favourable indicators than the Czech Lands in some respects; for example, in the total number of the working population in education, medical services, science and research, or in the share of university undergraduates in the younger generation.

In April 1985 it was officially announced (by the Federal Premier L. Štrougal on the occasion of the 40th anniversary of the Košice Government Programme) that the process of equalization of the two republics had reached its target. The great differences in the economic level and the standard of living between Slovakia and the Czech Lands had been overcome and the economic and social structures of the two territories had become closer to one another. From Table 3.7 above, it can be seen that in 1989 Slovakia's share in the principal economic indicators equalled 30–34 per cent, with 33.7 per cent of the total population of the federation. As far as the consumption of the population and investment were concerned, this share was higher than the national income created, which testifies to a transfer of funds from the Czech Lands to Slovakia even towards the end of the 1980s. In the course of the economic reform launched at that time the financial flows between the two republics of the federation were to have

Table 3.8   Occupational distribution of the workforce in the principal sectors, 1948–89[a]

Indicator		In per cent					Index 1989 (1948=100)
		1948	*1960*	*1970*	*1980*	*1989*	
Agricultuture	CR	33.1	20.3	14.6	10.9	9.4	38.4
(excluding forestry)	SR	60.6	36.1	23.5	14.8	12.2	33.1
Manufacturing	CR	38.8	48.9	48.6	47.9	47.4	165.7
industry and							
building industry	SR	20.8	34.5	40.8	43.9	43.8	347.7
Transport	CR	4.3	4.8	5.3	5.2	5.0	159.6
	SR	3.8	5.2	5.5	5.3	5.2	229.7
Communications	CR	1.1	1.2	1.5	1.4	1.4	177.3
	SR	0.5	1.2	1.3	1.2	1.2	418.4
Trade[b]	CR	8.4	7.8	8.5	9.7	9.8	158.2
	SR	4.7	6.1	7.5	9.3	9.6	335.5
Banking and	CR	0.9	0.5	0.5	0.5	0.5	72.3
insurance	SR	0.3	0.4	0.4	0.4	0.4	215.6
Science, research	CR	0.4	1.8	2.5	2.3	2.3	855.9
and development	SR	0.2	1.2	1.5	2.1	2.4	1,868.1
Education and culture	CR	2.6	4.3	5.5	6.7	7.4	377.3
	SR	1.5	4.7	6.7	7.3	8.3	910.0
Health service	CR	1.9	2.9	3.6	4.5	5.0	366.5
and social care	SR	0.8	2.6	3.9	4.5	5.4	1,085.0
Administration and	CR	2.5	1.6	1.6	1.6	1.5	79.7
justice	SR	1.8	1.6	1.6	1.6	1.4	131.3
Others[c]	CR	6.0	5.9	7.8	9.3	10.3	230.9
	SR	5.0	6.4	7.3	9.6	10.1	332.3
Total of those	**CR**	**3,984**	**4,450**	**4,923**	**5,148**	**5,402**	**135.6**
employed	**SR**	**1,514**	**1,555**	**1,948**	**2,288**	**2,498**	**165.1**
(in thousands)							
Share of female	CR	36.5	43.7	46.5	45.8	45.8	–
employees	SR	39.7	38.7	42.8	44.6	45.5	–
(in per cent)							

Notes:
[a] Excluding the armed forces, women on maternity leave; 1980 and 1989 including secondary-job workers.
[b] Home trade, foreign trade and purchase of agricultural products.
[c] Forestry, water provision, geological and designing activities, publishing, housing, services to tourism, municipal, commercial and technical services, and other activities.
Sources: Historická statistická ročenka ČSSR, 1985, pp. 429, 460–63, 630, 661–4 (1948–70); *Statistická ročenka ČSFR*, ('Statistical Yearbook of the CSFR'), Prague: 1992, pp. 51, 67, 194–5 (1980–89). Mostly calculated from absolute data.

been made more transparent, and transfers in favour of Slovakia were to have been ended.

There is no doubt that in the whole postwar period economic development up to 1989 exhibited a greater dynamism in Slovakia than in the Czech Lands. However critical our attitude to the economic development of the country under the Communist regime may be, and even though great reservations about the method of industrialization of Slovakia may be voiced, the reduction of economic and social differences between the two parts of the country in the course of several decades is an undisputed fact, which was also reflected in the social consciousness of that time. Public opinion polls undertaken in the 1970s and 1980s and also in the post-communist period show that the population of Slovakia judged postwar economic and social developments much more favourably than the Czechs, and that until the end of 1989 the Slovaks were more optimistic about the future prospects of the country. But among the Czech population there was some differentiation on this issue. In big cities, particularly Prague, and partly in the ecologically highly afflicted regions, the population was more critical, whereas in smaller towns and in the rural districts people were relatively more content.

It is paradoxical that Czechoslovakia should have broken up at a time when, in contrast to Yugoslavia or the Soviet Union, the differences between the economic and the living standards of the Slovak and the Czech nations were reduced to a minimum and when the branch structures, social structures and the educational level of the populations in the two parts of the federation had already been brought closer to each other than ever before.

Notes

1 B.R. Mitchell, *International Historical Statistics: Europe 1750–1988*, third edition, Basingstoke: 1992.
2 Ľ. Lipták, *Slovensko v 20. storočí* ('Slovakia in the Twentieth Century'), Bratislava: 1968, p. 11.
3 *Československá statistika: Pramenné dílo* ('Czechoslovak Statistics: A Source Book'), vols. 20–23 and 104, on various pages.
4 *Historická statistická ročenka ČSSR* ('Historical Statistical Yearbook of the CSSR'), Prague: 1985, pp. 868–70.
5 *Economic Survey of Europe in 1948*, Geneva: UN, 1949, p. 235.
6 Data on the damage quoted by the official report on German criminal acts against Czechoslovakia. See *Československo a norimberský proces* ('Czechoslovakia and the Nuremberg Process'), Prague: 1946, pp. 210–12 (herein also the itemization of the damage).

7 *Svět hospodářství* ('The World of the Economy'), 29/1992, p. 4.
8 These issues were commented on by the then Slovak Premier M. Číč as follows: 'In the existing jungle of distorted statistical and other data and greatly deformed economic relationships, one can hardly try to prove with some degree of exactitude and a clear conscience who is actually the benefactor and the beneficiary ... This process of evaluation should certainly also take account of the problems of the input raw materials entering the process of manufacture, the finalization of the products, their sale on foreign markets, the balance of the mobility of the labour creating national income between the two republics ... On the other hand, we should also note what the Czech Republic provides for Slovakia. I would like to mention only some examples: the supply of energy and income for the metallurgical industry, some of the more interesting textiles, and of course also a certain volume of consumer goods (e.g. cars). Neither should we forget the assistance given by the Czechs in the industrialization of Slovakia in the postwar period and the foundation of Slovak universities, cultural institutes and the education or instruction provided for the Slovak intelligentsia as far back as the era of the First Republic.' (M. Číč, 'Who is the benefactor and who the beneficiary?', *Tvorba* 16/1990, p. 6 – in Slovak).
9 Collected papers: *Rozvíjanie socializmu na Slovensku v prvej polovici šestdesiatych rokov* ('The Development of Socialism in Slovakia in the First Half of the 1960s'), Bratislava: 1979, p. 36.

4 Czech and Slovak Society

JIŘÍ MUSIL

Czechoslovakia disintegrated in spite of the fact that the two societies, at the time of the split, had substantially more in common – at least in sociostructural terms – than they had had at the time of Czechoslovakia's formation. At the beginning of the 1990s, both featured similar economic and social structures, and demographic behaviour, and nearly identical legal, technical and educational systems. Slovakia's level of urbanization approached that of the Czech Lands and economic interdependence was very high. In spite of these shared characteristics, the state broke up. In view of the fact that the predominant theory of European integration is based on the concept of economic interdependencies and increasing social homogeneity between parts of Europe, the history of the break-up of Czechoslovakia takes on new importance and merits close analytical attention.

The following study is a comparative analysis of the social structure in the Czech and Slovak parts of former Czechoslovakia. It explicitly assumes that in Czechoslovakia the differences and the similarities between the two parts of the country remained all the time an important aspect of their integration. The growing structural homogeneity, however, never became a sufficient basis for a lasting unity. It is also presumed that the underlying reason for the division of Czechoslovakia was that 'Czechoslovak society' as such had not been established during the seventy years of the existence of the common state, regardless of the efforts of parts of the Czech and Slovak population.

Comparative Models of Structural Changes

Most of the existing studies on the division of Czechoslovakia are principally descriptive. Historical methods for identifying particular events that led to the decline of the federation appear to predominate. In some sociopolitical studies, more general phenomena which do not just depict the character of events, and which are labelled by terms such as 'Czech paternalism' and 'Slovak separatism', are assumed to be the cause of the failure of Czechoslovakia. But even in these cases, the sociological and long-standing causes of this separation, with a few exceptions, are not investigated. Even though historical analysis and sociopolitical interpretations are essential, they are not sufficient to fully explain the break-up of the common state. This is not, under any circumstances, to underestimate the importance of single, even accidental events. It would be just as inappropriate to fail to state the role of certain political attitudes and movements. An interpretation of Czechoslovakia's division cannot avoid analysis of the role of social structures and of cultures and, in particular, of their differing nature in Czech and Slovak society.

One of the basic hypotheses of this study is the view that processes of modernization in Czech and Slovak society proceeded asynchronously and, in some respects, differently. The modernization of Czech society was implemented, to a considerable extent, within the framework of the capitalist system and had, except for some specific features, such as a low degree of urbanization coupled with a relatively high degree of industrialization, the standard features of modernization processes in Western Europe. Modernization processes in Slovakia took place not only later than in the Czech Lands, i.e. after 1918 with a rapid growth of the educational system, but also mainly during the socialist era and according to a Soviet model. This different systemic context was not without significance.

In this context it is necessary to stress the fact that, when applied to questions of ethnic relationships in a common state, modernization theory assumes that interaction and communication among the inhabitants of the territory in question is going to have a positive impact.[1] Their interaction, caused by economic development, urbanization, literacy, etc., is presumed to lead to cultural homogeneity, which, among other things, implies that differences decrease, leading to a kind of amalgamation of ethnically different societies. In both their Marxist and non-Marxist forms, modernization theories are implicitly based on evolutionist optimism. There is no doubt that the theory of modernization is one of the bases for a policy of integration in Western Europe. It is assumed that a certain degree of economic and social similarity is the necessary condition for political integration. From this point of view, a sociological analysis of the Czechoslovak experiences might have even greater significance.

The Economic Transition in the Czech Lands and in Slovakia

A simple way to describe economic transition processes is to analyse the population structure according to the following three economic sectors: (1) agriculture, forestry, fishery; (2) industry and the building industry; and (3) services.[2]

If we are to follow Friedrichs's three economic transition periods we may distinguish the periods as follows:[3]

(1) A period before the transition during which more than 50 per cent of the population belongs to the primary sector and during which the proportions of the secondary and tertiary sectors increase;
(2) A period of real economic transition during which the proportion of the primary sector decreases, the secondary sector reaches its maximum and the proportion of the tertiary sector increases; and
(3) A post-transitional period during which proportions of both the primary and secondary sectors decrease and the proportion of the tertiary sector exceeds 50 per cent and continues to increase.

Data for the Czech and Slovak territories based upon data for an economically active population testify to the fact that the Czech Lands finished the first period soon after 1900, while Slovakia did not do so until 1950. In other words, the Czech Lands ceased to be an agricultural society by early in the twentieth century, whereas Slovakia did so only in the middle of this century. Both societies, however, are now in the second period of economic transition according to the results of the 1991 census. However, the proportion of the tertiary sector has not yet exceeded 50 per cent (Czech Republic – 43.5 per cent; Slovak Republic – 43.7 per cent. Compare Tables 4.1 and 4.2.)

From data on the development of the economically active population in regard to their division into the three sectors, we can deduce the following further differences within the process of the economic transition:

(1) Whereas, before the First World War, Slovakia belonged to the category of agrarian countries, the Czech Lands, by that time, ranked amongst considerably industrialized territories, and the differences between both parts of Czechoslovakia during the interwar period of 1918–39 increased even more in this respect.
(2) The years of socialism caused a swift loss of the primary sector in Slovakia, and similar, yet more moderate processes occurred in the Czech Lands.
(3) Socialism experienced an unusual phenomenon: the loss of the tertiary

Table 4.1   The beginning and the end of economic transition in selected European countries

Country	Year of the beginning of the transition	Year of the end of the transition	Duration of the transition
England	1841*	1932	91*
France	1869	1974	105
Germany	1876	1981	105
Austria	1884	1980	96
Czech Lands	1900	1991*	91*
Soviet Union	1946	1980*	34*
Slovakia	1950	1991*	41*
Hungary	1951	1980*	29*
Poland	1957	1980*	23*

* The time series is not closed, i.e. either the economic transition started earlier than stated in the table (but there are no available data, as in the case of England) or the transition has not yet finished.

Sources: Data regarding the Czech Lands and Slovakia have been taken from *Demografická příručka* ('Handbook of Demography'), Prague: 1982. For other countries, they are taken from J. Friedrichs (see note 2). The author is grateful for the kind permission to reproduce the data in this volume.

Table 4.2   The peak of the industrial period and indices of the intensity of economic transition

Country	Maximum of the secondary sector		Intensity of transition		
	Year	Share (%)	I	II	III
England	1880	52.5	0.16	0.12	0.22
France	1970	40.6	0.38	0.13	0.26
Germany	1971	49.0	0.42	0.16	0.29
Austria	1961	43.5	0.42	0.19	0.29
Czech Lands	1980	55.9	0.45	0.28	0.32
Soviet Union	1980	39.0	0.88	0.40	0.48
Slovakia	1980	51.4	0.97	0.87	0.55
Hungary	1974	44.0	1.07	0.88	0.44
Poland	1980	39.9	1.00	0.48	0.44

Sources: See Table 4.1.

Note: Indices of transition intensity have been calculated in the following manner: The index for the primary sector is defined as the difference between the proportion of the primary sector at the beginning and at the end of the transition, divided by the number of years for the transition. The indices for the tertiary sector are calculated similarly. The indices for the secondary sector are defined as the difference between the greatest proportion of the secondary sector and its proportion in the last year of the transition. This difference is then divided by the number of years between the height and the end of the transition. This means, in general, the higher the index value, the faster the transition.

sector. This was somewhat more dramatic in the Czech part of the state, and the Czech Lands had not reached its 1930 standard even by 1980. Slovakia, on the other hand, had achieved, by 1961, a higher proportion of the tertiary sector than it had had in 1930.

(4) The Slovak economic transition proceeded substantially faster compared to the Czech Lands and was accomplished during the socialism period.

(5) The sector structure of Slovakia caught up with that of the Czech Lands in 1991, while retaining a slightly higher proportion of agriculture. The swiftness of such levelling between both parts of the state is, according to K. Mihailovič, of special significance in modern European history.[4]

Slovak industrialization proceeded not only unusually rapidly but also with further features that can be mentioned briefly here. The establishment of rather large industrial plants, placed, in numerous cases, in relatively small localities (Detva, Senica, Turzovka) was typical of this process. The location of these plants depended upon the large resources of labour in each particular place. These enterprises now often have the position of sole employers in these locations and the dependence of the localities upon such plants, both in the economic sense and in the social and political sense, appears to be considerable. Slovak industry was designed with the economic and strategic targets of the federation and of the Soviet bloc in mind. This has led to a well-known one-sidedness of new Slovak industry today and, consequently, to a high rate of unemployment in many of its branches. Czech industry, on the other hand, characterized from its very origins in the nineteenth century by its notoriously widespread network, by a relatively diversified structure and by a proportionally high contribution from the consumer goods industry, has maintained a characteristically high number of enterprises located in small and medium-sized towns with relatively short distances between them. (This particularly applies to east and north Bohemia and partially to west Bohemia.) The link between workplace and residence was much more flexible in those settlements with old industries than in regions that were industrialized or re-industrialized during the socialist period (the Ostrava region, the north Bohemian coal basin).

The concept of Slovak industrialization was implemented on the basis of large new enterprises and was imposed upon a network of agrarian settlements with limited resources for building houses and for the technical and social components of urban infrastructure. This led to a phenomenon which Ivan Szelenyi calls 'under-urbanization'.[5] This arises when the state creates a high number of employment opportunities but lacks sufficient resources to build housing close to the sources of employment, and thus forces new industrial employees to commute from the surrounding municipalities and to build private housing themselves. In Slovakia, the statistics for the proportion of the construction of private housing and for commuters prove Szelenyi's hypothesis. Both these phenomena occurred more frequently in Slovakia than in the Czech Lands. Of the total number of housing units built during the period 1946–85, in Slovakia 40 per cent of them were private family houses while in Bohemia and Moravia only 22.7 per cent of them were.

Demographic Transition and Family Changes

Changes in a population's reproductive behaviour, which are described by the terms 'demographic revolution'[6] or 'demographic transition',[7] constitute an important component of modernization in European countries. Demographic transition is a process caused by reduced child mortality, to which a population reacts, in the short or long term, by a reduction of the birth rate.

In the Czech Lands, demographic transition began around 1870, and its first phase ended around 1900. The second phase ended around 1930. According to some studies,[8] in the Czech Lands the gross fertility index had been in decline as early as 1820 (from 42 to 38 births per 1000 inhabitants). This change was the result of postponing marriages to an older age and of fertility changes. A marked fertility decline came about after 1890, and then a radical change came after 1900. In the year 1900, the general fertility index showed that 140 out of 1000 married women were at a reproductive age; however, within a period of ten years, it fell to 117 and then kept falling until the 1940s. In the Czech Lands, therefore, demographic transition proceeded relatively slowly and resembled the Anglo-French type. In Slovakia, the first signs of declining fertility were registered after 1900. Its index decreased considerably during the First World War, then increased substantially only to fall again sharply after 1930. In Slovakia, demographic transition was completed by 1950. It is noteworthy, however, that during the period of Czech and Slovak rapprochement, i.e. during the decade of 1920–29, the fertility differences between both parts of the new state appeared larger than at the beginning of the century and appeared even larger at subsequent stages.

As a result of late demographic transition, and of the sustaining of a relatively high fertility level, Slovak society, in comparison with Czech society, is younger. In 1991, the average age of women in the Czech Lands was 38.0 and that of men, 34.6; in Slovakia the average ages were 34.9 and 32.1 respectively. These differences are quite considerable.

A consequence of differing population processes, i.e. of natural increase and migration, is the fact that from 1921 to 1991, the percentage of those living in Slovakia of the total number of Czechoslovak inhabitants increased from 23 per cent to 34 per cent. Although the 1921 figure included the German population, and even considering European regional changes, this is an extraordinarily fast growth, which indicates dynamic economic and social development in Slovakia.

In a historical context too, Slovak society differed structurally from Czech society regarding family models and property relations. This concerned primarily agricultural families in which some basic features of the social organization of both societies took shape. The traditional Slovak family belonged, according to J. Hajnal's classification, to the so-called 'East European' type.[9] In such families a high correlation between a low marriage age, a low number of domestic staff and a higher fertility index (contrary to the West European type) is distinctive. This is connected with the fact that the inheritance of a father's land was shared by the majority of brothers and sisters, and that primogeniture did not apply. This led to the splitting of agricultural land and to the creation of very small farming units and therefore to a stagnation of technical progress in agriculture and, at the same time, to limited migration to and from towns.[10] In Western Europe and in the Czech Lands, property was acquired by one sole heir who generally postponed marriage until he inherited the farmstead. This directly caused only a slight breaking up of lands and a higher male migration from villages to towns. In Slovakia extended families and patriarchal families prevailed, whereas Czech families were smaller and the position of the father was weaker. These traditions changed swiftly as a result of Slovak industrialization and urbanization when migration to towns began, yet they persisted, albeit in a reduced and modified form, in rural areas. They led to different types of social cohesion in both societies, to differing interpretations of roles, of social status and of relations between individuals and groups. There is no doubt that legal, political and economic unification launched by the First Republic, the process of stringent homogenization and 'levelling' pursued by the centralized communist regime, and industrialization and urbanization processes all combined to reduce the differences between both parts of the federation. Nevertheless, all sociological research concerning family relations, the importance of neighbourhoods and localities, social structure, household structure, etc., refers to the variances in the structure and in the functioning of both societies.[11]

Urbanization and the Sociospatial System of Society

Processes of urbanization have led, since the beginning of this century, to the gradual assimilation of both parts of Czechoslovakia, yet this assimiliation started during a phase of considerable differences between the Czech Lands and Slovakia. It is necessary to stress that the rate of urbanization in Slovakia has been, in recent decades, constantly higher than in the Czech Lands. This applies even to the 1980s when the percentage of people living in cities of more than 10,000 inhabitants (according to preliminary and not quite accurate estimates) increased only by 2 per cent in the Czech Lands, whereas in Slovakia it increased by 22 per cent. This corresponds with the fact that the Czech Lands were already in a phase of a slow urbanization, whereas Slovakia only reached the middle of a steady and rapid process of population concentration in cities during the 1980s. A whole range of inevitable and correlated phenomena reflects the fact that Slovakia was still in the middle of a rapid urbanization process. With respect to the standard of living, to the rate of industrialization and urbanization and to the way of life, regional differences within Slovakia were larger than those in the Czech Lands; the latter were in the final phase of urbanization transition and were, as a whole, socially more homogeneous. On the basis of these data, the geographic mobility of the Slovak population should theoretically have been higher during the period of socialism, and particularly in its last decade, than the mobility of the Czech population. Statistical data, however, show that this holds only for daily commuting, while from the point of view of migration, the Slovak population was less mobile than that of the Czech Lands.

For many Slovak towns, including Bratislava, the main problem remains, paradoxically, their swift expansion and the resulting devastation of many of their old parts. From a sociological point of view, serious problems have also been caused by the ruralization of cities and by swift suburbanization by numerous municipal agglomerations.

Literacy and Changes in the Structure of Education

The high level of literacy of the Czech population under the Austro-Hungarian monarchy has been described in detail many times. Similarly, descriptions of the state of the Slovak educational system at the end of the nineteenth and the beginning of the twentieth century, and of the relatively high proportion of illiterates in Slovakia, abound. All this was still true at the time of the census in 1921. Among the population over 14 years of age,

15 per cent of them were illiterate. By the end of the 1860s there were 1,800 primary schools in Slovakia and by the beginning of the war in 1914 this figure had declined to 250, out of which 233 were just single-class schools. Only 17 per cent of 256,000 children whose native tongue was Slovak were able to attend primary schools where Slovak was the language of instruction.[12] The situation in secondary education was much worse. After 1874/5, when the three existing grammar schools were closed, anybody wanting to acquire secondary education had to attend a Hungarian secondary school. There Slovak students formed only 3.2 per cent of the total number of all students. At university or at other institutions of higher education in Hungary, Slovak students represented just 1.4 per cent of the student population. The social and professional consequences of such a situation have been described many times.[13] In regard to our hypothesis on the rapid process of Slovak modernization, a more important fact is that, during the lifetime of the First Republic, illiteracy in Slovakia was virtually eliminated and the foundations for a secondary and higher educational system were laid down. The dynamic process of modernization in the field of education continued even during the period of the communist regime. Nowadays, indices of educational structure in Slovakia are slightly superior to those in the Czech Republic.

The Democratization of Society

The differentiation of political movements and the formation of political parties is also an element of the modernization process. The creation of a pluralist structure of political interests may be considered to be an integral aspect of modernization. A more favourable political setting, highly developed capitalism and the differentiated structure of the Czech Lands towards the end of the nineteenth century in comparison with the Slovak situation after 1867 also became evident within the political structures.[14] During the 1890s and during the years before the First World War, when there was already a widely developed structure of political parties in the Czech Lands, the situation in Slovakia was quite different. A. Štefánek characterizes it as follows: 'In Slovakia, political activity before the formation of Czechoslovakia did not show any deeper differentiation. After the creation of a national consciousness it became nationalist and, more or less, autonomistic, albeit conservative and panslavistic. Slovaks actually had, until 1918, just one single party, the so-called Slovak National Party.'[15]

Štefánek emphasizes the fact that there existed considerable differences among the nationalists, but during elections and any political action, the various strands came together. The Czech situation, as is generally known, was quite different, for political parties had already entered into completely open competition, which turned gradually into normal political life. The political life of the First Republic in the Czech Lands was, in regard to the parties' structure and to a certain extent to political culture, a resumption of prewar life. Radicalization occurred both of the left and of the right. Eight political parties took part in the first Slovak elections in 1920. By 1925, there were 18 of them. Slovakia rapidly adopted the structure of political parties in the Czech Lands and added to it Hlinka's Slovak People's Party, the Slovak National Party and Hungarian parties. The transition from the simple prewar structure to a complex one was realized in a relatively short period of time. In this respect, the integration of both sections of the republic proceeded quickly, and from a structural point of view there were no substantial differences between the Czech Lands and Slovakia. The political pluralism both of the Czech Lands and of Slovakia was subsequently suspended during the war and then, obviously, during the period 1948–89. The political culture of both areas, however, remained traditionally different.

Sociocultural Modernization

Modernization does not only have structural features. In theories of modernization, emphasis is always placed on the importance of changed attitudes towards work, on labour motivation, on the restriction of the influence of tradition, on the strengthening of the importance of the individual, on a rational orientation of behaviour, on a strengthening of secondary social relationships and a whole range of sociopsychological and sociocultural elements of behaviour.[16]

The Slovak population, unlike that of the Czech Lands, was less satisfied with the political, economic and social changes that came after November 1989 and had a 'qualitatively lower degree of confidence in the current social transformation'.[17] Part of the dissatisfaction of the Slovak population is, according to Machonin, tied to the perception of an excessive deepening of social differences and of the growth of social injustice. The Czech population attaches considerably greater importance to efficient and effective circumstances for success, such as one's own education, one's own endeavours, talent, diligence and willingness to take risks. The Slovak population, on the other hand, attaches greater importance to ascriptive circumstances such as extraction, family, coincidence, but never to the performance of an individual. These factors also include the parents' wealth and education, social contacts, political connections, national and racial origin, one's religion, place of birth, etc. The Slovak population, when evaluating itself on a political left-to-right scale, aligns itself more to the left. Slovaks, often substantially less than Czechs, rank themselves as 'Liberals' (18.1 per cent to 40.4 per cent) and as 'Conservatives' (13.1 per cent to 25.4 per cent).

From the published research, one can see that a lower degree of urbanization, the way of life in Slovakia and other circumstances led to the divergent life styles of both populations. In Slovakia there is evidently greater population sociability, a greater emphasis on family and on neighbourhoods. This corresponds to older surveys of R. Roško, who stressed the great importance of 'a local working radius' in Slovakia.[18] To use the known differentiations and classifications for populations designated either as 'locals' or as 'cosmopolitans', as introduced by M. Stacey,[19] Slovaks are more 'locals' whereas Czechs are more like 'cosmopolitans'. Slovak society is more solidaristic and more communal (*gemeinschaftlich*), Czech society is more associative (*gesellschaftlich*).

It should also be added that Slovak society consists of a population that is not secularized to such a degree as the Czech population and as Bohemia in particular. It is well-known that the Czech population, along with that of Sweden, belongs to the most secularized populations in Europe.

Therefore, it is possible to claim with some certainty that the Czech Lands, from sociocultural points of view, may be seen to be in a more developed phase of modernization than Slovakia. It is possible to state, too, that the differences between the two parts of the former federation are more than just structural, such as the stage of industrialization, of urbanization, of educational advancement, of the standard of living, of the gross national income, etc. This fact has important sociological and political consequences.

Some Features of Social Interaction Between Both Societies

The rate of integration of societies and their components depends on the exchange of people, information, capital and commodities. In the case of Czechoslovakia, there exists a whole range of other indicators that measure these features of integration. Indirect indicators are, for example, data on migration, on the number of students from Slovakia studying in the Czech Lands, the number of graduates returning to Slovakia or remaining in the Czech Lands, etc. The majority of such sociological indicators, in contrast to economic indicators such as the exchange of goods, cooperation between enterprises, capital flow, etc., indicate a mutual long-term closure of the federation by both parts. Migration movements between Slovakia and the Czech Lands appear to be a very important symptom of this closure.

At the beginning of the 1950s, 37,000 to 40,000 people migrated annually from Slovakia to the Czech Lands. Such large-scale migration was caused, among other things, by the additional settlement of the Bohemian and Moravian border areas in progress at the time. The numbers involved had already started to decrease by the second half of the 1950s and ranged around 21,000 per annum. The relatively high index of migration from Slovakia to the Czech Lands was connected with the expansion of the mining industry and metallurgy in the Ostrava region and in other Czech regions. In the 1960s, migration decreased further to 13,000, a fall of 19,000. The decline continued and in the 1980s the number of migrants fell below the level of 10,000 per annum. A similar trend is found when regarding migration from the Czech Lands to Slovakia. Both parts of the republic became more isolated and their interaction continuously declined. The political decision of the Slovak administration to restrict migration into the Czech Lands appears to be one of the factors in this development. But there were other causes, too. The decline in the volume of migration from Slovakia into the Czech Lands appears to be a reflection of the industrial development and, in general, of the economy of Slovakia. The more developed Slovakia became and the more labour opportunities arose there, the less necessary it was to migrate to Bohemia and Moravia. Migration from the Czech Lands also declined rapidly, especially that of more qualified workers. The greater the number of Slovak technical and creative intelligentsia, the fewer people from Bohemia and Moravia were needed to cover the demands of developing Slovak industry and other sectors. An important aspect in the relationship between both parts of the state is the fact that the degree of qualification of the migrating population from Slovakia into the Czech Lands was, especially before the formation of the federation, lower than the degree of qualification of the Czech migrants moving to Slovakia. Unskilled workers and agricultural workers from Slovakia moved to the Czech Lands in greater numbers than vice versa.

The process of the division of both parts of the state is also shown by an analysis of data on persons mentioned in the publication *Who's Who in Czechoslovakia*, the first volume of which was published by Václav Brož in 1969. The number of Slovaks who acquired their education in Bohemia from the time of the First Republic until the formation of the federation had gradually decreased. Furthermore, the number of young Slovaks working in Slovakia while acquiring their education at Czech schools had also fallen. On the other hand, the proportion of Slovaks acquiring their education in Slovakia and working there at the same time was gradually growing.[20] It is clear from this analysis that, with the development of the Slovak educational system, which proceeded simultaneously with the growth of labour opportunities, the circulation of the population between both parts of the state continuously declined. Thus, it is possible to agree with the opinion of the geographer K. Kühnl when he says that Czecho-slovakia consisted of two 'relatively closed' migratory subsystems: the Czech Lands and Slovakia.[21]

The interpenetration or the closing of both societies can also be investigated with the help of further data on the number of concluded Czech-Slovak marriages, tourism, the allocation of soldiers in military service, the volume of cultural contacts, and the mutual knowledge of language, culture and history. From a structural point of view, the alienation of both societies from each other seems to be quite clear.

Conclusions and Alternative Interpretation

There is no doubt that throughout the history of the common state there existed two relatively separated societies. Different historical developments and starting points, and the different courses of their respective processes of modernization resulted in sociocultural variations. Both societies, from certain points of view, converged and yet, from other standpoints, remained separated.

A large part of the modernization processes proceeded more quickly in Slovakia, albeit at a later stage than in the Czech Lands. This obviously was not purely the result of industrialization, urbanization and demographic transition but was also due to the pace of education and democratization. In addition, in the Czech Lands processes of modernization based on Austrian capitalism were imposed on a system full of feudal elements and did not attain the form of liberal democratic capitalism until the First Republic, whereas a considerable part of Slovakia's swiftly realized modernization proceeded in the context of socialism. To a certain extent, it should be stressed that Slovakia modernized with such speed because of external pressures. It was not so-called 'organic growth', as in the case of the Czech Lands.

Moreover, some processes in Slovakia were dissociated and they did not proceed simultaneously. This is true, in particular, of the relationship between industrialization and urbanization. Slovakia is probably the case that has confirmed the Szelenyi theory of under-urbanization. The process of concentrating labour opportunities in towns proceeded faster than the concentration of inhabitants in towns. This under-urbanization meant, at the same time, the indirect exploitation of the newly formed social stratum of workers and of service sector staff. In Slovakia there also existed, to a lesser extent, a time lag between industrial processes and changes in demographic behaviour. For a considerable time Slovak demographic behaviour maintained features of reproduction of agrarian-industrial or even of agrarian societies. Thus, unlike the Czech model, Slovak social modernization showed a wide gap between technical and economic features of modernization on the one hand, and cultural and social processes of modernization on the other.

Slovakia, in contrast to the Czech Lands, secularized itself more slowly, and it is well known that religion remained an important component of life in Slovak society. Some historically determined phenomena, such as family structure, the great importance of communal bonds, a rural lifestyle, the high incidence of farming, and great emphasis placed on socialist society and on collective forms of life (the transition from non-industrial and late pre-industrial living evolved straight into socialist collectivism) created a situation in which new industry and even towns existed in a society that lacked the standard features of other modern industrial societies.

The fact that the pace with which technical and economic modernization proceeded was swift, while the social and cultural structures of Slovak society moved at a much slower pace, created tension and discordance among the subsystems of Slovak society. Czech society, on the other hand, suffered from a syndrome of social stagnation, from a certain introversion and from self-satisfaction. Here numerous features of anomie and of the disintegration of social cohesion also appeared. This was, however, a different form of anomie from that found in Slovakia.

Despite the variance in the respective courses of the modernization processes, both societies became more and more alike. The analysis of our data points to the fact that Czechoslovakia had been formed during a period in which these macrostructural differences, differences in demographic behaviour and a whole range of other parameters were at their greatest. Czechoslovakia split up during the period in which these differences were at their smallest.

In the postwar period, the Czech Lands and Slovakia developed, despite increasing technical and economic integration, into two separate geo-demographic and migratory regions. This was essentially caused by the reduction of dissimilarities between the Czech Lands and Slovakia and by industrial and economic development in Slovakia. The development of Czech-Slovak relations thus challenges those modernization theories which stress that similar standards of living, similar socioeconomic structures of the population and similar or identical systems of social security and law are the most reliable factors to suppress ethnic tensions and to stimulate social integration.

In order to interpret the sociological separation of both societies and the failure of the federation, it is not sufficient to describe Slovak society as unstable owing to internal tension caused by the asynchronous processes of modernization of the respective Slovak social subsystems. This asynchronicity may also have resulted from societal disruptions experienced by the Slovaks and from the fact that the Czechs had not been able to interpret social and cultural processes occurring in Slovakia correctly. Traditional modernization theory also tries to explain the separation of Czechs and Slovaks by pointing to the fact that Slovakia was a 'retarded' society, which was not able to converge with the more developed Czech society. However, neither theory in isolation has been able to explain what really happened.

Clearly even a modified form of modernization theory, which refers to both the 'internal asynchronism' and the 'instability' of Slovakia, should be complemented with other interpretive theories. This theory should be compared with a model of 'internal dependence', which was formulated by M. Hechter while analysing the development of Celtic territories in Great Britain.[22]

This theory, in essence, refers to a more sophisticated structural analysis, which pays attention not only to macrosocial quantities such as GNP or to Fourastié's sectors of a national economy, but also to concrete relations within industry in various parts of a state inhabited by various ethnic groups. For example, it analyses the effects of enterprises producing industrial semi-finished products in one part of the country, while in other parts of the country there are enterprises processing those semi-finished products, as in the sphere of mechanical engineering or the food industry. With such an approach, hierarchic integration may be discovered. The social structure of migration is also important. The migration of a less qualified labour force from one part of the state to another also appears to be an indicator of 'internal dependence'.

In addition to this theory, modernization theories should be complemented both by the theory of ethnic socialization and, in particular, by the élite mobilization theory. This latter theory, associated today with the name of J. McKay, combined with the internal dependence theory may explain, to a considerable extent, the separation of the Czechoslovak Federation.[23] The theory of the mobilization of the élite assumes that a movement leading towards the separation of ethnic groups from a common state must have a mobilized élite to interpret both its ethnic background, i.e. its essentially cultural background such as language and cultural patterns of behaviour, and the various forms of economic inequalities, possibly internal dependence, through the medium of politics. Without the existence of such an élite, which connects ethnic background with a political interpretation of internal dependence, the separation could not have taken place. The connection of all these factors only arises, however, after some great systemic shock, as happened in the case of Czechoslovakia with the collapse of the communist regime.

Thus, the comparative analysis of Czech and Slovak societies has shown that, in spite of the fact that, due to the rapid modernization of Slovakia, both parts of the country had become similar in macroeconomic and macrosocial aspects at the beginning of the 1990s, modernization brought many internal strains for Slovakia. It also changed the relationship of Slovakia to the Czech Lands. For a great proportion of the Slovak population, modernization meant an improvement in economic and social opportunities, but at the same time it destabilized Slovak society. On the other hand, Czech society did not undergo such major structural changes. Here the socialist transformations were not linked to such dramatic changes in socioeconomic structure nor in the regional distribution of the population. All the time the Czechs were also aware of their dominant position within the Czechoslovak Republic and were mostly unable to understand the motives of Slovak nationalism.

The modernization of Slovakia, which began after the First World War and was accomplished mainly during the socialist era, was a necessary but not a sufficient condition for the disintegration of Czechoslovakia. Neither the rapidly diminishing structural differences between the two parts of the country, nor the hidden asymmetries, can explain the end of Czechoslovakia. Differing sociopolitical value orientation – the Czechs preferring individualism, the Slovaks laying more stress on communal values – were seemingly more important. But even these differences do not sufficiently explain the break-up of the state. Nor would the split have happened without two further occurrences: the collapse of the communist system and the rapid formation of a new Slovak political élite for which the establishment of a sovereign national state became the main mobilizing objective. Clearly the phenomenon of the break-up of the Czechoslovak state, at this particular point in history, can be explained only by a more sophisticated, multifactorial theory.

Notes

Some of the material contained in this paper was previously published in J. Musil, 'Czech and Slovak Society: Outline of a Comparative Study', in *Czech Sociological Review*, vol. 1, no. 1 (1993), pp. 5–21. The author is grateful to the publishers for their kind permission to use it in this volume.

1 See also H. van Amersfoort, 'Nationalities, Cities, and Ethnic Conflicts: Towards a Theory of Ethnicity in the Modern State' in H. van Amersfoort and H. Knippenberg, *States and Nations: The Rebirth of the 'Nationalities Question' in Europe*, Amsterdam: Nederlandse Geografische Studies 137, 1991.

2   C. Clark, *The Conditions of Economic Progress*, New York: 1940; J. Fourastié, *Le grand espoir du XXe siècle*, Paris: 1949; and J. Friedrichs, *Stadtentwicklungen in West- und Osteuropa*, Berlin and New York: Walter de Gruyter, 1985.

3   J. Friedrichs, ibid.

4   K. Mihailovič, *Regional Development: Experience and Prospects in Eastern Europe*, The Hague: Mouton, 1973.

5   I. Szelenyi, *Urban Inequalities under State Socialism*, Oxford: Oxford University Press, 1983.

6   A. Landry, *La révolution démographique*, Paris: Librarie du Recueil Sirey, 1934.

7   F.W. Notestein, 'Population Theory: Long View', in T.W. Schulz (ed.), *Food for the World*, Chicago: University of Chicago Press, 1945. See also W.S. Thompson, *Population Problems*, London: McGraw Hill, 1930.

8   See L. Fialov, Z. Pavlík and P. Vereš, 'Fertility Decline in Czechoslovakia during the Last Two Centuries', *Population Studies*, 44 (1990), pp. 89–106.

9   J. Hajnal, 'Household Formation Patterns in Historical Perspective', *Population and Development Review*, vol. 8, no. 3 (1982), pp. 449–94.

10 S. Švecová, 'Dva typy tradičnej rolnickej rodiny v Československu' ('Two Types of Traditional Agricultural Families in Czechoslovakia'), *Český lid*, 76 (1990), pp. 110–22.

11 Compare R. Roško, K. Podoláková and J. Jančovičová, 'Sociálna štruktura slovenskej a českej společnosti' ('The Social Structure of Slovak and Czech Society'), in P. Machonin et al., *Československá společnost*, Bratislava: Epocha, 1969, with P. Machonin's 1992 essay 'Česko-slovenské vztahy ve světle dat sociologického výzkumu' ('Czech-Slovak Relations in the Light of Sociological Research Data'), in F. Gál et al. (eds.), *Dnešní krize česko-slovenských vztahů*, Prague: Slon, 1992.

12 A. Štefánek, *Základy sociografie Slovenska* ('Principles of the Sociography of Slovakia'), Bratislava: 1944.

13 See, for example, L. Holotík, 'Die Slowaken', in A. Wandruska and P. Urbanitsch (eds.), *Die Habsburgenmonarchie 1848–1918*, Vienna: Verlag der Österreichischen Akademie der Wissenschaften, 1980.

14 Cf. O. Urban, *Česká společnost 1848–1918* ('Czech Society 1848–1918'), Prague: Svoboda, 1982.

15 A. Štefánek, 'Slovensko: Přehled politický' ('Slovakia: A Political Survey'), in *Slovník národohospodářský, sociální a politický*, Prague: O. Janáček, 1933.

16 A study comparing the Czech Lands and Slovakia in these aspects, highlighting the mutual relations between both societies, has not yet been carried out. For our purposes, we utilize data provided by P. Machonin's 1992 research on the transformation of Czechoslovak social structure carried out by the Institute of Sociology of the Academy of Sciences of the Czech Republic and by the Institute of Social and Political Sciences of the Faculty of Social Sciences of Charles University.

17 Machonin, 1992, p. 94.

18 R. Roško, 'Zbližovanie robotníkov a inteligencie' ('Bringing Closer the

Intelligentsia and the Working Class'), in *Studie/Pramene*, Bratislava: Slovak Academy of Sciences, 1986.

19 M. Stacey, *Tradition and Change: A Study of Banbury*, Oxford: Oxford University Press, 1960.

20 Cf. C. Skalnik Leff, *National Conflict in Czechoslovakia*, Princeton: Princeton University Press, 1968, pp. 289–91.

21 K. Kühnl, *Migration and Settlement: 16, Czechoslovakia RR-82-32*, Laxenburg, Austria: International Institute for Applied Systems Analysis, 1982.

22 M. Hechter, *Internal Colonialism: The Celtic Fringe in British National Development*, London: Routledge, 1975.

23 J. McKay, 'An Exploratory Synthesis of Primordial and Mobilizationist Approaches to Ethnic Phenomena', *Ethnic and Racial Studies*, 5, pp. 395–420.

II *National Consciousness*

5 National Consciousness and the Common State (A Historical– Ethnological Analysis)

JAN RYCHLÍK

The disintegration of Czechoslovakia was certainly a surprise for many people. Foreign observers in particular tried in vain to find an answer to the question as to how two nations so close from a linguistic, cultural and historical point of view could split up. Advocates of the common state – both in the two successor states and abroad – tended to emphasize the economic aspects of the problem, pointing at the material losses that would arise as a consequence of the disintegration of Czechoslovakia. In reality, however, the material factor played an inferior role.[1] The reasons for the break-up of Czechoslovakia must be sought in the principles of the development of the modern nation, i.e. in the process of the formation of a separate national awareness of Czechs and Slovaks.

First we must consider the question as to what a nation is and in what conditions the permanent coexistence of various nations in one state is possible. We have to recognize the difference between a nation in a political sense and a nation in an ethnic sense. A political nation is understood as 'all citizens of one state' and it is mostly in this way that the word 'nation' is used in Western countries, e.g. in France, Great Britain or the USA. However, in Central and Eastern Europe the word 'nation' is treated more as a cultural-ethnic unit, as the consequence of different developments in this part of the continent. It is impossible to prove that the ethnic nation exists objectively, since the criteria cannot be determined according to which peoples would be classified as separate nations. In Central Europe it is mainly language which is understood as the criterion of allegiance to a particular nation, but this classification is often misleading. A literary language is always more or less a standardized fiction that nobody speaks:

children are born into a dialect and they learn the literary language only at school. Today more and more ethnologists share the view that an ethnic nation is created purely by our collective consciousness. This so-called subjectivist theory states that a nation is a group of people who share a sense of unity.[2]

Understanding a nation as collective awareness means that people belong to the same nation if they share the same cultural values.[3] In practice this means that people realize their allegiance to a nation only on the basis of a dissimilarity to other people. Thus, the definition of a nation is a negative one, and this definition can be briefly expressed as the contrasts 'we – you' and 'our – your'.[4] This awareness of similarity may be defined, for example, on the basis of language (the Czechs – the Germans) or on the basis of religion (the Serbs – the Croats), but there may be cases when the distinctive features cannot be defined and the awareness of difference has arisen only as a result of the long-term existence of a political frontier (the Austrians – the Germans). However, it is beyond doubt that, in general, due to the influence of family and education, national allegiance is taken for granted (except, for example, in the cases of children from mixed marriages and people from boundary areas). Normally we do not think about our nationality too much.

People became aware of their ethnic differences a long time ago, but throughout history these have been of varying importance. We can say, for example, that in the Middle Ages ethnic allegiance had little importance. Religious and state allegiances were much more important in feudal society. The process of the foundation of a modern nation, described in reference to Central Europe as the 'national revival', to some degree took the form of a return to pre-feudal times. It had to be explained to people that being Catholics or Protestants, nobles, serfs or burghers was not of primary importance; what was most important was whether they were Czechs, Slovaks, Germans, Hungarians, etc. The positive aspect of this process was that it helped to establish civic society. It is also of note that its protagonists in the first half of the nineteenth century imagined the future world as a kind of freely cooperating community of nations, a notion very close to that of modern federalism.

The formation processes of the Czech and Slovak nations ran parallel. Within the area known after 1918 as Czechoslovakia the same process of 'national revival' of the Hungarian (Magyar), German, and later Polish populations took place. Czech or German (or Polish in Silesia) orientation in the Czech Lands was, in fact, a matter of the personal decision of an individual, made, in many cases, regardless of their ethnic origin. This also explains the large number of Czech surnames among German inhabitants and vice versa. The same applies to the division of Slovaks and Magyars in 'Upper Hungary', the present territory of Slovakia. However, there the emancipation process was rather limited and a relatively large part of the population remained indifferent to the question of nationality, especially in the mixed territories of southern Slovakia.

While the Czech-German and Slovak-Magyar separation was relatively fast and simple, differentiation between the Czechs and Slovaks was more complicated, because there was no language barrier. Within Czechs and Slovaks there existed both a sense of affinity and a sense of difference. The affinity was caused not only by the complete mutual comprehension of their languages but also strengthened by the usage of archaic Czech (*biblična*) as a liturgical language by the Slovak Lutherans and by the lack of a standard form of the literary Slovak language before 1843.[5] The feeling of difference was caused by the fact that both nations had developed separately: the Czechs in the Kingdom of Bohemia, the Slovaks in the Kingdom of Hungary. Although both countries had been united by a personal union since 1490,[6] the political border between them resulted in a different historical consciousness and social structure between Czechs and Slovaks. Gradually, the awareness of being different predominated. In the nineteenth century the process of the formation of both nations was more or less completed and – as was proved later – was irreversible on both sides. Increased Magyarization after the Austro-Hungarian Compromise in 1867[7] managed to slow down the process of Slovak emancipation and even to forcibly assimilate the Slovaks, but did not succeed in changing their Slovak consciousness back to a joint 'Czecho-Slovak' one.[8]

Once a nation is constituted, its people start to feel the necessity of its statehood, and this naturally applies to the Czechs and Slovaks as well. Due to their historical development, the theoretical and philosophical bases for Czech and Slovak statehood differed. Czech politicians (with a few exceptions) operated the so-called Bohemian 'Historical' or 'State' Right, which has its origins in the sixteenth century. In 1526 the Bohemian estates,[9] by their own free will, elected the Austrian Archduke Ferdinand of the Habsburg dynasty their king. Thus, the Bohemian Lands and Hungary were united with Austria by a personal union into one empire. This, however, did not mean that the Lands of the Bohemian Crown had lost their political independence. Neither the events after the battle of White Mountain in 1620,[10] nor the gradual dissolution of the Bohemian state authorities after 1749 and the end of the special position of the Bohemian Lands, meant the forfeiture of their independence. Czech political leaders struggled for an enforcement of the so-called Bohemian Historical Right within the framework of the Habsburg monarchy. The Lands of the Bohemian Crown – Bohemia, Moravia and Silesia – were, in principle, to form a single unit. This single unit was to be more or less independent and only essential matters were to be solved together with other parts of the monarchy. The Czech programme of the Bohemian Historical Right appeared in a detailed form during the revolution of 1848, after the restoration of constitutional life in Austria in 1861 and finally as the so-called fundamental articles (*fundamentální články*) in 1870–71. None of these suggestions was accepted because they always met with opposition from the German inhabitants of Austria (including the Germans in the Lands of the Bohemian Crown), from imperial Germany and, after 1867, from the Hungarian government.

The Slovak programme, on the other hand, was not based on any historical rights but only on natural ones. The Slovaks were to be given a semi-independent state within the framework of Hungary, i.e. Hungary was to be federalized on the basis of nationality. This programme was presented during the 1848 revolution as the Demands of the Slovak Nation (*Žiadosti slovenského národa*) and later in 1861 as the Memorandum of the Slovak Nation (*Memorandum národa slovenského*).[11] Naturally, the Slovak demands were absolutely incompatible with the aims of the Hungarian ruling circles, which were to transform Hungary into a modern Magyar state gradually breaking away from Austria. Therefore the Slovak demand for an autonomous territory (*okolie*) was rejected. After the Austro-Hungarian Compromise of 1867, it became evident that the realization of the Slovak programme within the framework of Hungary was impossible. Slovak politicians even stopped discussing it.

The First World War brought Austria-Hungary unequivocally under the influence of its stronger ally, imperial Germany. The positions of German and Magyar chauvinists strengthened and it became clear that, had the German-Austrian-Hungarian bloc (the so-called 'Central Powers') been victorious, the position of the Czech and Slovak nations would have been even worse. The Czech and Slovak plans to realize their own statehood within Austria and Hungary were gradually abandoned and the question arose as to whether, in the case of the victory of the 'Entente', it would not be better to break up Austria-Hungary and to establish a common state of the Czechs and the Slovaks – Czechoslovakia. The campaign for this programme was started as early as 1914 with the presentation of a special memorandum to the British Foreign Office by T. G. Masaryk, who was later to become the first Czechoslovak President. This liberation movement, which was organized from abroad, was joined by Masaryk's disciples Edvard Beneš and the Slovak astronomer living in France, Milan Rastislav Štefánik.

Here the question arises as to under what conditions the coexistence of two nations is possible. In principle there are two possibilities. An ideal solution is if ethnic nations, regardless of their origin, acquire an awareness of belonging to a common state, as the result of long coexistence, and if this awareness becomes a primordial and determining factor for them. In this way one political nation is formed from several ethnic nations. Such a process took place in the USA, Australia, partly in Canada (where the francophone population of Quebec remained intact) and in Switzerland. The formation of a political nation in no way restricts the cultural development of the individual ethnic nations concerned.

Another solution to the coexistence of nations in one state is the existence of national state units with their own political state structure unified in one supranational state organization. This means the coexistence of political nations that lack complete individual statehood. In other words, the state units are not completely independent but united into a composite state, within the framework of which they have a certain autonomy. Such forms of coexistence (mostly based on a federation) are, as a rule, not very stable because they continuously have to face two problems emanating from the nation's behaviour. Firstly, as the national allegiance of a people is felt only on the basis of their dissimilarity to other nations, each national unit tries to make itself very 'visible'. This is very difficult in a multi-nation state because accepted thinking follows the pattern 'one state – one nation'. Secondly, individual state units usually are not of the same size and power. So although they have the same rights and duties, in practice the weaker are restricted (both economically and politically) in comparison with the stronger ones. This effective inequality is usually considered to be a stronger unit's hegemony over the weaker one. Each national unit struggles to get as much jurisdiction as possible but at the same time – aware of its weakness – does not want to lose any advantages connected with the membership of a common state. In short, it makes an effort to leave maximum responsibility to the state authorities while it maintains maximum rights.

Each state represents a subject of international law and is characterized by an internal common market. Subsequently each composite state must have at least three authorities, the decisions of which must be able to be executed directly. These are the authorities for foreign policy, defence (which is closely connected with foreign affairs, because the army must be under somebody's political control) and finance as an implement of the common market. Elimination of any of these three factors signifies the end of the common state. It is not possible for national member units to have, for example, their own international legal status or their own sovereignty in economic affairs. If they do have these we can speak only of a confederation, which is not a common state but only a union of independent states striving to reach a certain goal. A confederation cannot exist permanently – it tends either to develop from totally independent states into a federation (for example, the German Confederation (*Bund*, 1815–66) or from a federation into totally independent states (the Commonwealth of Independent States replacing the former USSR). The coexistence of several nations in one state where the citizens have no awareness of allegiance to this state (or where only a minority have it) consequently requires the permanent equilibration of jurisdiction between the centre and the national units. The central authorities cannot leave any of the three fundamental matters previously mentioned out of their range of responsibilities, because if they do, the country or state will disintegrate. The national units, on the other hand, frequently try to get some of the cornerstones of authority under their control and in this way they undermine the basis of the common state.

These principles must be considered when analysing the formation of Czechoslovakia and the background of the Slovak-Czech disagreement. Unlike the older Czech politicians, who had based their policy only on the Bohemian Historical Right and who had wanted to pursue only cultural relations with Slovakia, T.G. Masaryk had, even before the First World War, counted on Slovakia to counterbalance the German minority, while in return the Czechs were to give support against the Magyars in Slovakia. Masaryk did not bring up the question of language at all, although attempts to substitute Czech for Slovak still existed in some Czech philological circles, which considered Slovak not a separate language but only a dialect of Czech. According to Masaryk the Slovak language was to be recognized as equal to Czech and used parallel with it.[12] As far as the existence or nonexistence of the Slovak nation is concerned, Masaryk, whose father was Slovak, never doubted the existence of the Slovak ethnic nation, unlike a considerable part of the Czech public. His aim was not to make Slovakia Czech but to create a Czechoslovak political nation, within the framework of which the Czechs and Slovaks would develop independently.[13] Ostensibly, it was, of course, necessary to present the Czechs and Slovaks to the Entente Powers as one nation, because otherwise they would not have agreed to the division of Austria-Hungary which they finally accepted in spring 1918.

The birth of Czechoslovakia on 28 October 1918 was of immense importance for the Czech and Slovak nations, especially for the Slovaks, who were saved from complete Magyarization. Nevertheless, the two nations entered the new state with different historical experiences. Consequently, though both nations welcomed the new state, each had a different concept of it. From the Czech point of view the new state was the climax of the Czech national liberation effort, and for many Czechoslovakia was the restored ancient Bohemian state, whose independence had been lost in 1620. Thus Czechoslovakia was a realization of the Bohemian Historical Right in an 'improved' version, i.e. extended over Slovakia and

Ruthenia.[14] From the Slovak point of view the situation was completely different. In the new state the old programme for autonomy which had not been realized within Hungary was now to be implemented. In other words, Slovakia was to be loosely connected with the Czech Lands. There were to be two states, each with sovereignty in some areas but having joint arrangements in others.[15] The dual state was to be modelled according to former Austria-Hungary: Czechoslovakia was to be 'Czecho-Slovakia' – as the Slovaks always spelled it. The truth is that, initially, by no means all political parties in Slovakia supported this. However, this idea, advocated by the Slovak People's Party under its leader, the Catholic priest Andrej Hlinka, gradually predominated.

The possibility of creating a Czechoslovak political nation, which evidently would have been the best form of protection for the Czechoslovak state, was not realized for three main reasons. Firstly, the official ideology of the Hungarian state before 1918 was so-called 'Hungarism', i.e. the theory claiming that all nationalities in Hungary formed one political nation. The historical experience of Slovaks with Hungarism was negative because in practice it degenerated into the forced assimilation of non-Magyars. This was the reason why many Slovaks had no confidence in the idea of a Czechoslovak political nation which its opponents called 'Czechoslovakism',[16] fearing a possible assimilation by the stronger Czech partner. Secondly, the Czech population itself did not feel any necessity to give up its Czech identity for the benefit of a higher, Czechoslovak one. For the majority of Czechs 'Czech' and 'Czechoslovak' were more or less identical, and this was not acceptable for the Slovaks. However, the main reason why a Czechoslovak political nation did not come into existence has to be seen in the fact that the first Czechoslovak Republic existed for only twenty years (1918–38). Neither the international political situation nor domestic economic affairs were favourable conditions for the new state, and so the coexistence of the two nations lacked stability. The existence of the independent Slovak state (1939–45) – even though its independence was illusionary because the new state came to existence at the demand of Nazi Germany and was absolutely dependent on it – meant the clear formation of two separate political nations. The renewed existence of Czechoslovakia after 1945 was possible only by a constant balancing of the relations between the two nations. The ethnic and cultural proximity of both communities did not become a sufficient link to create an awareness of an allegiance to a common state, the existence of which would be a *conditio sine qua non* for its inhabitants.

Thus the potential factors of Czechoslovakia's destruction were laid down in the very basis of the common state. Nonetheless, it could not be said that their activization in 1989–92 was inevitable.

Notes

1   The fundamentalist adherents of the Slovak state regarded the independence of Slovakia as an absolute value for which no economic prosperity could compensate. In private discussions, some of them made no secret of their conviction that an independent Slovakia would be in a much worse economic situation than it had been in within Czechoslovakia, although for political reasons they claimed the opposite in public. (Author's discussion with Mr Roman Zelenay, one of the leaders of Mečiar's Party, the Movement for a Democratic Slovakia, in Brno, 17 April 1993.)

2   W.E. Mühlmann, *Rassen, Ethniken, Kulturen: Moderne Ethnologie*, Berlin: 1964, p. 57; M. Maget, 'Problèmes d'ethnographie européenne', in *Ethnologie générale*, Paris: 1968, p. 1326.

3   E. Gellner, *Národy a nacionalismus*, Prague: 1993, p. 18. Available in English as *Nations and Nationalism*, Oxford: 1988.

4   A more detailed analysis of this problem is to be found in my unpublished Ph.D. thesis, J. Rychlík, 'Folklorna i nefolklorna kultura' ('Folkloric and Nonfolkloric Culture'), Sofia: 1984, pp. 9–24 (held in The National Library 'Kiril i Metodij' in Sofia, in the Slovak National Library in Martin and in the archives of Charles University, Prague).

5   The Slovak literary language was standardized by Ľudovít Štúr in 1843. See M. Hodža, *Česko-slovenský rozkol* ('The Czech-Slovak Split'), T.S. Martin: 1920, pp. 168–95.

6   In 1490 Vladislav II, King of Bohemia, was also elected King of Hungary.

7   In 1867 the Austrian empire was divided into two semi-independent parts – Austria and Hungary – having a common monarch, army, currency and common foreign affairs.

8   See detailed analyses in J. Rychlík, 'Etnické uvědomění a národní vývoj Čechů a Slováků' ('Ethnic Consciousness and the National Development of the Czechs and Slovaks') in *Kulturní tradice a nacionalismus* ('Cultural Tradition and Nationalism'), Brno: 1992, pp. 17– 21.

9   'Bohemian' meant an inhabitant – either Czech or German – living within the boundaries of the Kingdom of Bohemia. 'Czech' is an ethnical expression which in the past referred to ethnic Czechs only.

10 After the battle of White Mountain, absolutism was introduced in the Lands of the Bohemian Crown.

11 K. Čulen, *Memorandum národa slovenského z r. 1861* ('The Slovak Nation's Memorandum of 1861'), T.S. Martin: 1941, pp. 10–32.

12 The parallel usage of both Czech and Slovak (i.e. the right to use one or the other language) was introduced in 1918 and it continued during the whole existence of Czechoslovakia. The possibility of using either language was not abolished even after Czechoslovakia split at the end of 1992. See J. Rychlík, 'Teorie a praxe jednotného československého národa a československého jazyka v I. republice' ('Theory and Practice of the Unitarian Czechoslovak Nation and Language in the First Republic'), in *Masarykova idea*

československé státnosti ve světle kritiky dějin ('Masaryk's Idea of Czechoslovak Statehood in the Light of Historical Criticism'), Prague: Ústav T.G. Masaryka, 1993, p. 69–77. Of the following laws: paragraph 4 of No. 122/1920 Sb. (Sb. = Sbírka zákonů, Collection of Laws), article VI of No. 143/1968 Sb., No. 428/1990 Sb. and No. 460/1992 Sb.

13 In the nineteenth century the Czechs usually considered Slovaks to be a branch of the 'Czecho-Slavonic' ('*českoslovanský*', at that time not yet 'Czecho-slovak') nation, not a separate nation. See, for example, *Encyclopedia Ottův slovník naučný*, 23, pp. 406, 418–20. Cf. also the view of Karel Havlíček Borovský, in T.G. Masaryk, *Karel Havlíček*, 2nd edition (Prague: 1904), pp. 99-101.

14 Cf. J. Kapras, *Český stát v historickém vývoji a v dnešní podobě dle kongresu pařížského* ('The Czech State in History and in the Present Form According to the Paris Congress'), Prague: 1920.

15 This idea first appeared among the Slovaks in America, who discussed it with American Czechs and even with T.G. Masaryk during the war. Cf. K. Čulen, *Pittsburghská dohoda* ('The Pittsburgh Agreement'), Bratislava: 1938, pp. 45–6.

16 The expression 'Czechoslovakism' ('*čechoslovakismus*') was invented as a pejorative word by the Slovak autonomists from Hlinka's Slovak People's Party. It was later used by the communists.

6 *Slovakia in Czech National Consciousness*

ZDENĚK SUDA

In the discussion that follows an attempt will be made to identify the place Slovakia and the Slovaks have taken in modern Czech national consciousness. It will be undertaken with the purpose of determining to what extent the specific perception of the Slovaks by the Czechs and of the links between the two ethnic groups contributed to what eventually became the so-called 'Slovak problem' for the Czechs and was responsible for the dissolution of a political home shared over three-quarters of a century.

The concept of national consciousness in general is not easy to define. This may be the reason why it has not been addressed too often among the academic community. Its reality and importance have nonetheless been proven by the acuity of the crises that have erupted whenever the perception of collective identity has been in doubt. The case of Slovakia is one of such occurrences, which have been characteristic of Central and Eastern Europe. As will be shown later, it has been, among other things, the lack of clarity of Slovak national consciousness that rendered Czech-Slovak relations difficult to the point of intractability. National consciousness as such could best be described as a set of points and coordinates in space (the geographical situation of a nation) and time (a common historical experience), serving individuals in modern societies in expressing their identity as members of a national collective. Naturally, this definition also applies to the Czech case.

The Characteristics of Modern Czech National Consciousness

The subject of Czech national consciousness as such would no doubt merit a more extensive treatment than allowed by the present volume, which focuses upon the causes and the circumstances of the disintegration of Czechoslovakia. Here, the author has to restrict himself to this narrow and precise focus. Yet considering the fact that the crisis of Czech-Slovak relations was to a large extent due to a clash between two distinctly different views of historical reality (if not between two different political cultures), a closer look at the nature of Czech national consciousness, as an introduction, is called for. For the reasons cited already it must remain very brief. Some of the statements contained in it may therefore appear rather apodictic, which the reader, we hope, will kindly excuse.

Modern Czech national consciousness (*české národní povědomí*) appears to have included two principal properties at its outset: it was restorative in the sense that it not only sought to legitimate the existence of the Czech nation by its reportedly great and glorious past (this, after all, was typical of most national movements in Europe at the time), but that it also made one of its main objectives the recognition of the former Kingdom of Bohemia as a distinct entity in political terms and in terms of the restitution to this entity of a place in the central European geopolitical system; it also put particular emphasis on language as the principal sign of collective identity. Both these traits betrayed close affinity and common roots with the idea of a nation based on the nineteenth century German philosophy of history. Nevertheless, Czech national consciousness developed in opposition to the German culture and to the national aspirations of the German-speaking population of Austria, of which the provinces of the Czech Crown then formed a part. The anti-German ingredient in Czech national consciousness was very pronounced; many leaders of the national movement saw in Czech-German confrontation the meaning of the existence of the Czechs as a self-contained national group

The wilful nature of the Czech national movement, the zeal with which its leaders, called 'the awakeners', pursued their goals in the face of almost insurmountable difficulties, have puzzled many foreign observers and analysts. The movement may, indeed, have had deeper roots than the 'awakeners' themselves were aware of. A case can be made for interpreting the intense efforts of the Czechs to set themselves apart from the German culture of Austria-Hungary as a disguised, subconscious search for a means to express their erstwhile nonconformist Protestant religious beliefs which they had not been allowed to profess since the Counter-Reformation of the seventeenth century. Having been prevented from openly declaring their adherence to a different Church, they all the more vehemently emphasized their membership of a different nation. The religious element in Czech national consciousness was later brought up by T.G. Masaryk, philosopher and sociologist, leader of the successful liberation campaign during the First World War and Czechoslovakia's first president, in his interpretation of Czech history. Another important contribution by Masaryk, purporting to modify the nature of Czech national consciousness, was the stress he put on the consensus on social and political values, which he called the 'national programme', as an indispensable condition for an ethnic group to become a nation.

The two concepts of a nation – on the one hand, a collectivity linked together by a common past and language and, on the other hand, a community based on moral and political consensus – and the two interpretations of Czech history – i.e the struggle with the Germans and the implementation of the values of the Czech Reformation – coexisted in Czech national consciousness from the end of the nineteenth century, including the critical period of the statehood shared with the Slovaks. The joint state would have best been protected if the national consciousness of the two ethnic groups could also have been shared or if they had blended into one. There were, however, serious obstacles in the way of such a development. Despite great linguistic similarity, the general culture, the historical experience and the lifestyle of the Slovaks were notably different from those of the Czechs. For the Slovaks and the Czechs, language was the most important sign of national affiliation, but language affinity, in this case indisputable, did not bring the two any closer to each other.

Unlike the Czechs, the Slovaks had no past to which they could have referred as a separate nation. Their history was part of the history of Hungary, a multi-ethnic polity where Latin had been used as the means of official communication until the mid-nineteenth century, when it was replaced by Hungarian and aggressive Magyarization set in. Yet perhaps an equally important factor preventing the rise of a common national consciousness was the peculiar place which Slovakia occupied in the collective awareness of the Czechs. This place changed somewhat over time but never enough to facilitate the growth of a common national consciousness.

Early Beginnings of Czech-Slovak Solidarity

The Czechs had been aware of the existence of the Slovak ethnic group, as well as of its cultural and political aspirations, since early modern history. They had been linked to the Slovaks by a common literary language; the Slovaks, although speaking various dialects of their own, wrote and read in Czech until 1844. This tie had been of a long standing, dating back to the time of the Protestant Reformation in the fifteenth and sixteenth centuries, when Czech translations of the Bible and other Protestant religious literature were introduced into northern Hungary. There they enjoyed a more hospitable environment than in Austria proper, since Hungary had not been subject to a Counter-Reformation of comparable harshness and duration to that which had taken place in the Czech Lands after the fateful battle of White Mountain, lost in 1620. Protestant faith there survived until the Tolerance Edict of Emperor Joseph II restored freedom of religion in Austria and in Bohemia in 1774. The 'truly Czech' Reformation Churches, the Hussite and the Czech Brethren Church, however, were then considered to be mere 'sects' and as such not legalized by the Edict. At that point, as a substitute, some Protestant ministers and preachers were recruited among the Slovak Lutheran and Calvinist communities to lead the newly constituted congregations in the Czech Lands. However, this particular link between the Czechs and the Slovaks was denominationally coloured and its significance therefore limited, especially considering that the Protestants, after the Thirty Years War, represented only a minority among both ethnic groups, notably among the Czechs. The prominent place given in contacts between the Czechs and the Slovaks to the links between the Protestant groups of the two nations could – and in fact did – become a handicap, impairing the chances of winning the mainly Catholic Slovak population over to the idea of a Czechoslovak state. On the other hand, these influences should not be entirely dismissed, given the fact that Masaryk's thesis of the meaning of Czech history reserved the Czech Reformation an important place. It was precisely this trend which generated the literary and cultural legacy that the Slovaks later shared with the Czechs.

Some Slovak intellectuals, especially in the pre-March period (the period before the 1848 revolution), joined the ranks of the Czech 'awakeners' – such as the poet Jan Kollár (1793–1852) and the ethnographer Pavel Josef Šafařík (1795–1861) – and participated in Czech political life during the 1848–9 liberal revolution. The revolution, which brought about important changes within Czech society, also marked a turning point in Czech-Slovak relations. The virulently nationalist orientation of the revolutionary leadership in Budapest, bent on the 'homogenization', i.e. the Magyarization, of the entire population of Hungary, the majority of which was non-Magyar and which had been using Latin as a means of official communication up to that time, provoked strong resistance everywhere. It also pushed, regrettably, the non-Magyar ethnic groups into the arms of the Austrian conservatives, and deprived the Hungarian liberal revolution of much sympathy and support.[1] The Czech leaders then began to worry about the future of the Slovaks as a distinct ethnic and cultural entity, although the most violent onslaught, from a different Magyar quarter, was yet to come.

The situation of the Slovaks in 1848–9 might have been one of the reasons why František Palacký, the leader of the Czech Liberals at the

Constituent Austrian Assembly in Kroměříž, and chairman of the subcommittee charged with the preparation of the draft of the constitution, submitted a project for the territorial reorganization of Austria-Hungary along ethnic lines. The parts of the Lands of St Wenceslas's Crown inhabited by the Czech-speaking population – about two-thirds of the geographical area – were to be united with the northern part of Hungary inhabited by the Slovaks. Applying consistently the ethnic principle meant also that the regions of Bohemia, Moravia and Silesia, inhabited by the German-speaking citizens, would have formed a self-governing unit with other regions of Austria populated by the same ethnic element. Thus Palacký spelled out an idea which did not have much chance of being implemented on account of the number of economical and technical problems it posed, but which nobody at the time could have suspected would be rediscovered first by the extreme-right nationalist Austrian movement of the *Deutschnationalen*, under the leadership of Georg Schönerer (1842–1921), who advocated the incorporation of the German-speaking part of Austria into Germany, then by the German opponents of Czechoslovakia in 1919, who proposed to create an independent state out of the German-speaking regions of Bohemia and Moravia, and finally be used as a Trojan horse against the post-Versailles alliance system in Europe by Adolf Hitler, who saw it implemented in the Munich Treaty in 1938.

The Constituent Assembly was dissolved in the spring of 1849, so that Palacký's proposal could not even seriously be considered. Palacký himself admitted later in his memoirs that the draft had been a compromise about which he had not been happy. He claimed that under the circumstances this would have been the best settlement for the Slavic parts of Austria. However, Czech involvement in the Slovak national struggle and the help offered to the Slovaks, especially after 1867, did not fail to reinforce Hungarian suspicions that Czech politics aimed also at the division of Hungary along ethnic lines. Palacký's constitutional project of January 1849 appeared to provide some evidence of such intentions. This perception may have motivated Hungarian insistence on an Austrian commitment never to grant any other component of Austria-Hungary the status bestowed upon Hungary in the 1867 Austro-Hungarian Compromise (*Ausgleich*). Some historians even infer that the failure of the agreement with the Czechs, negotiated by Prime Minister Karl Hohenwart in 1871, on the territorial rearrangement and the recognition of the Lands of St Wenceslas's Crown as a distinct, self-governing kingdom, should not be attributed solely to the opposition of the German-speaking minority in these areas and to the Viennese Liberal Party but also to external intervention, notably that by the Hungarian Prime Minister Gyula Andrássy (1823–1890), who perceived such an agreement to be a 'breach of promise' on the part of the emperor. If this is true, it would suggest that Czech-Slovak relations may have had a direct impact upon the political fate of the Czechs in Austria-Hungary. While the Czechs may not have been subjectively aware of it, the objective significance of these relations for them was considerable. Certainly the cost for the Czechs of Czech-Slovak 'mutuality' would appear quite high in this light.

Czech-Slovak Relations Before the First World War

Before the First World War, the Slovak national reality did not seem to enter very distinctly into the Czech political field of vision. The interest in all things Slovak, the sympathy with the Slovak struggle for national survival, even the assistance given to the Slovaks in this struggle by the Czechs, all these things seemed to increase the distance between the two, rather than to bring them closer together.[2] It was already evident at the time that mere language similarity would not amount to much in this respect. The fact that the two ethnic groups could understand each other without the use of a dictionary or a grammar book was an indisputable advantage to Slovak students who attended Czech colleges or the University of Prague after all Slovak educational institutions above elementary level had been closed by the Hungarian government. However, looking closer at the possibility of a true understanding between the Czechs and the Slovaks, a keen observer might have been reminded of a semi-facetious dictum applied to relations between the British and the Americans: 'two peoples divided by a common language'. A significant fact highlighting the special relationship of the Czechs to the Slovaks can be seen in the use and the development, over 150 years from the time of the French Revolution, of the meaning of the term 'Czecho-Slovak' or 'Czechoslovak'. It was not an invention of the founders of the First Republic in 1918. Then, as compared to the pre-March period, the term had a completely different connotation. For the 'awakeners', it referred to a cultural and linguistic orbit. In this particular sense, the idea of 'Czech', i.e., of what could be called 'Czechdom', was dominant, not unlike the component 'Anglo' in the term 'Anglo-American' or 'French' in 'French-Canadian'.

This interpretation can be supported by the fact that the term was used alternatively with the term 'Czecho-Slav', (*československý* and *českoslovanský*). The latter was in use until the First World War, and was chosen by the Czech socialists, after the multi-ethnic Austrian socialist movement split into its national components, in the title of their political party: Českoslovanská sociálně demokratická strana dělnická – The Czecho-Slav Social Democratic Workers Party. In the First Republic, the terms 'Czechoslovakia' and 'Czechoslovak' were understood to convey rather an idea of equality between the two components. This was consistent with the official thesis anchored in the constitution, according to which there existed one Czechoslovak nation with two branches and two languages, Czech and Slovak. It is worth noting, though, that Milan Rastislav Štefánik (1879–1919), the chief representative of the Slovaks in the 1914–18 liberation campaign, advocated a different notion, one which was much closer to the nineteenth century use. For him there was only one Czechoslovak nation, not subdivided into any branches. Czech and Slovak, in his opinion, were but two different versions of one and the same language. He also urged migration and inter-marriage as the means to achieve a single national community. His early death, however, prevented this concept from becoming a serious alternative.

Thus, at the turn of the nineteenth century, the Czechs' understanding of the nature of the relations between themselves and the Slovaks may not have been without ambiguity. However, lack of clarity, if indeed there had been such, did not cause any major problems for the national consciousness of the Czechs themselves. They could afford some ambiguity in this respect, since at that point they did not face the need to define the roles and the place of the two ethnic groups in one state. The real challenge to their complacency was to come much later. It came as the need to anchor the principles of the mutual relations between the Czechs and the Slovaks in the constitution of the Republic created in 1918. This need was never fully satisfied, and it eventually became the Achilles' heel of the new state. The issue was overshadowed, and at the same time aggravated, by another serious problem, namely that of the situation of the German-speaking minority.

The Concept of a Czechoslovak Nation

The founders of the First Republic and most Czech political leaders in the period between the two World Wars were aware of the importance for the young state of good relations with Germany. They also knew, from their prewar experience, that the quality of these relations would depend, in one way or another, on relations with the German-speaking ethnic group in the Czech provinces. However, the opportunity to arrive at a workable solution of this problem, available only until the rise of the Nazi regime in neighbouring Germany, was missed.

The apprehensions of the Czech leaders about the possible misuse of greater autonomy by the German-speaking ethnic element also had an impact in the area of relations between the Czechs and the Slovaks. A constitutional arrangement recognizing the right of the Slovaks to regional self-government was contemplated on several occasions during the twenty years after the First World War, partly inspired by the Pittsburgh Agreement signed by T.G. Masaryk and the American organizations of Slovak immigrants in May 1918. Yet no such reform was carried through. It has to be emphasized, however, that in the constitution of the First Republic, the Slovak ethnic group was considered to be equal to the Czechs. Slovak was the official language in Slovakia, so that, for example, Czech parents living there had to send their children to Slovak schools. It is true that Slovakia was treated as one of the provinces of Czechoslovakia, with no separate legislative organs, but this was because, at the time, Czechoslovakia was not a federation. The Czech Lands, too, were merely administrative provinces with no self-government of their own. Fears that the same right would have to be granted to the regions inhabitated by the German-speaking population paralysed all initiatives. Only after Munich, when the German problem disappeared, was a constitutional reform introduced which gave legislative autonomy to Slovakia in the form of a locally elected diet. This proved to be too late. The unresolved question of Czech-Slovak relations became the most immediate cause of the disintegration of the first Czechoslovak republic – something that hardly anyone would have anticipated in 1918. Instead of sharing a common fate, the two nations embarked upon different paths to follow during the highly critical years of the Second World War and the gap between them, due to their different historical experiences, widened further.

The scene for the ultimate break-up had in part already been set prior to German intervention. A very serious obstacle to a satisfactory settlement between the Czechs and the Slovaks was the very concept on which their joint political home was built, namely the idea of the two ethnic groups forming 'one nation with two branches and two languages'. There has been a tendency among historians to attribute this idea exclusively to Czech initiatives, which sometimes even implies accusations of 'expansionist' or 'imperialist' drives on the part of the Czechs. Adolf Hitler tried to capitalize on this assumption in a speech broadcast in 1938, when he claimed that Beneš (then the president of Czechoslovakia) had fabricated the 'whole nonsense about a Czechoslovak nation'. Documentary evidence, however, shows that things were not that simple by far. Slovak deputies and senators in the Provisional National Assembly, 1918–20, urged, more strongly than their Czech colleagues, the adoption of the concept of the Czechoslovak nation in the draft of the constitution. Some even pressed for using the term 'Czechoslovak language', i.e. for dropping the distinction between Czech and Slovak. Close association, the closest possible, with the Czechs appeared to them at the time to be the condition for the survival of the Slovak ethnic group, and the only reliable means to prise this group loose from the Hungarian social and cultural body.

Although also partly intended as a symbol of total equality on the point of identity, the concept of a Czechoslovak nation was increasingly perceived by the Slovaks as a disguise for Czech prevalence and domination. Of the two ethnic groups, the Czechs were more numerous and more developed in all respects. The initial assistance given to Slovakia when there were no literate cadres among the Slovaks to staff the administrative and educational institutions, and tens of thousands of Czech officials and teachers had to be transferred from the western part of the republic to Slovakia, began to be felt as a disadvantage during the Great Depression, namely as the withholding of economic opportunities from the younger Slovak generations which had been educated and trained in the meantime by Czech teachers and professionals. This feeling added to an earlier resentment concerning the behaviour and the lifestyle of the Czechs as observed by their Slovak hosts, and which the Slovaks regarded as alien to their established ways. The Czechs were often seen as 'immoral' and 'godless'. Much of that was due to the fact that religious belief was distinctly stronger in Slovakia than in the Czech Lands. The disharmony between the two ethnic elements and the clash of social values was also, perhaps to an even larger extent, caused by the typical contrast between a predominantly industrial and a predominantly rural society. Whatever the sources of these misunderstandings and clashes may have been, they led some Slovak circles to believe that the concept of one Czechoslovak nation was a clever gimmick making it possible for the agnostic and atheistic forces in the western provinces, especially in the capital city of Prague, deemed evil and corrupt (a common provincial stereotype of capitals in modern times), to subvert the pristine virtues of Christian Slovak society.

Yet apart from the negative feelings and suspicions evoked among the Slovaks, the most damaging aspect of the concept of the Czechoslovak nation was its ambiguity. The idea that a nation could consist of two nations, both of them distinct and with separate identities, was difficult to conceive of in any circumstances. However, it was particularly hard in the context of central European social and political philosophy where 'ethnic group' and 'nation' were understood to be synonyms, and the apparent contradiction could not be bridged by making the former subordinate to the latter. Also, the paramount importance in central Europe of language as the characteristic of a nation made the notion of a national collective with two languages a contradiction in terms. A way out of this paradox might theoretically have been found if the architects of the First Republic had consistently applied the principle of a political nation, thus defying prevalent central European beliefs. However, the term 'Czechoslovak' was unsuitable for such a purpose because of its semantic bias. It suggested precisely the opposite: namely, the ethnic nature of the nation. Moreover, if Masaryk's yardstick of a political nation had been applied, a programme would have had to be postulated for the two-headed Czechoslovak whole. But was the programme, as formulated by the republic's first president, really shared by both components? To the Catholic majority of the Slovaks, among whom Catholicism had a very pronounced conservative tinge typical of a pre-modern society, a common programme with the Czechs based on the traditions of the Protestant Reformation must have been almost an anathema.

The call for a redefinition of national identity, implied in the concept of a Czechoslovak nation, came at a time when the Slovaks were ill-prepared to handle it. They had barely emerged from centuries of a semi-dormant status, during which they had seen themselves as part of a multi-ethnic Hungarian culture but had been exposed to intense Magyarization during the decades preceding the war. They were hardly certain about who they actually were; in a survey undertaken in 1919, two-thirds of the respondents identified themselves as 'Slovak-speaking subjects of Hungary' – whereby all they stated was that they were not Hungarian-speaking. For them to develop an awareness of their distinct ethnicity, with all the necessary attributes, would in itself have required considerable time. The complicated notion of a double nation was too difficult to be internalized by them at that point. It only rendered their latent identity crisis, which was to continue all through the twentieth century until the post-communist period, more acute.

The Czechoslovak Concept and Czech National Consciousness

The negative response from so many Slovak quarters to the idea of a Czechoslovak nation often makes the analyst overlook the fact that this issue was not without problems on the Czech side either. Seen from the subjective perspective of those Slovaks who believed themselves to be at a disadvantage whenever this concept was implemented, it might have appeared logical that the Czechs stood only to gain in such a situation. The reality was different. The notion of 'Czechoslovakism' also constituted a serious challenge to Czech national consciousness. It challenged, above all, the Czechs' perceptions of the continuity of their own history. The merger of the two ethnic groups into one nation called for an important adjustment of these perceptions. This could have been accomplished in two different ways: either the creation of the Czechoslovak state could have been defined as a completely new beginning, comparable in its impact to the differentiation of the Czech tribe from the Slavic racial stock at the dawn of Middle Ages and representing a complete break with the Czech past up to 1918, and, indeed, representing the end of Czech history as it was then understood; or the unity of the two peoples, the Czechs and the Slovaks, could have been projected back into the past, with an inevitable need for a reinterpretation of both Czech and Slovak history.

The first approach, the more logical of the two, would have put an enormous burden on Czech national consciousness. We have seen how important a role the image of a shared continuous historical experience played in maintaining the cohesion and solidarity of modern Czech society. In fact, there may have been few nations in nineteenth-century Europe – perhaps with the exception of the Poles – as heavily dependent as the Czechs on historical tradition for the awareness of their identity. It could be argued that, at the time, the Czechs were the most historically minded people, possibly even overly so. To require this nation to consider its long past, glorious as well as tragic, to be a closed chapter and to make a fresh start with a junior partner, focusing its attention on the future, must have seemed to many of its members tantamount to an invitation to the loss of collective memory. Other, less emotional, nationally conscious Czechs might have wondered whether the concept of one nation with two branches and two languages, which they were called upon to espouse, was not a patent recipe for inducing collective schizophrenia.

The second approach, having the merit that it preserved some of the continuity of history so highly prized by the Czechs, was not any easier for it. In these terms, the unity of the two ethnic groups was viewed as given from the very start. The Czechoslovak nation, following this interpretation, had existed, so to speak, since the beginning of time. It was admitted that the two branches might not have always shared the same historical experience, but this had supposedly been due to external factors. Some historical facts, indeed, could have been invoked to support such a claim. In the period of the Great Moravian Empire, from the eighth to the tenth century AD, Czechs and Slovaks did live in one political configuration. Their separation is blamed upon the collapse of this empire, due to the invasion of the Hungarian plains by the Magyars. From that time, the lands inhabited by the Czechs led a separate existence from that of the Slovak component of the Czechoslovak nation. This, according to the proponents of the Czechoslovak concept, was unfortunate, but the unity of the two was not questioned by them even then.[3]

Another, relatively short, period of Czech and Slovak common history opened after the Hussite wars in the mid-fifteenth century, when the Hussite armies operated in northern Hungary to secure the Hungarian crown for the Bohemian king, Ladislas the Posthumous. On the heels of this army, later called *Bratrstvo* ('Brotherhood'), the ideas and the literature of the Czech Reformation came to Slovakia. A new powerful tie was then established between the two nations, which, however, was limited to Protestant circles. The fact that the Lands of St Wenceslas's Crown and Hungary had been unified, for four and a half centuries, under one sceptre, first of the Jagellonian, then of the Habsburg, dynasty, provided another, rather loose, link. However, it was for less than one hundred years during this period that the two ethnic groups were actually ruled by the same government: from the era of Emperor Joseph II in the 1780s, till the Austrio-Hungarian Compromise in 1867. Nevertheless, those reinterpreting Czech and Slovak history from the perspective of the Czechoslovak concept found a significant body of evidence in this temporary political cohabitation.

It is possible to say that on the whole the second approach prevailed, despite the contradictions which it contained; resistance against the first was too strong. The historiography of the First Republic used to apply the appellation 'Czechoslovak' even where it was an indisputable anachronism. So, for example, the historian Kamil Krofta entitled his concise, well-written academic manual of Czech history *Malé dějiny československé* ('A Short History of Czechoslovakia'), although 90 per cent of the text was devoted to the events that had occurred prior to the First World War, i.e. before Czechoslovakia had even been established. Given a fairly good knowledge of facts relevant to national history among the Czech public at large, these misnomers could be neutralized, and did not cause too much confusion. The Czechs quickly acquired the habit of reading 'Czech' whenever the term 'Czechoslovak' did not quite seem to make sense.

The consequences, however, were more serious where foreign observers, journalists and diplomats had to face similar situations. Not having the necessary background or experience, they chose a safe path: they either consistently used the term 'Czechoslovak' in any and all cases, or equally consistently substituted 'Czech' for 'Czechoslovak'. This had two results, none of them fortunate. Serious distortion of Czech and Slovak historical perspectives which in the domestic environment continued to be only a risk, became reality in the international arena. The anachronisms took almost grotesque forms when Western commentators (especially Anglo-Saxon ones, who had been socialized into perceiving the words 'nation' and 'state' to be synonyms) in all earnest referred to the fifteenth century Hussite religious movement as the 'Czechoslovak Reformation' or to Charles IV of Luxembourg as 'the most prominent Czechoslovak king'.

On the other hand, the use by foreign writers and media of the abbreviation 'Czech' in which the Slovak component was obliterated, could not but exacerbate Czech-Slovak relations. Whenever anything of this kind was brought to the attention of Slovak public opinion it reinforced the latter's suspicions that, in the eyes of the Czechs, the Czechoslovak state was just Greater Bohemia. How else could the complacency be explained with which this practice was registered on the part of the official bodies responsible for the representation of the state abroad? It must have appeared to the Slovaks that these agencies, primarily the Ministry of Foreign Affairs, were neglecting their duties and had failed to make the world aware of the existence of the second nation-forming ethnic group in Czechoslovakia. This was the origin of the Slovak grievance which was to become part of the Slovak ammunition in the post-1989 dispute, namely the complaint that the leadership of the Federal Republic, notably President Václav Havel, had not ensured the 'sufficient international visibility of Slovakia'.

The peculiar cognitive mechanism developed by the Czechs to translate the artificial and complicated modifier 'Czechoslovak' into the more familiar 'Czech' proved to be quite effective in the end. It helped to preserve the continuity of Czech national consciousness and reduced the threat of confusion that the idea of two nations in one would have caused if it had been taken literally. An indicator of its effectiveness can be seen in the apparent paradox that the Czechs managed to internalize the Czechoslovak perspective better and faster than the Slovaks, although this perspective was a much more serious challenge to their sense of national identity and its historical moorings. In the minds of the Czechs, the notions of 'Czech' and 'Czechoslovak' had blended into one by the end of the Second World War at the latest. What a superficial observer then may have mistaken for a sign of the success of the political resocialization of the Czechs in the First Republic was in reality nothing but a change of labels. The supposedly new Czechoslovak national consciousness was merely the continuing traditional Czech consciousness. A significant consequence of this psycho-social operation was the removal of the Slovaks as a distinct ethnic entity from the Czech field of vision. The Slovaks eventually began to be perceived as part of the same national organism – almost as the advocates of the Czechoslovak concept would have liked to have it – only this organism was not Czechoslovak but Czech.

The Slovak State of 1939 and Czech National Consciousness

The peculiar way in which the majority of the Czechs resolved the apparent contradictions of the concept of a Czechoslovak nation was indicative of the relatively low degree of their involvement in this issue. However, the most serious test of the importance of the place Slovakia and the Slovaks occupied in their collective awareness came only at the very end of the interwar period, literally in the last days and hours of the republic. Apart from the two major traumas of the late 1930s – Munich and the Nazi occupation – Czech national self-image suffered an additional shock on the eve of the Second World War: the secession of Slovakia and its passage to the enemy camp. The intensity of the shock was not comparable with that produced by the amputation of the border territories or by the imposition of a German protectorate over Bohemia and Moravia. The 'inadequate presence of the Slovak element' in Czech collective awareness (due to whatever reasons) may have mitigated its impact. Nevertheless, the separation of the two ethnic groups in March 1939 prompted some soul-searching among the hapless Czechs, and left a trace in Czech national consciousness. It was here, too, that the seeds of the 1993 separation were sown.

Understandably, the establishment of a Nazi satellite state in Slovakia was generally felt by the Czechs as treason, a stab in the back from the nearest of kin. The on-the-whole bitter commentaries sometimes included wry, tongue-in-cheek compliments to the Slovak leaders who allegedly had given proof of great political realism – greater than that shown by their 'naïve', 'idealistic', or 'overscrupulous' Czech brethren – in that they had put the interests of their nation above everything else, even if it meant helping in the enslavement of their former partners and closest allies.[4] It was only at this point that the Czech public realized that the social and political value system of the First Republic had not been shared by the Slovaks, or had only been shared by a minority among them. In certain Czech quarters, the validity and the cogency of the concept of a Czechoslovak nation was submitted to scrutiny and its inconsistencies were exposed. Although these various 'post-mortems' were undertaken in many circles and at many levels, it was chiefly the right and the extreme right who manifested the most zeal in this respect.

With hindsight, however, it appears rather striking that none of those who then bemoaned the Slovak secession gave much thought, be it even in the abstract, to an alternative approach to Czech-Slovak relations which could have prevented the disintegration of the joint political home. No lesson concerning possible future institutional arrangements seemed to have been drawn from this painful experience, in case another historical opportunity presented itself to both ethnic groups to form a common state. As a consequence, the Czechs entered the renewed statehood in 1945 in a 'business-as-usual' (read: 'pre-1939') frame of mind. (They were to commit the same mistake, or were to succumb to the same misperception, in 1989, when they would take for granted that post-communist Czecho-slovakia represented a simple return to the pre-communist *status quo ante*).

Since on the Slovak side the situation had been defined quite differently, the purely restorative Czech approach could not prevail. An important factor had been the Slovak uprising of 1944 which, in the eyes of the Slovaks, not only redeemed their nation from the stigma of pro-fascist collaboration, but also legitimated their claim to equal representation in the re-established republic. This morally based claim was sometimes implicitly, sometimes explicitly, supported by a pragmatic but apparently incompatible argument, namely that the experience acquired in the puppet state of 1939–45 – i.e. in the political configuration which the uprising had aimed at destroying – was proof of the maturity of the Slovak people and their ability to govern themselves. These two historical facts, offering two diametrically opposed interpretations, were supposed to make the case for a new start of Czech-Slovak cohabitation, on the basis of parity (*rovný s rovným* – 'equal with equal').

These two lines of argument were indeed incompatible; however, the claim *per se* that the six years of the Slovak state had been a test which Slovak society had passed to satisfaction was not devoid of validity, although Czech public opinion was reluctant to acknowledge this. This reluctance was more deleterious to Czech-Slovak dialogue than the sporadically aired suspicion that the uprising might have been a last-hour alibi venture; the latter could easily be countered by inferring that it might betray an inferiority complex on the Czech part, due to feelings of powerlessness *vis-à-vis* the German occupying regime during the war. The refusal to see, objectively and without undue moralizing, the period of the Slovak state as a perhaps unplanned, but nonetheless real, political apprenticeship for the Slovak population was also one of the factors of the disharmony of historical perspectives adopted by the Czechs and the Slovaks, respectively, after the collapse of communism 45 years later.

The reconstructed Czechoslovakia of 1945 met the Slovak demands only halfway, so that they kept hoping for more, somewhere down the road. An unmistakable sign of the lack of enthusiasm on the Czech side was the curious asymmetry of the new state form. There was a central government and two Slovak autonomous bodies, but there were no corresponding Czech legislative and administrative organs to match the Slovak National Council and the Board of Commissioners. The situation was found to be disquieting not only by the Slovaks; a young Czech journalist observed sarcastically that the republic was apparently composed of two parts, Czechoslovakia and Slovakia, where Czechoslovakia comprised only Bohemia and Moravia. It would be unfair, however, not to grant that the inconsistency was primarily an instrument of the overall communist strategy aimed at securing decisive power in the country. Anticipating, wrongly, that the pattern of the vote for the Communist Party known from the prewar elections, where the Slovak and Ruthenian rural proletariate constituted the mainstay, would be reproduced after 1945, the communists initially promoted and supported this asymmetric decentralization. Their weaker showing in Slovakia than in the Czech provinces in the election of May 1946 made them reverse this course.

The ambiguous and slightly uneasy feelings of a large part of the Czech public concerning Slovakia and its role during the world crisis and war perfectly fitted communist plans. This psychological disposition prevented the only logical coalition for the salvation of democracy and national independence from coming into existence: that of all non-communist parties both in the Czech Lands and in Slovakia. The election results in the former were alarming – about 40 per cent for the Communist Party – but the single most critical element of the situation was not the absolute size of the communist victory. In Slovakia, too, communist gains were considerable: over 30 per cent. However, the Communist Party was not the strongest party there; the Slovak Democratic Party was returned with 60 per cent, while in the Czech provinces the non-communist vote – in itself also representing a clear majority – was split between three major parties, thus making the Communist Party the largest fraction in the parliament. A timely agreement between the three parties in the Czech Lands and the Slovak Democrats, or at least an understanding not to render each other's situation more difficult, would have gone a long way towards thwarting communist designs, although it certainly could not have eliminated the mighty external factor, i.e. Soviet interests and plans in the incipient Cold War. Instead, the Czech non-communist politicians passively watched the Communist Party develop the various schemes and manoeuvres of the 'salami tactic' (i.e. the gradual elimination of representatives of other parties) against their natural Slovak ally.

It is of particular interest to determine how much the experience of the first Czech-Slovak separation affected Czech national consciousness. It has already been pointed out that its impact could not be compared with that of other calamities visited upon Czechoslovakia at the time. This circumstance in itself testifies to the relatively low rank of importance of Slovakia in Czech political awareness. What it demonstrates above all, however, is the weak and shallow effect of the First Republic's attempt to resocialize the Czechs into a sense of a new, Czechoslovak collective identity. Had the operation been successful, Slovak secession in March 1939 would have been perceived as by far the most lethal blow, but this was not the case. A common state with the Slovaks was soon no more than a fleeting memory of an unsuccessful experiment or, rather, of a bad investment.

122   *Zdeněk Suda*

The Lessons of the Divorce

The shared life of the Czechs and the Slovaks in one political home, which
had lasted, with a brief interruption during the Second World War, for three-
quarters of a century, came to an end in January 1993. The dissolution of
Czechoslovakia was carried out as an agreement between the governments
of the two republics, then parts of the Czechoslovak federative state. No
constitutional amendment to this effect has ever been submitted to public
vote; no such vote has even been proposed in the legislative bodies. The
smoothness and the speed of the operation even aroused suspicions about
its legitimacy. World media sometimes referred to it as 'an end that nobody
really wanted'. Yet an end it was. What were its causes? The parallel drawn
with divorce could be pursued a little further in this case: there had been a
kind of incompatibility of the character make-up between the two ethnic
groups. However, the explanatory value of this rather witty image is not
great; it belongs to the category of entertaining speculations about the so-
called personality types of various nations.

Somewhat more useful would appear the theory according to which
there had been a chronic discrepancy between the stages of the development of the two partners. Paraphrasing the Swiss journalist Herbert Lüthy,
who once compared France with other West European societies and wrote
that 'the French clock shows a different time', we could perhaps say that
the Czech clock kept showing a different time from the Slovak clock.
Indeed, the level of social and political development in the two cases had
been very different when the two ethnic groups embarked upon coexistence in one state. The differences, although notably reduced by the time
the communist system collapsed, were still considerable. One factor,
however, is often cited as critical: the national aspirations of the Czechs
were satisfied when the first Czechoslovak republic was established, while
the aspirations of the Slovaks fell short of their goal even after the 'velvet
revolution' of 1989. Hence the attainment of sovereignty, even if only for
the purpose of later surrendering to a larger political unit, either to a federation with the Czechs or to the European Union, had ranked very high on
the list of Slovak objectives.

Although the differences in the levels of development can hardly be
denied between the Czechs and the Slovaks, they in themselves – whatever
form they might have taken – need not have made the cohabitation of the
two under one government impossible. In order to grasp fully the true
nature of the Slovak drive for self-government, it is necessary to point out
the peculiar formula the Slovak leaders were proposing. The seemingly
irrational, contradictory goal they professed to follow, namely 'sovereignty

without independence', is a key element here. It will be even more helpful in an understanding of the situation before the break-up of Czechoslovakia if it is considered in connection with another issue the Slovaks then raised, and to which they appeared to ascribe great importance: namely their concern about the 'greater international visibility of Slovakia', which has been mentioned earlier in this discussion. The emphasis on 'visibility' provides the observer with a clue as to why the Slovaks rejected the near-perfect federalist formula for Czech-Slovak relations after November 1989. This rejection thwarted a whole series of negotiations on a new constitutional arrangement. Eventually the terms 'federation' and 'federal' became almost dirty words in the Slovak political vocabulary. The Czech partners felt deeply frustrated, as they could not understand why the Slovaks, if they desired full equality, would not accept a federalist solution which objectively was the most suitable to bring about such equality. Here precisely was the misunderstanding: it was not equality that the Slovak leaders sought, but 'visibility'. There is little doubt that a federative state form, like any state form including more than one nation, reduces the international visibility of its individual components.

But why, Czech politicians and Czech public opinion would ask, this logically untenable concept of sovereignty without independence and the stress upon 'visibility'? The dialogue of the deaf between Prague and Bratislava not only testified to two completely different 'wavelengths' on which the two national entities communicated; it also pointed to the very root of mutual misperceptions and to one of the principal causes of their ultimate separation: a profound crisis of collective identity on the Slovak side.[5]

The question as to whether and how the Slovak collective identity crisis could have been managed or resolved, and whether any such resolution would have saved the common political home of the Czechs and the Slovaks, is not easy to answer. More relevant is the question as to why the real motives for the Slovak desire for greater visibility escaped the attention of the Czechs, i.e. why this profound identity crisis could have continued unnoticed by them for such a long time. This fact seems rather surprising when considering the historical experience of the Czechs. The fact *per se* that they were not capable of sufficient empathy should not be astonishing; nations, not unlike individuals, tend to forget how it feels to be in a development phase once they have passed into another phase (a kind of 'collective post-adolescent amnesia'?). However, the Czechs in their relations with the Slovaks were not just one society observing and assessing another society. They themselves had been, in a certain respect, the architects of Slovak nationalism and had directly participated in developing Slovak national consciousness. Thus much of what occurred in Slovakia from the second half of the nineteenth century, but especially since the end of the

First World War, was also of their doing. After the separation of 1993, they may well ask themselves what actually the role was that they had played in this respect – that of Pygmalion or of Dr Frankenstein?

In Lieu of a Conclusion

Three-quarters of a century of Czech and Slovak cohabitation came to an end at a time when the prospects for democracy in Central Europe had brightened. This was regrettable, because within a democratic framework a viable solution to ethnic and national problems could have been found more easily – or so it would seem. It is often pointed out that the separation was the work of a minority on both sides, the majority – as is so often the case – remaining silent. Yet this fact tends to support the claim that something substantial was missing that prevented this silent majority from speaking up, namely a common collective consciousness in both nations.

It can be asserted that in general multi-ethnic polities are compelled to lead a risky and precarious existence in times where a racially homogeneous, consistently inclusive as well as exclusive nation-state is the most attractive model. This climate appears to have prevailed since the proclamation of the principle of self-determination at the end of the First World War, especially in the contemporary, post-communist stage of development. None of the ethnically and culturally heterogeneous configurations, not even the most solid among them, with centuries of history, have been spared serious challenges to their cohesion. The Czech and Slovak Federal Republic, too, fell victim to this trend, although it disintegrated under conditions and in a form which do not allow a simple equation with the case of Yugoslavia or the Soviet Union.

No one can safely predict the future of Czech-Slovak relations since the break-up of 1993. Many circumstances suggest that these will be rather unique, different and somewhat closer than typical rapports between two nation-states. However, a *rapprochement* that eventually would enable the two nations to resume common statehood does not appear to be likely. On the contrary, it is to be expected that the experience of living in separate political units will set them even farther apart. Their national consciousness will inevitably be marked by this experience. Among the Czechs, the sense of the continuity of their history will be reinforced, as the ambiguity marking the idea of Czechoslovakism and the resulting problem posed to Czech collective identity will have completely vanished. If the Czechs and the Slovaks ever live again in one political home it will probably not be thanks to common national consciousness. The separation between the two will be overcome only when the universal disintegrative nationalistic current, which has reached a new, unprecedented high in post-communist Central and Eastern Europe, is overcome, when political nationality takes precedence over ethnic nationality and when European consciousness supplants ethnocentric consciousness, which at the same time will be the time of a triumph of democracy in this crisis-ridden region of the world.

Notes

1   It was the stand of the majority of Austrian Slavs, but especially of the Czechs, on the Hungarian liberal revolution that infuriated Karl Marx and inspired him to the most vicious attacks upon the Czech leader František Palacký, and the Czech national movement in general. In a commentary in the *New York Tribune* of 5 March 1852 (omitted in the Czech translation of Marx's collected works published under the communist regime) he intimated that the Czechs were traitors to the revolutionary cause. Also of note is his branding them to 'a dying nationality, dying according to every fact known in history for the last four hundred years' and calling Palacký 'nothing but a learned German run mad'. The wilful and voluntaristic character of the Czech national renascence obviously did not fit into his social theory, which may have angered him even more than any Czech position on the concrete political issues of the time. He could not understand why the Czechs, when all the circumstances – political, social and economic – were hostile to their survival, did not abandon themselves to the irresistible forces of history and did not lie down and die. Thus he laid bare a fatal weakness of his political sociology: the underestimation of the need for collective identity other than that based only on class, i.e. on shared material interests. His followers, who never noted his mistake and continued to dismiss nationalism as an instance of 'false consciousness', contributed in a significant measure to the failure of the most extensive socialist experiment, the first – and probably the last – of its kind.

2   In certain respects, the feelings of large sections of the Czech public *vis-à-vis* Slovakia at the time resembled those shown towards the Lusatian Zorbs, a tiny Slavic ethnic group on the point of extinction, the remainder of a large settlement of the so-called Elbe-Slavs who in the early Middle Ages had extended from the Baltic Sea to the Bohemian border. However, Czech contacts with the Slovaks had been too long-standing and of too great variety to allow an unqualified comparison.

3   It is interesting to note that the episode of the Great Moravian Kingdom was also cited by those who radically opposed the Czechoslovak idea and/or any coexistence of the Czechs and the Slovaks in a common political framework; these 'separatists' brought it up as proof that the Slovak nation – which here is identified with the population of the Great Moravian Empire – had existed as a distinct entity for 1100 years, and had enjoyed independent statehood.

4   It was suggested, at the time and afterwards, that the Czech leaders learn from this example of political realism and act likewise in similar situations, i.e.

dump their partners whenever they prove to be a burden. An opportunity for taking such a course of action seemed to arise immediately after the war, in the short period before the Cold War front hardened and the two superblocs, East and West, solidified. It did not appear absurd at that time to imagine – in fact, it sounded quite plausible – that Stalin's view of the geopolitical importance of Czechoslovakia should be a reversed copy of that of Hitler. While for Hitler the Czech provinces were of vital significance, to the point that they had to be incorporated in the Third Reich, and Slovakia was located more on the periphery, for Stalin it was precisely Slovakia that could not be left out of the Soviet satellite system if the two already firmly held pawns – Poland and Hungary – were not to be separated from each other. The control of Bohemia and Moravia was not nearly as essential for the Soviet Union at that time; on the contrary, the Iron Curtain could have been drawn more 'tidily' had it followed the White Carpathian mountain range (the Moravian-Slovak border) than if it protruded, as actually was the case, some four hundred miles into central Europe and placed Vienna, an indisputably Western metropolis, two hundred miles *east* of the now 'eastern' capital of Prague. Shortly after the war, too, there was a powerful trend in the Communist Party of Slovakia, not only towards national independence and separation from the Czechs, but also towards the inclusion of Slovakia in the Soviet Union as 'the eleventh Union Republic'. This movement had started already during the war (*'Za sovietske Slovensko!'* – 'For a Soviet Slovakia!'); one of its most prominent representatives was Gustáv Husák, later Secretary General of the Communist Party of Czechoslovakia and President of the Czechoslovak Republic after the Soviet invasion of 1968. In the second half of the 1940s, therefore, a 'deal' or some horse-trading might have appeared conceivable, whereby Stalin would have relinquished his grip on the Czech part of Czechoslovakia in exchange for a more solid control of Slovakia. The Czechs would then have had their chance to pay the Slovaks back in kind for their defection in 1939. The main problem with this scenario is that it overlooks the internal political conditions in Czechoslovakia at the time, especially the distribution of power in the Czech provinces. Hitler chose his solution in March 1939 because the issue of Czechoslovakia was otherwise intractable. With the Communist Party in the lead in Bohemia and Moravia in 1946, Stalin had more than one option; the one which he chose did not lack appeal, since it provided him with the resources of the second most industrialized nation in central Europe (80 per cent of whose invested assets were located precisely in the Czech provinces).

5   It can be historically documented that the concern about 'visibility' is a symptom of collective insecurity and an identity crisis. A prominent example would be imperial Germany under Wilhelm II. Naturally, the importance of Germany in world politics at the turn of the century was much greater than that of today's Slovakia, but this is not essential for the sake of our argument. What matters here is that the frantic efforts of Wilhelm II, especially after the dismissal of Chancellor Bismarck, to secure Germany a say, however small, in all issues and conflicts of the time – Czech historian Josef Šusta remarked caustically that Wilhelm 'eagerly collected tips from all world political dining

tables' – betrayed an abnormal concern about Germany's 'visibility' and likewise was a sign of deep-seated collective insecurity and of an identity crisis.

Further Reading

Edvard Beneš, *Reč k Slovákom* ('The Address to the Slovaks'), Bratislava: 1934.

Eva Broklová, *Československá demokracie 1918–1938* ('Czechoslovak Democracy 1918–1938'), Prague: 1992.

Ludovit Holotík (ed.), *O vzájomných vzťahoch Čechov a Slovákov* ('On Relations between the Czechs and Slovaks'), Bratislava: 1956.

Oskar Jászi, *The Disintegration of the Habsburg Empire*, Chicago: 1929.

—— *Revolution and Counterrevolution in Hungary*, London: 1924.

Hans Kohn, *The Idea of Nationalism*, New York: 1961.

Karel Lisický, *Problém česko-slovenský a problém česko-německý* ('Czech-Slovak and Czech-German Problems'), London: 1954.

Hugh Seton-Watson, *Nations and States*, Boulder, CO: 1977.

R.W. Seton-Watson, *A History of the Czechs and Slovaks*, Hamden: 1965.

Helmut Slapnicka, *Die böhmischen Länder und die Slowakei*, Stuttgart: 1970.

Zdeněk Suda, *The Origins and the Development of Modern Czech National Consciousness*, Prague: 1994.

Wolfgang Venohr, *Aufstand für die Tschechoslowakei*, Hamburg: 1969.

7 Mutual Perceptions in Czech-Slovak Relationships

PETR PŘÍHODA

Introduction

In the spring of 1990, a controversy developed concerning the future name of our joint state in the Czechoslovak parliament. It was obvious that we could not be the 'Czechoslovak Socialist Republic', but Slovak members of parliament were also not satisfied with the name 'Czechoslovakia' because it did not adequately emphasize Slovak individuality, but even concealed it. This was the claim of Slovak cultural representatives and journalists, and also the feeling of the majority of the Slovak public. The Czech public did not understand this.

Just at that time, a minor incident occured. A group of Czech tourists in the Slovak mountains got into a quarrel with some local people, and several Slovak teenagers beat up one of the tourists. The mass media spread information about this event throughout the country and influenced the public mood, including the mood in the editor's office of the daily paper *Lidové noviny*, where I happened to be paying a visit. *Lidové noviny* is a liberal daily newspaper, which especially appeals to well-educated readers. It was published monthly as a samizdat during the communist regime and was read mainly by dissidents.

The incident created a debate in the editor's office, and one agitated commentator declared with contempt that the Slovaks were not even a nation. He did not elaborate further, whether they were an ethnic group on a tribal level of organization, or some other group. No one from the editor's office contradicted him.

The main point of this episode is the following: at the time *Lidové noviny* wrote about the attitude of Slovak parliamentary members and the Slovak public in a very critical, often controversial, manner, but still correctly. Contempt could be found only behind the scenes.

Sometimes similar contempt manifested itself openly. When I was doing military service, one Slovak soldier remarked after a very tiring day that he was 'at the end of his strength'. He said it in Slovak. The Czech and Slovak languages are so similar that translation is not necessary, but some Slovak words sound peculiar to Czech ears, even if they are intelligible. This was true of the sigh of the exhausted Slovak soldier. His Czech colleagues started to laugh, even though they were just as tired, and the Slovak felt humiliated.

If we want to explore the conflictive aspects of Czech-Slovak relationships, and especially the role of mutual misperception and misinterpretation, it is not sufficient to have publicly available information. We also have to remember events which happen on an ordinary and private level of communication, when the censorship of the conscious ego is relaxed. These are manifestations of the psychopathology of everyday life.

The critical attitude of *Lidové noviny* towards Slovak reality is more understandable if we know about the emotions of their chief commentator and how his emotions are accepted by the editorial team in private. We can also understand the attitudes of some Slovaks better if we know about their experiences during their military service in units with a Czech majority. Czech soldiers in Slovakia also met with manifestations of aversion, but less often, and this Slovak aversion did not take the form of contempt.

Similar facts could be found and quantified by sophisticated sociological methods, but this kind of research has never been done and probably never will be. We have to be satisfied, therefore, with more simple methods of investigation, which use, for example, an informed journalist as he goes to an unfamiliar country and only observes and listens.

Mutual Expectations

In some respects, Czechs and Slovaks are similar to the point that they are indistinguishable. In other respects, they are completely different. One can read about this in other chapters of this book.

A hundred years ago, not even an astute observer would have been able to find out from external manifestations where Czech (in this respect, Moravian) society ended and where Slovak society began. The lifestyle of village communities on both sides of the geographical border was identical, the transition of dialects unnoticeable. However, the intensity of communication between both groups was minor for centuries: less than that between Czechs and Germans, and between Slovaks and Hungarians.

It was not until the process of the formation of nations began that the Czechs and Slovaks were stimulated to new self-awareness and their mutual expectations were aroused. Instead of using terms like 'Czechs' and 'Slovaks', I should refer to their intellectual élites, who gave a louder voice to the ideology of nationalism.

The more both sides realized their handicaps in competition with other nations, the more necessary it was for them to expect something from each other. Just one example of such a handicap was the relatively small number of Czechs compared with Germans, and of Slovaks compared with Hungarians. Whole Czech and Slovak social classes were missing, notably the wealthier classes. For this reason both societies lacked the economic, political and cultural institutions which these had created elsewhere. In this respect, Slovaks were even more handicapped than Czechs.

This reminds me of a story about two medieval rulers: the Czech king, Jan of Luxembourg, and the Austrian archduke, Albrecht of Habsburg. They met in 1336 for a confidential political conference alone in a room with a secret entrance. King Jan was blind and Archduke Albrecht was lame. Their problem was, therefore, that neither was able to open the secret door, because neither could successfully manipulate the mechanism. Finally, lame Albrecht directed blind Jan, and the door was opened. Both were amused and confessed that only together could they 'function as a complete man'. Czech and Slovak dispositions and indispositions at the beginning of the age of modern nations can be seen in a similar light.

The initiators of Czech-Slovak relations were nationalistic intellectuals, and the development of this relationship was dictated a priori by expectations on both sides, which were often followed by disappointment. For this reason, realistic perceptions and mutual recognition were rare.

Misperceptions and misinterpretations, therefore, frequently arose, and became stereotypes, because of the lack of opportunities and willingness to correct them. It seems that these stereotyped misperceptions and misinterpretations have created a complex, which has a layered structure. The formation of each layer corresponds to successive stages in the history of Czech-Slovak relationships. Each successive stereotype on one side or the other naturally had its *fundamentum in re*. As realistic corrections were not made, prejudice persisted. The question as to the actual importance of these stereotypes can lead to a never-ending academic debate. The split of our joint state in 1993 was not provoked by external force, so the importance of these stereotypes may be greater than it seems at first glance.

I will try to describe the forms of misperception, misinterpretation and stereotypes in people's minds on both sides, Czech and Slovak. I am Czech, I live in a Czech environment, and I can only observe our joint history from this point of view. That is why I will devote greater attention to the Czech side. This I cannot change, and I apologize in advance for this unbalanced approach.

Courtship

At the beginning of the twentieth century, Slovakia was an underdeveloped agricultural region. The only Slovaks whom Czechs had a chance to meet were wandering tradesmen such as tinkers. The original Czech image of Slovakia corresponded to this lack of familiarity.

The intellectual élites of the awakening Slavic nations of the Habsburg monarchy were dissatisfied with their economic, cultural and political underdevelopment. To compensate for this handicap, therefore, a vague ideology was created: panslavism. From this was derived the imperative for Slavic cooperation to create a better Slavic future, which was anticipated by the German philosopher Johann Gottfried Herder (1744–1803). The result of this ideology was that the Czechs started to need the Slovaks. The Czechs were frustrated by German superiority, and there was suddenly an opportunity to expand into the Carpathians. As early as the first half of the nineteenth century, it had been perceived that Slovaks were Czechs, although less developed, that the Slovak language was a complex of Czech dialects, and that, in fact, Slovak existence was a less developed variation of Czech existence.

If the Slovak situation had been less complicated, Slovaks would have unanimously rejected this concept. But in Slovakia there was a Protestant minority of around 12 per cent who were convinced that Czechs and Slovaks were one ethnic group. Slovak Protestants even used the Czech version of the Protestant Bible, and supported Czechs in their illusory concept. The majority of Slovaks, however, were Catholic, and the Catholic clergy rejected this notion. Slovak Protestant intellectuals later realized that Slovaks were not Czechs and that this concept was illusory, and, after an agreement with the Catholics, created the literary Slovak language in the 1840s. The Czechs were greatly dissatisfied with this, because to them it seemed a 'betrayal'. They did not want to give up the stereotype of Slovak inferiority. Slovaks were looked on as poorer, less educated, less technically skilled, less enterprising, politically immature, etc. This perception could have been considered realistic in the nineteenth century, and later it became a prejudice which functions to this day.

Even though after a time this perception was overshadowed by different Czech conceptions of Slovaks, it did not become extinct and still often manifests itself in its original appearance in conflict situations today. This can be illustrated by the statement of the commentator from *Lidové noviny* mentioned previously.

Certain advantages of Czechs compared with Slovaks cannot be denied. Czechs are more numerous, economically more efficient, their land is more fertile, and their contact with the European West is stronger. The stereo-type of Slovak inferiority, however, functions in the Czech mind automatically, a priori, even before experience of the Slovak environment.

While from the first half of the nineteenth century the Czechs naïvely hoped that through the 'annexation' of Slovakia they would gain an advantage over the Germans, the Slovaks just as naïvely relied on the unselfish help and protection of the luckier Czechs to strengthen Slovak resistance to the pressure of Hungarian assimilation. The Czech reaction to the creation of literary Slovak caused disappointment and shook Slovak self-confidence. It was necessary for the Slovaks to protect themselves against this, and thus a Slovak stereotype of Czech haughtiness and expansionism was created, which continues to exist to the present day. In the 1870s, Slovak intellectuals reacted to the failure of independent Slovak policies by a nostalgic escape to the dream world of Slovak patriarchal ideals. It was in this period that their perception of Czechs as 'not true Slavs' and as being 'corrupted by the West', a stereotype which has also survived up to the present, was formed. This manifested itself in the 1990s in the apprehensions of the Slovak politician Ján Čarnogurský concerning 'Czech liberalism'.

Marriage

While in the second half of the nineteenth century the Czech Lands blossomed economically and culturally, Slovak society was in constant decline due to progressive Magyarization, supported by the state adminis-tration. They therefore sought a new understanding with the Czechs. This suited the Czechs, because their endeavours to federalize the Habsburg monarchy had not been successful. This mutual *rapprochement* culminated in the formation of the independent Czechoslovak state. Another layer was added to Czech perception – the stereotype of Slovak complementarity. It was a more suitable instrument for the joint life of both ethnic groups in a united state than the notorious Czech conception of Slovak inferiority.

In this new perception, the Czechs endowed Slovaks with a certain one-sidedness which was the opposite pole to Czech onesidedness and which therefore 'balanced' it. The Czechs attributed an analytic rationality to themselves and perceived the Slovaks as intuitive and emotional beings. Earlier, the Czechs had perceived their position as adult while the Slovaks were infantile; now they perceived themselves as masculine and the Slovaks as feminine. The Czech environment was seen as an urban or industrial civilization, while the Slovak environment had agricultural characteristics.

At first glance, this stereotype seems to be more kind to Slovaks than the previous one. It implied that only both together, i.e. Czechs and Slovaks, could create a complete organism, similar to King Jan and Archduke Albrecht. This stereotype gained sympathizers even in Slovakia, and still exists on both sides, even after the division of our joint state. This variation can be conceived as the relationship between an older and a younger brother, or as the idea of a Czech-Slovak marriage, where the Czech side plays the role of husband and the Slovak side that of wife. The break-up of the state, in fact, was perceived as a divorce.

The idea of two ethnic groups in one state, their positions complementary, contains a snag: their future is set to follow a certain course. This idea ascribes a role to each of the partners and assumes that they will not deviate from it. Even though this complementary model was accepted in Slovakia, conflicting views soon appeared concerning the correct form of this 'marriage'. The Slovak demand of 'equal to equal' came up against the simple and unchangeable fact of the inequality of the two ethnic groups, demographically and economically speaking, and met with Czech incomprehension. In these controversial situations, Slovak expectations sometimes led to the concept of Czechs as the sponsors of Slovakia, and the sensitive Czech side reacted by creating the concept of Slovakia as a parasite of the Czech Lands. Thus the old stereotype of Slovak inferiority was restored.

The stereotype of complementarity is one of the sources of so-called Czechoslovakism, or, by another name, 'the theory of a united Czecho-slovak nation'. However, its title is ambiguous and the theory itself was never sufficiently explained. Czechoslovakism can be interpreted as the idea of one political nation, like the nation in an American sense, where it is not important how many and which ethnic groups it consists of. It can also be interpreted, however, as the idea of one ethnic group created by the fusion of Slovaks and Czechs; in other words, this is a concept of gradual convergence, the result being in fact the 'Czechization' of Slovaks. It is a very unrealistic concept, but it was the belief of many educated Czechs. Czechoslovakism as a programme of the formation of a political nation did not succeed because it did not shed this unrealistic Czech concept.

Enemies

The joint existence in a united state after 1918 was harmonious for only a short time. The first manifestations of disappointment on the part of conservative Slovak politicians were evident by the end of 1918. In the next few years, many Czech professionals went to Slovakia. This help was necessary from the beginning, as Slovaks recognize even today. In Czech eyes, this was unselfish help, a view which still exists today, but it had a paternalistic motivation which Slovaks perceived even then. Thus was formed the present-day ambivalence towards the Czechs.

With Czech help, the process of the formation of a modern Slovak nation continued, faster than before, aided by the Slovak emancipation movement, which was founded in Slovak Catholic circles. It is not surprising that its programme was autonomy even at this stage, as the conception of the Czechoslovak state as a unified nation in which Czechs (representing about half of the state's population) were hegemonial, was problematic. In spite of this, a unified Czechoslovakia became the official state doctrine, threatening Slovak autonomy. The state powers, within the possibilities of parliamentary democracy, resisted moves towards such autonomy. Nationalistic Slovak journalists restored the stereotype of Czech expansionism. The argument about the Pittsburgh Agreement added a new characteristic, that of Czech perfidiousness, and, because a part of the Slovak public was strongly Catholic, yet another characteristic appeared: Czech impiety.

When Czechoslovakia came under pressure from Nazi Germany, Slovak autonomism transformed into separatism. Czechs, therefore, formed the stereotype of the Slovak betrayal. This is reminiscent of the German *Dolchstosslegende*, which was created by nationalistic German journalists after Germany's defeat in the First World War. From the late 1930s onwards, there was a fear on the Czech side that 'in a moment of extreme jeopardy, Slovaks will stab you in the back'.

With Hitler's help, Slovak separatism was successful. For the first time in history an independent Slovak state was founded. This episode of Slovak history (1939–45) is both infamous and tragic. Almost without exception, Czechs consider it purely infamous; the Slovak press and public opinion are ambivalent on this point. The official propaganda of the Slovak state at the time was both anti-Semitic and anti-Czech.

Czech-Slovak misperceptions also compounded events after the Second World War, above all after the parliamentary elections of 1946, when the structure of the political spectrum on both sides was polarized. The majority of Slovaks disagreed with the execution in 1947 of the president of the former Slovak Republic, the Catholic priest Jozef Tiso. The communist seizure of power in February 1948 was a Czech, rather than Slovak, matter, because the strong position of the communists was the result of the elections in the Czech Lands. The conviction quickly spread in Slovakia that 'communism was brought by the Czechs'. Communist centralism, too, was perceived in Slovakia as 'Czech'. Czechs did not understand these Slovak perceptions and misperceptions, and did not concern themselves much with Slovakia, because, in the eyes of many, it was considered merely a province.

'A United Path To A Brighter Future'

The communist terror of the 1950s afflicted Slovakia as much as the Czech Lands. Followers of the Tiso regime were also affected. Communist propaganda identified all Slovak anti-communists, expecially Catholics, as Nazi collaborators. This communist persecution was also perceived as 'Czech'.

Anti-Czech feeling, therefore, persisted in Slovakia, and so at the time of the Prague Spring of 1968 the aspirations of both nations were different. Czechs sought the democratization of public life, while Slovaks objected: 'First federalization, then democratization.'

The communist programme of the industrialization of Slovakia paradoxically permitted the modernization of the country. This was carried out 'from above', in Slovak eyes from the centre, from Prague. The consequence of this modernization was a vast increase in the standard of living in Slovakia, made possible at the cost of the redistribution of economic resources which were created in the Czech Lands. The Slovak mind refused to perceive this. Slovak thinking (political, published and public) did not adequately respect economic logic and repressed economic problems. This attitude could also be observed among Slovaks after November 1989. The motive for this repression is possibly the fact that, at that point, in the light of economic rationality, the fatal unequal position of both nations was evident, and this was unacceptable to most Slovaks. Only after the division of the joint state did Slovaks realize the extent of the damage caused by this lack of realism.

Still, there existed one area where both the Czech Lands and Slovakia became closer in the symbiosis with the communist regime. Its repressive, centralized, uniform and levelling politics imposed a Czech and Slovak lifestyle, which was practically identical on an everyday level. For both, passivity, submissiveness, dependence and corruption reigned for forty years, and determined the behaviour of three generations. One might have assumed that this togetherness would have made it possible for both Czechs and Slovaks to forget the harm done to each other in the past.

When the breakdown of the communist bloc started in the 1980s, Western experts produced prognostic hypotheses. The French political analyst Jacques Rupnik presented a classification of these hypotheses and postulated two types. The first type is the 'theory of purgatory': a communist dictatorship would liquidate all problems, aversions, complexes and resentments of the past in Eastern Europe, and these nations would step into an open future with a clean slate. The second type is represented by the 'theory of a badly functioning refrigerator': unsolved problems were only partly frozen, the refrigerator stopped working, and everything that was deposited there retained its original or even a slightly rotten appearance. The character of Czech-Slovak relationships after November 1989 is reflected more accurately in theories of the second type.

The Velvet Divorce

The communist regime in Czechoslovakia collapsed due to its own weakness; the mass demonstrations in November 1989 were only the *coup de grâce*. For a short time, in the town squares of bigger cities, Czechs and Slovaks found a common cause. It soon became apparent, however, that the involuntary symbiosis with the former regime, which was perhaps the only joint experience, was not a sufficient bond. The Czech and Slovak motives for the rejection of the communist regime were only partly the same. Their perceptions of moving beyond the communist heritage were also rather different.

Attitudes of Slovak journalists to this heritage were less differentiated and on the whole more conciliatory than Czech attitudes. There are two reasons for this. Firstly, Slovakia gained much during socialism. In contrast to the Czechs, few Slovaks looked on the Communist era as lost decades. The need to greatly distance itself from communism was less strong in Slovakia than in the Czech Lands. Secondly, Slovakia had reason to look at the post-communist future with apprehension. The modernization of Slovakia was designed socialistically, and its achievements were suddenly almost useless. In other words, the problems of the post-communist future worried Slovaks more than Czechs. Because of this, the traditional misperception and misinterpretation that 'all innovations which come from Prague endanger Slovakia' prevailed among the Slovaks. One of these innovations was economic transformation.

Czech traditional ignorance of Slovakia resulted in an irritable reaction by Czech journalists. Slovaks were blamed *en bloc* for crypto-communism and 'national socialism'. The hostile Czech reaction in the years 1990–91 discredited Slovak followers of the united state and joint economic transformation in the eyes of the Slovak public. For this reason, very few were represented in the parliamentary elections of 1992.

The mass-media war liberated populist emotions on both sides. Apart from its primary significance, the Czech-Slovak controversy had another side: the Czech post-communist (and crypto-communist) political left tried to slow down the economic transformation and to preserve the common state. In this conflictive atmosphere, all Czech and Slovak stereotypes created during the previous two centuries returned in full. There were also some blows below the belt: Czech journalists recalled the precarious position of the Hungarian minority in Slovakia, and Slovak journalists wrote about the postwar expulsion of the Sudeten Germans, which taints Czech-German relations to this day. After November, political exiles returned to Czechoslovakia. There were two kinds of Slovak political exile: one was above all democratically oriented, pro-Czechoslovak, and anti-communist; the second was oriented towards nationalism and maintained the traditions of the independent Slovakia of 1939–45. Members of this second group significantly influenced the Slovak emancipation process. A small but vocal part of the Slovak public started openly heralding the representatives of prewar autonomy, separatism and the independent Slovak state. The Czech reaction to this reminiscence was hostile. It has to be said that the Czech public and Czech journalists were never very familiar with Slovak affairs and saw only a negligible nuance in a significant differ-ence. The figures of more recent Slovak history, such as Andrej Hlinka, Jozef Tiso and Vojtech Tuka, were therefore seen in Czech minds as being practically the same.

At the time, I had the opportunity to talk privately with several Slovak politicians. When a memorial plaque appeared in the city where Jozef Tiso had practised as a Catholic priest, the then chairman of the Slovak parlia-ment, who did not support this act, told me: 'In the time of the communist dictatorship you Czechs remembered prewar Czechoslovakia as an old, sentimental time. Slovaks, however, did not have such feelings for this time. Therefore the illusion of the independent Slovakia of 1939–45 was created, even if people knew very little of this period.'

After the death of the last communist president, Gustáv Husák (an ethnic Slovak), in 1991, the participants at his funeral included some of the highest Slovak political representatives. Czech journalists accepted this with distaste, voicing the suspicion that in Slovakia it did not matter if one was a communist, only that one was Slovak. At that time, the Slovak premier told me: 'Before the majesty of death, hostile politicians should be silent. We wanted to make a conciliatory gesture. Slovak journalists today cannot afford such internal conflicts, which would be destabilizing. You Czechs are more resistant in this regard.'

In December 1991, the break-up of our joint state was already very probable. At the time, the deputy chairman of the Slovak parliament reacted to my prognostic scepticism in this way: 'Maybe you are right that Slovakia will not prosper after secession, but we must try it in spite of all the risks which you refer to. We must test our ability to rule our own independent state for the sake of our self-confidence. If we miss this opportunity, we will suffer from a feeling of inferiority for generations. Maybe we will founder, maybe not, but we have to try …'

In my view, the division of our joint state was against the principles of geopolitical and economic rationality. But mutual Czech-Slovak alienation had reached a stage where no other conclusion was possible. In itself, the act of divorce was very decent. The economic consequence of the divorce fell incomparably more on the Slovak side than on the Czech side. The Slovak government press blamed the Czechs for any difficulties, but by the start of 1994 the majority of Slovaks had realized that the reasons lay elsewhere. In Slovakia, I often come across nostalgia for the joint state; on the Czech side I rarely find it. Immediately after the break-up, Czechs largely felt relief and a certain satisfaction. Today, indifference predominates, and communication between both societies is weakening. Already many bus and rail links between them have been discontinued, because Czechs and Slovaks visit each other less. Both countries are becoming more distant from each other, and I intuitively feel that this is not good.

8 Slovak Exceptionalism

MIROSLAV KUSÝ

The 'Slovak question', or the question of 'Slovak exceptionalism', became the focus of domestic and foreign analyses of the process of disintegration of the Czech and Slovak Federal Republic a long time before 1 January 1993. The inevitability of the break-up, the impossibility of further coexistence between Czechs and Slovaks, was argued in many cases on the very basis of this 'exceptionalism'. Slovakia was too different, it was claimed: it was oriented in quite a different direction from the Czech Lands; Slovaks were too different from Czechs, and so their joint state was only an artificially and forcibly maintained entity, incapable of an independent and democratic life.

At the time stereotypes abounded relating to the specific position of Slovakia and of the Slovaks in the Czech and Slovak Federal Republic. Some of these stereotypes described reality truthfully, but only superficially, while others distorted or simply contradicted reality. Many of these stereotypes dated back a long way – as can be seen in the case of the 1943 study of the Slovak national character by a well-known Slovak professor of psychology, Anton Jurovský.[1]

Jurovský analysed primarily the psychological side of the Slovak character, and specifically the allegedly higher degree of emotionality or over-sensitivity of the Slovak national character. He came to the conclusion that 'emotionality', i.e. the ability to experience emotions, was greater in Slovaks than in the case of other ethnic groups. 'It is a sign of a higher emotional 'stimulativeness', of a higher sensitivity, which means that the subject needs relatively fewer stimuli to put all of his emotional life in motion ... This emotional vitality also becomes emotional expressiveness, i.e. the ability to manifest emotions by gestures, by speech and by other actions. Slovaks are quite outstanding in all of these respects.'[2]

According to Jurovský, the so-called 'legend of Jánošík' (very similar to the Robin Hood legend) had a special influence on the Slovak national character:

'It is extraordinarily important in this question that the fabled Jánošík was created from the historical Jánošík by the imagination of a subservient and suffering nation ... We can conclude that through Jánošík's features we can see in the Slovak national character a heroic feature which shows that Slovaks suffer for justice, and that those people who venture to do so can attain glory and honour among the broad masses of the people.'[3]

The main aim of this discussion is not to analyse the Slovak national character, but to study the political characteristics of the modern Slovak nation, which can be seen in many interpretations and views of the situation in the Czech and Slovak republics in the 1990s. Some, but not all, of these views are the product of Czech prejudices against Slovaks.

There existed several stereotyped views of the position of Slovakia and the Slovaks in the last days of the Czech and Slovak Federal Republic. Some of these stereotypes were undoubtedly an accurate reflection of reality, but only on a very superficial level. Others distorted reality to a greater or lesser degree, or were simply false. Five areas of such standard characteristics of the Slovaks compared with the Czechs can be identified:

(1) Slovaks are more nationalistically oriented;
(2) Slovaks are more separatistically oriented;
(3) Slovaks are more Christian-oriented;
(4) Slovaks are more left-wing; and
(5) Slovaks are more eastwardly oriented.

This discussion aims to analyse these general characteristics in concrete terms to determine to what extent they are accurate and how they have arisen.

Are the Slovaks more Nationalistically Oriented?

Nationalism originates where membership of a nation begins to be seen as the decisive characteristic of a person and as being more important than other forms of classification, such as social class or political inclination. Specific national values (national language, national culture, national history, etc.) are then elevated above all other value systems, be they, for example, aesthetic or ethical: what is national, i.e. what originates from the nation concerned, is a priori better, more beautiful, more correct and more righteous.

No doubt there are Slovaks for whom this type of Slovak nationalism is typical. This is not to say that they are essentially more extreme in this respect than other similar nationalists in any other nation, including the Czechs (this is also borne out, after all, by the characteristic proverb *'Co je české, to je hezké!'* – 'What is Czech is beautiful!'

The situation changes qualitatively when such occasional, individual nationalism becomes systematic and communal. It manifests itself as a kind of one-sided, unidirectional fanaticism of values, deriving from the same principles as party or religious fanaticism.

During the 74 years of coexistence of Czechs and Slovaks in a common state, such group nationalism regularly appeared, especially on the Slovak side, as a political movement with an exalted national programme. This was the case in the time of the first Czechoslovak republic (1918–38), when this programme was adopted by the Slovak People's Party under the leadership of Andrej Hlinka. 'Christian nationalism' was a specific product of this time and went on to form the ideological starting point of the Slovak nationalist movement. In the 1925 parliamentary elections, Hlinka's Slovak People's Party won one-third of the votes.

This Christian nationalism was, at the time, the constituting principle of the Slovak state, which was formed and existed in accordance with Hitler's will during the Second World War. According to Stefan Polakovič, one of its leading ideologues, 'the mission and aim of the Slovak state is to give an example of 'Christian nationalism'.[4] In this state 'Slovak fascism and nationalism represent a completely new destination'. The destination is Christian totalitarianism, based on the assumption that 'our system will be further supported by one party as the bearer and representative of the will of the nation'. Equally, however, it is the arrangement of an 'authoritarian system', which is the assertion of the leadership principle, according to which 'the nation uses its leader's mouth to express its will'. This nationalistic programme also comprises a higher mission: 'To the Slovak state and nation falls the splendid historical role of showing the whole of humanity that nationalism may be a constructive power, and is not the bearer of injustice.'[5]

In reality Slovak totalitarian nationalism became militant intolerance towards the neighbouring nations, domestic nationalities and minority ethnic groups (except the Germans), who were all seen as the national enemies of the Slovaks. It was for this reason that the Czechs were expelled from their territory, 'so that by deporting the Czechs it would be purified of idle tramps'; that an aggressive war was fought against Poland in September 1939; that essential prejudices existed regarding the Hungarians, as it was said that 'an atavistic streak of ruthlessness and unrighteousness remains imprinted in the Hungarian character'; and that Jews were deported to Nazi death camps, since 'the Jews not only despised our culture, but were its destroyers'.[6]

Powerful resistance by the whole nation grew against the rise of Slovak nationalism and its implementation in the political arena. This led to the Slovak National Uprising of 1944. In the view of Ľ. Lipták, 'the Slovak

National Uprising was one of the greatest armed resistance activities carried out in German-controlled territory during the Second World War'.[7] Even in the 1990s, Slovak nationalist ideologues could not come to terms with the fact that the nation rose up against the nation-state and its representatives. According to F. Vnuk: 'This betrayal, the only one of its kind in the modern history of humanity, namely that the nation took up arms to destroy its own state, is in essence so monstrous that any self-respecting Slovak must reject the Slovak National Uprising, even if it had been organized and led by angels.'[8] In reality, this uprising is a source of national pride to the Slovaks, since they achieved it as a conscious, sovereign and resolute nation. Equally, this is significant evidence that the decisive majority of the Slovak nation were not adherents of the nationalist ideology of the Slovak state, but more its active opponents.

The total discrediting of this ideology was completed by the defeat of fascism in the Second World War, with the resulting dissolution of the Slovak state and the renewal of the Czechoslovak Republic in 1945.

Thus, for a relatively long period, Slovak nationalism was practically written off on domestic soil, but not in exile. In addition, from the beginning of the communist dictatorship in Czechoslovakia in 1948, communist totalitarianism began to suppress it as a rival totalitarian ideology. Only the interruption of this communist hegemony, in the short period of the Prague Spring of 1968, allowed a certain revitalization of the nationalist movement in Slovakia. One result of this was that federalization was given higher priority by the Slovaks than democratization. The external manifestation of this movement was the revival of national symbols suppressed by the communists, such as those traditions connected with Cyril and Methodius, Štúr (the 'father' of the Slovak language), the Matica Slovenská movement for Slovak revival, and M.R. Štefánik. It is not surprising that, at this time, many representatives of the communist regime also joined the nationalist revival, in the hope that, with the help of a nationalist programme, they could succeed in becoming a part of the new democratic order.

However, this change in regime was not achieved in 1968, and disciplined communists returned to the party's internationalist ideology, in the so-called process of normalization in Czechoslovakia, enforced through the Soviet occupation. It is symptomatic that in this normalization process, lasting more than 20 years, the opposition to the totalitarian communist regime included no element of Slovak nationalistically oriented dissent, but only civic dissent, represented by the Chartist movement (Charter 77), the cultural underground, samizdat literature and the secret Church.

Nationalists appeared in Slovakia long after the victorious peaceful revolution of November 1989, at a time when the definitive defeat of the communists was already decided. The first nationalists organized the Slovak National Party (SNP) in March 1990, and in the elections in June that year they gained almost 14 per cent of the votes and became the third strongest party in the Slovak parliament. As far as uniting all Slovaks behind the principle of nationalism was concerned, however, they still had very far to go. This aim gradually perished, as a series of small and insignificant nationalist parties appeared and obstinately rejected this integrative principle. The last of these was the Slovak Christian Democrat Movement, formed shortly before the 1992 elections, and whose ideas were not unrelated to the Christian nationalism of the period of the Slovak state. This movement was formed by the breakaway nationalist wing of the former Christian Democrats. There was a similar nationalist wing in the left-wing Movement for a Democratic Slovakia, which broke away from the civic movement, Public Against Violence, winner of the 1990 elections, and was the strongest political group in 1994.

The final policy aim of the Slovak nationalists was the establishment of an independent nation-state, but their activity concentrated on emphasizing national symbols: renaming or preventing the renaming of towns, streets and squares; establishing Slovak as the official language 'without exception' (by means of the 'language law'); repeated attempts to declare sovereignty in the Slovak National Council; and seeking and detecting enemies of the Slovak nation among people who were not 'one of them' or 'renegades'. 'Therefore in the mass media, at demonstrations and press conferences, they are described as "enemies of society". In the Czech environment, these are, almost without exception, identified as enemies of the market and the right, i.e. as leftists, whereas in Slovakia they are enemies of the nation, i.e. "federalists".'[9] Just as in 1968, this nationalist wave included a whole series of former communist activists and members and agents of the former State Security.

In spite of all the nationalistic excesses which appeared in Slovakia after the 1989 revolution (for example, attacks on top government representatives, including those on the president of the republic, the breaking up of demonstrations of parties of the coalition government, and the public burning of the state flag), Slovakia did not suffer too severely from overexcited nationalistic passions: there were no wounded or dead, no looted shops, and there was no burning of state buildings. Hence, the Slovak nation as a whole remained relatively indifferent towards this movement; nationalism did not become a mass, nationwide movement. It seems that the nationalist wave reached its climax in the period of discussions about the so-called 'language law' in the Slovak National Council in October 1990. The concerns of the nation, according to public opinion research from this period, constantly differed from those mentioned by nationalist politicians at demonstrations, in the media and in parliament. Civic problems (unemployment, the standard of living, and the socially disadvantaged) were regularly deemed the most important, followed by problems of social pathology (crime, poor interpersonal relations, and alcohol and drugs); in third place were problems of the low quality of life (the environment, health care, and services), and after all these followed the question of Slovak sovereignty (in May 1991: 74 per cent, 68 per cent, 55 per cent and 45 per cent respectively). This latter proportion then gradually fell, to the disadvantage of the nationalist parties, which emphasized national values,[10] so that, for example, repeated provocative attempts to declare Slovak sovereignty on the floor of the Slovak National Council evidently passed without interest from the Slovak public. Public opinion research documents a growing weariness with obtrusive nationalistic propaganda.

Therefore it cannot be said that the Slovaks as a whole are much more nationalistically oriented than the Czechs or that the Slovak nation is a nation of Slovak nationalists. Exalted nationalism was never adopted by the nation as a whole, but only at a party political level by a minority of nationalistically oriented militant members of this nation.

Are the Slovaks more Separatistically Oriented ?

In practice separatism is usually connected with nationalism, and its main tenet states that an ethnic group will reach its ultimate self-realization only by forming its own sovereign state. To establish this, it must be released from its existing subordination to a constitutional union. In this sense the Czechoslovak Republic became the chief hindrance to Slovak separatists from the time of its foundation.

According to Jozef Lettrich, the escalation of Slovak nationalism went from a programme of autonomy for Slovakia, through Slovak separatism to the nationalist totalitarianism of the Slovak state.[11] Of these, separatism was a radical deviation from democratic lines of development, starting from the foundation of the Czechoslovak Republic. 'When the Slovak People's Party proclaimed a programme of autonomy for Slovakia, it took up a democratic position, but when it rejected this programme in favour of separatism, it also rejected democracy in favour of totalitarianism. Slovak separatism was not only anti-Czech, it was also anti-democratic.'[12]

Its form in the Slovak state was a clear demonstration of this. This state was neither founded nor maintained by democratic means, since the power of the separatist tendencies depended on the power of the nationalist movement, and, as has been shown, this movement has little support in Slovakia. Therefore the separatists could not rely on the democratically expressed will of the people, but had to force its separatist decision on them. 'The Slovak separatists were much less interested in the nation or the state than in gaining power. During the whole existence of the Slovak state, they governed without consent, against the will of the Slovak nation.'[13]

After the demise of the Slovak state, its fascist protagonists went into exile where, as individuals, they maintained the idea of Slovak separatism for life. In the domestic environment of anti-communist struggle up to 1989, this idea was not to be found among dissidents. After the velvet revolution, Slovak separatism gradually began to appear again in Slovakia, at first only as an import, introduced and spread by lobbyists for groups of Slovak emigrants and their organizations (the World Congress of Slovaks in Toronto and others). The only party in the parliamentary elections of 1990 with this explicit programme was the Slovak National Party, but gradually further nationalist parties and groups adopted a separatist solution to the question of Slovak statehood.

In spite of this gradual growth in separatism after 1989, according to public opinion polls undertaken at the time: 'It may be said unambiguously that representatives of the common state in the Czech Lands and in Slovakia have a long-term, and more or less stable, dominance. This is confirmed by the opinion polls carried out up to now ... The relation of national to anti-national positions from the point of view of the preferred form of constitutional arrangement may be stated as 9:1 in favour of the common state in the Czech Republic, and 8:2, or at least 7:3, in favour of the common state in the Slovak Republic.'[14]

The 20 to 30 per cent holding separatist positions in Slovak public opinion polls cannot, however, be explained away by the emigrant lobby, ex-communists, members of the former State Security, or lately roused ambitious politicians among 'those who sought power, but did not achieve it in, or shortly after, November 1989'.[15] All these no doubt represent certain groups determining the separatist movement, but its legitimation and basis must be sought outside these areas.

In this sense, Slovak separatism endeavoured to form links with the communist past, as well as with the new constitutional situation. In the first case it was based legitimately on the idea that: 'It is the very origin of sovereign national states, following the achievements of ending communist rule, establishing natural international relations, and instigating a new European integration, which, on the one hand, completes a healthy and demanding process of the decentralization (political, administrative, economic, cultural, military and other) of state power, and, at the same time, allows the natural needs of national identity to be satisfied. Opposition to hegemony and dominance, when it also has the form of a nationalist movement, is, from this point of view, the basis of deviation from the powerful principles of communism. According to the representatives of this view, therefore, this process is positive and natural.'[16]

This conception ignores the common totalitarian starting point of communism and nationalism; the common anti-democratic basis of the 'nation-state' and 'the dictatorship of the proletariat'; and the common mystic source of national and class unity, national and class identity, the common collectivist basis of both ideologies. In this sense, nationalism is not a deviation from the principle of communism, but a natural assertion of its totalitarian essence in another form. This nationalist separatism is only another form of the communist division from the rest of the world and of communist isolationism.

Slovak separatism was also a reaction to the lack of a continuing constitutional arrangement in the Czech and Slovak Federal Republic. The federation was a product of communist totalitarianism, and as such was significantly marked by communist constitutional ideology: the results of the assertion of the leading role of the party, the dictatorship of the proletariat, so-called democratic centralism, the omnipresent socialist state, etc. Therefore the democratic forces on the Czech and Slovak sides endeavoured from the first to complete the defeat of communism in the constitutional sphere as well, by constructing the basis of a new democratic federalism, on the principle of equality for both national republics, with a just and functional division of competencies between these and the federation.

However, the Slovak separatists started from the a priori viewpoint that the federation was useless in any form, that its survival, therefore, had no purpose, and that the only solution rested in the division of the existing federation into independent and sovereign national states. In the Slovak case the state was to be built not on the principle of citizenship, but on that of the state-forming nation, which was based on the division of the population of Slovakia into two categories of citizen: privileged members of the state-forming nation, whose language was the state and official language 'without exception', and members of the other nationalities and ethnic groups, as citizens of the second category.

Thus, as in the period of the Slovak state, the Slovak separatists were conscious that they did not represent the majority of the Slovak nation, and that, therefore, they could not rely on democratic and constitutional methods for their separatist aims. Their steadfast opposition to the acceptance and assertion of the constitutional principle of a referendum to solve this constitutional question was a result of this. There remained, then, only illegal and unconstitutional methods of breaking up the federation (the declaration of Slovak sovereignty, proclaiming the priority of laws of the Slovak Republic over federal laws, accepting a separate Slovak constitution, etc.), or introducing mechanisms into constitutional arrangements which immobilized the federation, paralysed it and made it unable to function. These obstructive methods used by the Slovak separatists were supported in the last days of the federation by the demagogic negotiating tactics of Vladimír Mečiar, victor in the Slovak parliamentary elections in 1992, who had been driven to an extreme position by the winner of the Czech elections, Václav Klaus.

Are the Slovaks more Christian-Oriented?

Naturally, this question does not concern the confessional composition of the Slovak nation: its composition is generally known, and is specifically enumerated in statistical yearbooks. It is more the question as to how the significant absolute majority of Catholics in Slovakia (60 per cent; 70 per cent together with other Christians) is manifested in the individual political orientation of the Slovaks. Can this phenomenon be considered to be a factor which qualitatively differentiates the Slovak from the Czech political scene, where the proportion of Christians is relatively low?

Christianity as the political programme of the Christian Democrat Movement (CDM) in Slovakia is based on the Christian traditions of the Slovak nation. Christian values form the basic content of this programme for the construction of 'the kingdom of God on earth'. The civic values of a democratic form of society are also subordinated to these values: one is a Christian first, and a citizen after. Christian principles are basic; only late in history do they accept democratic principles. In this spirit, individualistic civic principles, which form the starting point of European liberalism and the basis of traditional European conceptions of pluralist democracy, are essentially erroneous, and are criticized by the leader of the CDM and former prime minister, Ján Čarnogurský, who openly attacked liberalism as the source of all evil in the history of Europe generally, and in that of Czechoslovakia especially.

When the Slovak Christian Democrats agreed with the continuation of the Czech and Slovak Federal Republic, it was only in the sense that the national republics would be as sovereign as possible, less mutually dependent, and with Czech influence excluded as far as possible from Slovak development. Here, there was primarily an ideological defence of Slovakia as Christian territory – defence against destructive liberal and free-thinking influences from the Czech Lands. Therefore they opposed, for example, federal television, federal radio, and federal law-making in the fields of state administration, education, culture, health, etc. This also concerned the question of European integration: as a prospective participant in this integration, they preferred an independent Slovakia to a federation with the 'godless' Czechs. The Europe in which the representatives of the CDM wanted to be integrated, was to be above all a Christian Europe, and not the 'godless' Europe of the liberals.

This, then, was the Christian political programme, which presumed that the Christian-oriented majority of the Slovak population would naturally incline to support it. However, it is evident that this thesis of a Christian political orientation of a significant majority of the Slovaks is not valid for the 1990s, although earlier in Slovak history it had a certain justification, due to, among other things, the mostly rural character of Slovak society. Christian nationalism as the ideology of Hlinka's Slovak People's Party may also be recalled in this connection. However, Slovakia then underwent decisive changes, in the course of industrialization and urbanization, and thus entered modern European civil society, with all the implications of this for its political development.

The representatives of Christian democracy, headed by the former prime minister of the Slovak Republic, Ján Čarnogurský, directly relied on the religious feeling of Slovak voters when they were among the first to break away from the universal civic movement, Public Against Violence (PAV), which had brought about the velvet revolution in Slovakia. At the end of February 1990 the CDM was founded, with the clear aim of winning the first free elections in June 1990. The hope of winning a clear overall majority (the most optimistic estimates gave them up to 65 per cent of the votes) came from assumptions of 80 per cent Christian affiliation.

However, this hope of the Christian Democrats was not fulfilled. They did not take into account the factors of change in Slovakia mentioned previously, or the continuing discrediting of the linking of citizens' religious feelings with a political movement and its ambitions for power, as, for example, in the time of Hlinka's Slovak People's Party and the Slovak state. From the point of view of the expectations, the election result was a débâcle: with its 19.2 per cent of the votes the CDM was in second place after the victorious PAV, which won almost 30 per cent of the votes.

A sizeable proportion of Christian voters, therefore, cast their votes in the parliamentary elections of 1990 according to non-religious criteria, and scattered them among other political parties and movements. Many significant Christian personalities remained in the original civic movement, PAV (for example, the chairman of the Slovak National Council, F. Mikloško, and the Federal Minister of the Interior, J. Langoš) and attracted part of the Christian vote. A second part went to the ranks of the nationally oriented parties. The Evangelicals (Lutherans) generally felt some distrust towards the absolute Catholic dominance in the CDM, and preferred the renewed Democratic Party. The Slovak nationalist emphasis of the CDM dissuaded Hungarian Christians, and so they gave priority to establishing a Hungarian

Christian Democrat Movement.

Consequently, three-quarters of the Christian voters did not see Christian democracy as the most trustworthy representative of their political interests. During the election period, this discrepancy between Christian voters and Christian democracy grew still further. Leading personalities in the CDM gradually lost popularity, and the CDM itself lost part of its supporters. This trend culminated, as did the internal party quarrel, in the breakaway of the nationalist wing of the CDM. In March 1992, this wing registered itself as the Slovak Christian Democrat Movement, with a simple separatist programme, its Christian character relegated to the background.

All these factors led to the CDM, which, in its early stages, had had the mark of political Catholicism, gradually losing this position. In the 1990s the CDM appeared to be going through a process of becoming a modern European, civic Christian Democratic party, independent of the Church and the Church hierarchy, and linked with Christianity only by its ideas, not by its politics. This process, however, had not been completed by the pre-election period of the 1992 elections, and had no significant effect on the Slovak Christian vote.

Thus, the assumption of any significantly higher Christian political orientation of the Slovaks compared with the Czechs can be shown to be unfounded, and thus, in this respect, the Slovak voter behaved in basically the same way as voters in other developed European countries, including the Czech Lands. The Christian Democrat programme was judged primarily on its policies in areas such as economics, education, culture and health, and only secondarily on the basis of the voter's actual religious conviction or membership of a particular Church.

Are the Slovaks more Left Wing?

After the Second World War and the demise of the Slovak state, the Slovaks made their political position clear in the first free parliamentary elections in 1946. It was unambiguous: 62 per cent of the votes went to the Democratic Party. The communists, who scored highly in the Czech Lands, had to be content with 30 per cent of the votes and second place in Slovakia. These results allow no other interpretation than that in Slovakia it was the right which won, while in the Czech Lands it was the left.

In the 1990s, political analysis seemed to show the opposite situation. In the Czech Lands, the crystallization of the political scene from November 1989 tended towards a more significant dominance of right-wing groupings, but in Slovakia the opposite tendency prevailed, with a tendency to a more marked left-wing radicalization of trends in Slovak politics.

If this was indeed the case, it is necessary to seek the basic causes of this qualitative reversal of the whole political orientation of both nations.

In the Czech Lands in 1946, it was the prevailingly urban proletarian population, socially radicalized by wartime poverty and postwar shortages, that determined the result of the elections. However, Slovakia was still a prevailingly rural country, relatively untouched by the horrors of war, and over half of the members of the victorious Democratic Party were traditionally conservative private farmers. Their share in the overall structure of the Slovak population was still more significant.

In the Czech Lands, the process of industrialization and urbanization had, in essence, already culminated in the period before the First World War, within the framework of the industrial revolution in the developed European countries. The complete industrialization and urbanization of Slovakia began late, after the Second World War, and reached its peak sometime in the middle of the 1980s. From this point of view, the Slovak development curve of factors such as total economic prosperity, productivity of labour, gross production per capita and absolute growth of production for the whole of this period rose markedly and at a relatively high rate, as did the standard of living. It was not until the 1980s that their decline and final stagnation became more significant.

Paradoxically, this process of economic growth in Slovakia took place at the same time as the opposite process of the overall economic decline of Czechoslovakia, which had been one of the most industrially developed countries before the war, but was gradually brought down to the level of the developing countries. This downward trend, therefore, was primarily of detriment to the Czechs. Both these processes took place in the framework of the so-called socialist development of Czechoslovakia, which in Slovakia was connected with industrial and urban progress, but which in the Czech Lands was linked with the decline of the country, which had not undergone the post-industrial phase of its development.

In this sense, the 1989 revolution was an unambiguous liberation from the shackles of socialist economics for the Czech Lands. However, for Slovakia this revolution was connected with the end of an industrializing and urbanizing boom, and therefore with the exhausted possibilities of an extensive economy, with the arrival of economic stagnation and the end of development. This meant a qualitative deterioration of living conditions for a significant part of the Slovak population, a significant decline in the standard of living, and a resultant radicalization of political positions. This was observed in Slovakia, and the slogan 'We were better off under communism!', was widely accepted.

Industrialization and urbanization in Slovakia were inevitable processes, which also occurred in all the neighbouring European countries. However, the coincidence of these processes with the socialist 'development' of Slovakia meant that this was industrialization and urbanization significantly deformed, since they were not based on the optimal resources of the country and its population, but were subordinated to erroneous communist ideology, and its strategic and political intentions and aims. These included the preferential development of heavy industry, the strategic dispersal of work in relation to the western frontier (the east Slovak ironworks), the concept of mutual dependence within the framework of the countries of the Warsaw Pact (for example, an ironworks in east Slovakia using iron ore from Ukraine for products made in the Czech Lands, the aluminium works in central Slovakia, which was dependent on imported Hungarian bauxite, and the export of unfinished products for final processing abroad). The socialist urbanization of Slovakia certainly transformed the Slovaks in record time, from a mainly rural to a mainly urban population, but at the same time it brought a change from the harmony of a beautiful, rural country to barrack-like suburban blocks of flats in a country lacking an urban infrastructure and with a devastated environment.

In the mid-1990s Slovakia was beginning to suffer the increasingly disastrous results of this conception of industrialization and urbanization, at the end of its extensive, communist-directed development. Among these were the higher level of unemployment, urban social pathology, the existential uncertainty of a significant part of the population, the need for the relocation and requalification of much of the workforce resulting from the cessation of unproductive manufacturing, the conversion of the arms industry, and the limitation of the mining of low quality coal. These factors combined to form a second stimulus for the radicalization of a significant part of the Slovak population, and for the tendency towards a significantly more left-wing orientation.

This was fertile soil for various populist political parties and movements, which offered a discontented population quick and easy solutions to problems resulting from the economic and political situation in Slovakia. Three main solutions were proposed.

The first was *authoritarian demagogy*, according to which the required solution was to trust in a strong, decisive and all-knowing leader. This leader was to deliver the Slovaks from political quarrels, divisions and antitheses, and from the mutual annulment of political activity, and was to bring about the union of Slovakia into a functioning whole. The leader was to think and decide for the united mass, who would only carry out his will. The Movement for a Democratic Slovakia, headed by Mečiar, inclined towards this type of populism.

The second was *social demagogy* of the communist type. It stressed a class interpretation of social justice, inciting the poor to see the rich as the cause of their deteriorating social position, and calling for the social redistribution of national income, and for a strong welfare state, which this redistribution was to assure. It saw the solution in the unity of the working class and in the priority of solving their social demands 'at any price'.

The third was the *national demagogy* of the Slovak nationalist parties and institutions, which saw the solution in exalted national self-identification, in the strengthening of national pride, in the nation-state, in the unity of all 'chosen' inhabitants of the country, with the help of a national mystique and national symbols.

In fact all these three types of Slovak populism overlapped, so that it was only a question of the dominance of a particular type. A significant left-wing orientation was common to all, as is the case with populism in general. In this case it is especially important to recognize nationalism as being an unambiguously left-wing ideology. This was also true of the pre-Munich situation, when a contemporary analyst stated that the nationalist 'may not, at least definitely not among us, be known as rightist'.[17] Slovak populism, therefore, in all its forms, was a third 'back-door' source of the growing left-wing orientation of the Slovak population.

Are the Slovaks more Eastwardly Oriented?

In attempts to identify Slovak characteristics, it has been argued that, whereas the Czechs have belonged to Western European civilization for centuries, the Slovaks are, in this respect, more East European in provenance, and therefore look to the East. In the 1990s nationalists especially referred to this; they did so in an attempt to show that Slovakia belonged to a qualitatively different world compared with the Czech Lands. They argued that although Slovakia was temporarily linked to the Czech world, this was an artificial connection, which was without perspective, impermanent and unsustainable, and it was necessary for Slovakia to return to its natural position. This argument held that Czechoslovakia had no future.

A leading representative of Slovak separatism, the chairman of Matica Slovenská, Jozef Markus, turned to this argument in an interview with the Russian newspaper *Moskovskie Novosti*, when he stated that: 'Czechoslovakia is not a country consisting of two parts. It consists more of two political, economic and cultural orientations. We belong to Eastern Europe, to the Slavonic world. The Czechs are Slavonic Germans.'[18]

This is a grossly falsified view of Slovak history and of Slovakia's historical alignment in general. This territory has always been a natural part of the central European area, and beginning with Samo's state in the seventh century, Slovakia's Slavonic ancestors actively took part in it. Christianity was brought to this area by Slavonic apostles from Byzantium, but western, i.e. Roman Catholic, Christianity was accepted here. The fifteenth-century Gothic church at Bardejov in east Slovakia represents the last outpost of western European church architecture, and is accompanied by secular medieval and baroque urban architecture. In addition to bringing Christianity, Cyril and Methodius also introduced Slavonic Cyrillic letters, but the western European Latin script was accepted and took permanent root here.

Similarly, the Reformation was of a western type and arose naturally on Slovak territory, since it was brought by Slovak educators, enlighteners and national revivalists, who systematically looked for inspiration and education not to the East, but to the West. The ideological starting point for the process of the national renewal of Slovakia and the Slovaks came not from the Slavophiles, but from Herder. Slovak emigrants decisively headed towards the West, where they formed and maintained extensive enclaves of the Slovak population abroad, which had a 'westernizing' influence on Slovak domestic development. Despite attempts to Russianize many areas of Slovak life (the compulsory learning of Russian in schools, the renaming of streets, squares and institutions according to figures from Russian history), large parts of Slovak culture, literature, art, music and the dramatic arts are oriented towards the West, and this orientation is maintained by unbroken contacts and the search for sources of inspiration.

From the outset the clearly defined aim of the political changes after 1989 was the establishment of a pluralist democracy of the Western type, a modern economy, prospering on the principles of market economics, a fully equal share in European integration, based on the conception of a common market, and mutual checks on the respect for human and civil rights by the participating states. This pro-Western orientation of Slovak politics and economics was recognized in the 1990s by practically every component of the political spectrum, including the communists (the party of the Democratic Left). Therefore criticism of the reforms was not based on the desire to renew a totally discredited socialism, but was based on comparisons with other functioning Western social models (for example, the Swedish type of welfare state).

Thus it is evident that the theory of the eastern orientation of Slovakia and the Slovaks lacks justification. From the previous arguments it can be seen that there is no significant Slovak social group which has adopted this theory, apart perhaps from the occasional flirtation with it by the representatives of Slovak nationalist groups.

154   *Miroslav Kusý*

To sum up: a sober and critical analysis shows that the usual stereotypes of Slovak political and cultural attitudes distort or even contradict reality. Are the Slovaks excessive nationalists? Exalted nationalism was never accepted by the nation as a whole. It was always the ideology of a militant minority. Are the Slovaks separatists? After 1989 a gradual growth in separatism could undoubtedly be seen, but according to all opinion polls carried out in this period, only 20 to 30 per cent of respondents supported the separatist option.

As for excessive religious, explicitly Catholic, orientation in politics, recent history and the unexpectedly low position of the Christian Democratic Movement in Slovak political life show that the influence of Catholic political ideology is surprisingly small. The country has changed. The same can be said about the eastward orientation of the Slovaks. Groups which accept and cultivate such an orientation form an insignificant minority.

A decline in the standard of living and deterioration of living conditions – caused by the transformation of the inherited unproductive industrial structure – stimulated the radicalization of a significant part of the Slovak population and a move towards populism on both the left and the right. This can be considered one of the most important political phenomena in contemporary Slovakia.

Notes

1   A. Jurovský, 'Slovenská národná povaha' ('Slovak National Character'), in *Slovenská vlastivěda* ('Slovak Homeland Study'), vol. 2, Bratislava: 1943.
2   ibid., p. 357.
3   ibid., pp. 365–6.
4   Štefan Polakovič, *K základom slovenského štátu* ('The Foundations of the Slovak State'), Matica Slovenská, 1939, p. 139.
5   ibid., pp. 122–39.
6   ibid., pp. 164–79.
7   Ľ. Lipták, *A History of Slovakia and the Slovaks*, Bratislava: 1992, p. 15.
8   F. Vnuk, *Dedičstvo otcov* ('The Heritage of the Forefathers'), Bratislava: 1991, pp. 90–91.
9   M. Timoracký, 'Verejná mienka o československých vzťahoch' ('Public Opinion on Czech-Slovak Relations'), in F. Gál et al. (eds.), *Dnešní krize česko-slovenských vztahů* ('The Contemporary Crisis in Czech-Slovak Relations'), Prague: Slon, 1992, p. 89.
10   According to monthly research carried out by the Association for Independent Social Analysis (AISA).

11 See Jozef Lettrich, *History of Modern Slovakia*, Toronto: 1985; Part 2, 'Products of Slovak Radicalism', pp. 67–122.

12 ibid., p. 110.

13 ibid., p. 282.

14 M. Timoracký in F. Gál et al. (eds.), p. 89.

15 F. Gál, 'Problém česko-slovenskych vzťahov po novembri 1989 cez prizmu politiky' ('The Problem of Czech-Slovak Relations after November 1989 in a Political Context'), in F. Gál et al. (eds.), *Dnešní krize ...*

16 J. Alan, 'Česko-slovenské vztahy po pádu komunistického panství' ('Czech-Slovak Relations after the Collapse of Communist Rule'), in F. Gál et al. (eds.), *Dnešní krize ...*

17 Karel kníže ze Schwarzenbergu, *Obrana svobod* ('Defence of Liberties'), Prague: 1991, p. 84.

18 'Slovenský most', in *Moskovskie Novosti*, 19 January 1992.

III History of Czech-Slovak Relations

9 *Political Power-Sharing in the Interwar Period*

ALENA BARTLOVÁ

In the opening paragraphs of the American Declaration of Independence of 4 July 1776, it was emphasized that, at the point of separation of two nations which had hitherto shared one state and decided to 'dissolve the political bonds which have connected them', it is necessary to declare reasons for such an important emancipating step. The justification was needed not only for 'a decent respect to the opinions of mankind', as mentioned in the document, but also to remind later generations of important principles of liberty.[1] A similar task faces the intellectuals of the two closest Slavonic peoples, the Czechs and the Slovaks, in the wake of the dissolution of the Czech and Slovak Federal Republic into independent and separate Czech and Slovak Republics.

This study aims to contribute to the clarification of this problem. An attempt will be made to draw at least the broad outlines of some aspects of the differences in political and social conditions in the two territorial units of Austria-Hungary, while focusing specifically on the areas of state government, and local and regional administration; on the opportunities given to the Czech and Slovak population to participate in the government of their respective territories; and on the plans, intentions and aspirations of their political representatives. The main focus of this study will be the metamorphosis of the idea of independent state rights during the First World War, and in the initial period of coexistence of the two nations in one state. This longer time-span allows the changes to be sufficiently contrasted with the unifying and persevering themes of the important developments in the history and awareness of the two peoples.

An important milestone in the final decades of the existence of Austria-Hungary was the *Ausgleich* of 1867, which created the Austro-Hungarian Dual Monarchy. This was an agreement in which the imperial court in Vienna, weakened by heavy defeats in the Austro-Prussian war, acceded to the demands of a ruling group of Hungarian national-liberal politicians. The previously centrally governed and unified empire was transformed into a dualist state with two governments, two parliaments and two legislatures. In spite of the fact that both states were within the boundaries of the Habsburg empire, they were separated by a border which was far from a mere symbolic line on the map – it was a real dividing line between two distinct economic and territorial entities with discrete economies, a different social stratification of the population, a different level of capital investment, different traditions and religious affiliations, and also different attitudes to the principles of democracy and a host of other political values.

After the understanding, Austria and Hungary were united through the person of the emperor, and by three shared ministries (foreign affairs, finance and defence). Both states were within a unified customs and tariffs area which allowed for internal trade with a base of 55 million consumers. There was also a common currency and a central state bank. The two closely related Slavonic peoples, the Czechs and the Slovaks, found themselves in different parts of the empire: the Czechs in Austria and the Slovaks in Hungary. This retarded the opportunities for mutual exchanges, communications and cultural interaction, and the lines of their historical paths diverged tangentially both economically and politically. Due to a combination of several positive economic factors, towards the end of the nineteenth century the Czech economy was among the foremost and most progressive in the empire. It compared well with France, overtook Italy, but, at the same time, due to the overall structure of the national industry, lagged behind Germany, Great Britain, the Netherlands and Belgium.[2] The high level of activity in the Czech economy was also reflected in its above-average contribution to the Austrian state budget, the Czech population being responsible for 60 per cent of the overall taxation revenue. The economic, or rather financial, power of the Czech population was not rewarded by appropriate and equal political representation in the structure of the administrative and executive organs of the state government.

Austria was divided into 15 regional administrative units, each of which had a separate regional assembly. Three of them formed the Czech Lands. At the head of the regional assemblies, which sent their representatives to the Imperial Diet in Vienna, were chairmen nominated by the emperor. The executive power of the regional assemblies was exercised by regional committees. The regional assemblies wielded both legislative and executive powers. However, they were empowered to promulgate laws concerning only agriculture, public works (infrastructure), education, religious matters and some other, less important, social issues. While the state administration and decision-making were entirely in the hands of the central government, local government was, through the regional assemblies, more fertile ground for the development of Czech national ambitions and for the advancement of the objectives of Czech national emancipation.

The primary objective of the Czech national movement in the nineteenth century and at the beginning of the twentieth century was to achieve regional autonomy, including the unification of all areas inhabited by Czechs (Bohemia, Moravia and Silesia) into one political and administrative unit which would be governed by a separate regional government. The Czech regional assembly would thus be able to nominate Czech representatives to carry the will of the nation to the floor of the Imperial Diet in Vienna, and the emperor would be compelled to nominate a Czech national as the chairman. In other words, the Czech political leaders did not, at this stage, aim at the dissolution or dismemberment of the empire, but were merely trying to achieve fair representation within its power structures. They were striving to achieve a tripartite, instead of a dualist, empire through administrative reorganization. Their claims to the right of existence of a separate regional government and demands for the creation of a Czech state on a par with Austria and Hungary were based on the historical reality of the statehood of the Kingdom of Bohemia. At this juncture, there were no suggestions of the inclusion of Slovakia into a unified state within the empire. On the eve of the First World War, the Czechs were prepared and poised to realize their objectives.

The region which was inhabited by Slovaks in Hungary did not, at any stage before 1918, constitute an administrative or economic unit. It was inextricably interconnected, economically and administratively, with other parts of Hungary. The region comprised 20 administrative districts (so-called *župas*). Within post-1867 Hungary, only Croatia and Slovenia retained a semblance of independence; the rest of the country was governed strictly from the centre. In the Hungarian parliament, the combined non-Hungarian nationalities were represented by less than 10 per cent of members, in spite of the fact that the Hungarians were a minority within the overall population. The number of non-Hungarian full-time civil servants in the Hungarian state government and its organs was less than 6 per cent.[3] There was large-scale Magyarization (i.e. conversion to Hungarian nationality) of the Slovak youth, which was supposed to be achieved through the education system, where, for example, the laws of 1907 established Hungarian as the language of instruction in all schools. The precondition for a career in the relatively lucrative civil service and in the education system was assimilation through language and culture. The aim of Magyarization was to create an illusion of a unified and homogeneous Hungarian nation. In spite of the fact that the Hungarian government tried to create optimal conditions for economic growth and development by fostering industry, building railways, and by the electrification of the country, at the turn of the twentieth century, Hungary and Slovakia still had predominantly agrarian economies. They had not achieved anywhere near the level of industrialization of the western regions of the empire.

Under these difficult conditions, the Slovak political representatives and intellectuals concentrated mainly on the continuing existence of the Slovaks as a self-contained nation, through the preservation of the language, culture and unique traditions. The leaders of the Slovak national movement addressed memoranda and petitions to the emperor, asking for a demarcation of the ethnic borders of the territory which was predominantly inhabited by Slovak nationals. They proposed that this be called a 'district', and suggested that this new regional formation be divided into 16 administrative units.[4] They also demanded the establishment of a national assembly at Banská Bystrica. It was proposed that this national assembly should be headed by an executive committee which would be the highest national decision-making organ, and which would also provide for effective communication with the central government in Budapest.

After many unsuccessful campaigns for basic national, human and civil rights, the Slovak political representatives realized that, without outside help, it was beyond their abilities to bring about any positive change in the unenviable situation in which the Slovaks found themselves. They endeavoured to form an alliance with other nationalities, namely with the Romanians and the Serbs, with whose representatives the Slovak senators formed a faction in 1905. The leader of this faction was the Slovak senator M. Hodža. At the same time, the Slovak representatives sought help from their politically more sophisticated Czech counterparts and from the Czech nation at large. In spite of relatively intensive contacts at the turn of the century, cooperation between the Czech and Slovak national movements prior to the First World War did not go beyond the framework of purely cultural and business contacts. Up to that point, only a few hundred enthusiasts participated in such bilateral exchanges. Mutual awareness of, and information exchange on, important national concerns was not to reach a desirable level for some time to come.[5] The Slovak political leaders were painfully aware of the absence of historical claims to Slovak statehood and for this reason, when they worded their demands, their arguments were based on the natural right of all nations and communities to self-determination. '*Sumus, ergo postulamus*' was also stated in the most extensive prewar programme of the Slovak National Party, which united under its umbrella several independent political streams.[6] On the fertile soil of this party a plan was conceived, even before the First World War, for the establishment of a focus for the national movement – the Slovak National Council.

The onset of the war, which brought about radical changes in the international relations and individual economies of the participant countries, became an added stimulus for the leaders of the national movements to form national resistance centres at home and abroad. During the war, the relationship between the two political leaderships changed. It left the realm of purely cultural and business contacts, and was quickly transformed into mutual support in the political struggle for the achievement of basic national and democratic freedoms demanded by the Czechs and the Slovaks. The principal initiator of the joint campaign was the foremost representative of resistance abroad, T.G. Masaryk. He realized during the first months of the war that, given the complicated conditions of the geopolitical and spatial relationships in central Europe, neither the Czech nor the Slovak nation had much chance of independently ridding itself of the yoke of imperial power, and only concerted action held any hope of establishing an independent state. While both nations needed each other for the realization of their plans for statehood, they also depended on military and diplomatic actions, and on the overall moral support of the allies. It became evident that the states which were about to rise from the ruins of the empire would follow the line and principle of a nation-state. On this basis, Masaryk postulated the theory of a unified Czechoslovak nation as a natural foundation for the incipient independent Czechoslovak state. In London and Paris, as well as during several tours of the United States, Masaryk, Edvard Beneš and the Slovak astronomer, M.R. Štefánik, incited the Czechoslovak resistance movement in exile to fight for, and positively to engage itself in support of, the aspirations for national emancipation and self-determination of the Czech and Slovak nations.

The domestic centre for the movement was Prague. Vienna also played an important role, even shortly before the beginning of the war, as the meeting place of eminent personalities of the Czech and Slovak national fronts. To these two centres can be added Budapest, where there were active Slovak national leaders, and smaller Slovak towns, such as Martin, Skalica, Trnava, Ružomberok, Liptovský Mikuláš and others. The first official declaration from the internal resistance movement which favoured a common statehood for Czechs and Slovaks was read at the 30 May 1917 meeting of the imperial parliament, where the caucus of Czech MPs proposed a constitutional amendment dealing with a united approach to the self-determination of both Slavonic nations. This proposal voiced the views and desires for unification that Czech political leaders, and leading Slovak personages and representatives shared. A definitive decision of the Slovak political movements to sever all historical ties with Hungary and bind their future and fate with the Czech side was made much later (probably as a result of the complex political situation in Hungary), at a secret meeting of Slovak politicians in Martin on 24 May 1918. At the conclusion of their deliberations, regional delegates from Slovakia who were present at the

Martin meeting empowered the chairman of the Slovak National Party to take the following message to their Czech counterparts in Prague: 'The Slovak National Party strongly supports the unconditional right of the Slovak nation to self-determination and by this right expresses its full support for the Slovak nation to participate in the formation of an independent state consisting of Slovakia, Bohemia, Moravia and Silesia.' The participants also agreed that they would initiate a representative platform consisting of all political factions, with the aim of realizing the agreed declaration and programme.[7] The Slovak National Council became such a platform in the autumn of 1918. On 19 October 1918, F. Juriga, a Slovak MP representing this body, read a declaration from the floor of the Hungarian parliament, in which he demanded the right to self-determination for the Slovak nation and asserted that in those days of historical turmoil the Slovak National Council was the only body empowered to represent Slovaks in any negotiations and/or treaties.

By April and May 1918, the international political situation had matured sufficiently for the representatives of the internal resistance movement to start preparations for the takeover of political power and for making the initial decisions concerning the economy of the united state of Czechs and Slovaks. Commissions and committees were formed in Prague with the task of planning future administrative and legislative organs, solving fiscal and currency questions and problems of trade. The preparation of an administrative and political programme was entrusted to a committee under the experienced leadership of F. Pantůček, president of the highest imperial court in Vienna. The economic committee was led by the director of the Živnobanka (Commercial bank), J. Preiss, and E. Stodola in Budapest was charged with the task of making an inventory of all material and real estate claims which the Slovaks should present on behalf of the newly formed republic upon the disintegration of the empire.[8]

The problems of administrative organization in Slovakia were entrusted to M. Hodža, who at that time lived in Vienna. The choice of Hodža for this important part of the national programme was not accidental, as he was one of the most politically erudite Slovak personages and was a well-informed journalist. With his political wisdom, breadth of theoretical background and ability to communicate effectively, Hodža had by now gained the confidence and respect of both the heir to the throne, Prince Franz Ferdinand – being among his most trusted advisers – and his electorate of simple peasants. Just before the commencement of hostilities of the First World War, he was sentenced to 18 months of imprisonment and exiled from Hungarian soil for life for his sharply critical newspaper articles aimed at Hungarian, but also Czech, political trends. Hodža's close collaborator in Vienna, the chairman of the caucus of Czech parliamentarians, F. Staněk, later noted that the Hungarian courts could not have done anything more beneficial to the cause of unification of the Czechs and Slovaks, and for productive contacts between the two sides, than to confine and imprison Hodža in Vienna.[9] In all important documents issued by the caucus of Czech parliamentarians in Vienna, Hodža was the conceptual author of those parts which touched on Slovak interests and problems.

While preparing the framework for the future administrative organization of Slovakia, Hodža was assisted by several Slovak politicians, above all by I. Dérer. Being strongly aware of the importance of giving the nation a good start at the historical moment of its birth as an independent state, he took to the task with corresponding seriousness. His was not just editorial and stylistic work to be done in the preparation of the original versions of the documents; he was important in giving the national political aspirations a focus, one which would inspire the people of his day and at the same time embody and express the hopes, dreams and intentions of many generations of Slovak intellectuals and politicians of the past.

The Czech and Slovak legal experts faced a dilemma in the preparation of the political and administrative programme – they had to choose between the alternative of changing the Slovak system of law and local government to the Austrian model (which would bring it into line with the rest of the new state), and that of retaining the Hungarian legal and administrative system in Slovakia, while leaving the administrative divisions in local government in Bohemia and Moravia according to the Austrian model. Pantůček was inclined towards a uniform application of the Austrian model, with some modifications to reflect the needs of the new state in the whole territory of Czechoslovakia.[10] Hodža was in almost total agreement with this plan, which was to take the principle of regional administrative divisions as bequeathed to Bohemia by Austria and apply it to the Slovak part of the country, including the state (regional) parliament, and local government responsibilities. This was to bring about a fundamental change in the position of Slovakia. For the first time in a thousand years, Slovakia was to have its own regional self-government and thus, to a large degree, become an independent political unit. In his model, which he submitted to Pantůček, who was the main coordinator of the Czechoslovak political programme, Hodža anticipated that the Czechoslovak government would appoint, at the behest of the Slovak National Council, a 12-member regional committee which, in the initial period of the existence of the new common state, would work under the leadership of a 'secretary of state'.[11] Among the intended duties of the secretary was to be the appointment of temporary local councils.

The model of government also dealt with the preparation of elections, which were to be conducted by the regional committee. At the foundation of the new state, the MPs elected to the regional assembly were to be *ex officio* MPs in the National Assembly, and were to be charged with the task of conveying to the international community the commitment of the whole population of Slovakia to the unity and indivisibility of Czechoslovakia.[12] This deliberate campaign was obviously intended to signify that Slovakia was not just 'attached' to the Czechoslovak state, but that it had chosen to participate as one of two equal partners. Pantůček discussed Hodža's model with A. Rašín, who rejected it outright. Rašín supported a centralist model which would be better served by the continuation of the Hungarian local government system within the new Slovakia.

Pantůček's model, modified according to the wishes of Rašín, was tabled at the well-known historical assembly of about 200 representatives of Slovak political factions in Martin on 30 October 1918. The agenda of this memorable meeting was very full and the participants had little time to study and discuss in detail the model of the political structure as tabled by Dérer. The Slovak political representatives, assembled in the Tatra Banka building in Martin, agreed to and accepted the historically important document now known as 'The Declaration of the Slovak Nation'. In this document, representatives of all Slovak regions and political factions officially ratified the decision to enter into a joint state with the Czech nation, at the same time emphasizing that the participants in the proceedings 'insist on the principle of self-determination for all nations, as accepted throughout the world' and that only the Slovak National Council was to be empowered to speak and act on behalf of the Slovak nation.

The executive committee of the Slovak National Council was elected at this assembly and met for the first time the very next day, 31 October 1918. The main points for discussion on the agenda of this first meeting of the executive were the directives to effect the reorganization of the organs and institutions of local government. In reality, the whole discussion centred on the Pantůček model. A variety of opinions about the document and the prospective future position of Slovakia within the republic were signs of the future stratification of political factions. It was becoming clear that several participants were looking for a historical model for power-sharing arrangements. Thus Stodola suggested self-government for Slovakia according to the model which Moravia had enjoyed within the old empire, whereas Slavík proposed a solution resembling the position of Croatia in Hungary. Suggestions for partial autonomy were tabled, including independent control in the cultural and social spheres (in particular, separate school systems), but there were also voices which called for a fully equal federative system (Juriga), or at least for a special and separate national position for the Slovaks, which would be internationally guaranteed and ratified through a bilateral treaty.

Hodža demonstrated a characteristically realistic and practical attitude, realizing that the Slovaks had the best chance to control their future destiny if they showed, in those formative historical times, the ability to act and take the initiative in the areas of self-government, and law and order. He proposed to the executive that the Slovak National Council should start organizing local citizens' and workers' councils which should take charge of law and order in their towns and villages, at least until the arrival of the allied armies and/or the Czechoslovak legionnaires. He emphasized that it was important that these councils were 'to be seen as winning us independence and securing at the same time the rights and peaceful existence of the Hungarian minority'.[13] In spite of the fact that the members of the executive of the Slovak National Council voiced serious reservations about the Pantůček model, which they considered to be too bureaucratic, it was eventually ratified. They agreed that 'after the first phase of the transitional period, within ten years, the position in the state of the population hitherto living in Hungary will be resolved by an agreement between the representatives of Slovakia on one side, and of Bohemia, Moravia and Silesia on the other'.[14] It was a mistake that, in those formative and revolutionary times, the executive of the Slovak National Council did not insist on immediate finalization of an agreement on the mutual arrangements for power-sharing, a joint *modus vivendi*, and questions of administrative arrangements with the Czech political powers of the day. The executive used a delaying tactic in the hope that within, say, ten years, the national awareness of the Slovaks, who had been oppressed for a millennium, would receive a substantial boost and that they would be able to negotiate from a position of greater strength and confidence. Much misunderstanding and uneasiness over several decades may be traced to the absence of an early agreement which, if successfully concluded in the formative period of the nascent state, would have helped to crystallize the power-sharing arrangements, and the roles and responsibilities of the Slovak political institutions. Spelling out the 'rules of the game' even in those very complex and uncertain times, would have prevented and pre-empted many negative actions and feelings, and would even have taken the wind from the sails of the factions that opposed the central government soon after the birth of the republic.

The situation in which the Slovak National Council found itself was much more difficult and complicated than that of the Czechoslovak National Council in Prague. The government in Budapest, headed by Baron Károlyi, was prepared to use any means in its campaign for the preservation of the integrity of Hungarian territory. Its hopes for the realization of these ambitions were aided by the uncertain atmosphere of international relations, for which the allied countries bore the lion's share of responsibility. The allies were united until they achieved the capitulation of their arch-enemies, Germany and Austria-Hungary. There is no doubt that, through the disintegration of the empire, the allied countries had weakened their traditional adversaries for the future. At that point, however, their united front concerning the fate of the member nations of the former empire ended, and they did not have any constructive view as to how the territory should be divided. When this question gained some prominence on the agenda of the negotiations in the postwar period, the united front of the allies began to show widening cracks. Each of the allied powers naturally followed their own plans and pursued their own ambitions in the turmoil of central Europe. This meant that the allied powers were not suitable guarantors for any agreements, since they were increasingly becoming adversaries in the negotiations themselves. These differences in aims, and the 'hidden agendas' of the allied powers did not only make themselves felt at the time of the negotiations concerning the mutual borders between the successor states of the empire – they persisted during the following decades, contributing to the lack of stability in post- Versailles Europe. This instability provided fertile ground for the inception and growth of totalitarian systems.

Austria-Hungary signed the armistice on 3 November 1918. The text of this document, as published on 5 November 1918, did not, however, include the demarcation line between Hungary and Slovakia, and thus provided encouragement for the Hungarian government, which was interested in maintaining the status quo. Equally, the Belgrade Convention, signed on 13 November 1918, supported the legal position of the Károlyi government, since it left Slovakia under Hungarian jurisdiction.[15] Consequently, the Hungarian government prepared to put the question to a referendum. The situation was not completely resolved by the border designated in Paris in December 1918, mainly as a result of Beneš's campaign, nor even when the Czechoslovak and allied armies occupied Slovakia in January 1919. Ongoing sporadic battles throughout the Slovak territory caused the minister of defence to declare a state of emergency in Slovakia.[16] In the following offensive, the Hungarian army penetrated deep into Slovak territory. This called for further drastic action and the government of Czechoslovakia declared Slovakia to be under martial law. The military command had plenipotentiary powers and the garrison was responsible for law and order as well as for the supply of provisions to the population. The military ruled until 9 January 1922, in spite of the fact that the question of the Slovak-Hungarian border had, in the meantime, been settled by the Treaty of Trianon signed between Hungary and the allies on 4 June 1920.

Thus, it can be concluded from the above events that the entry of Slovakia into the united state was neither simple nor uneventful. It is understandable that these dramatic times also witnessed the almost total destruction of the economy of Slovakia, when whole factories and enterprises were removed to Hungary, when all government records were either destroyed or transferred to Budapest, and locomotives and carriages were expropriated to Hungary. All this had a profoundly negative and depressing influence on the vitality of the Slovaks at the time of the inception of the new administrative and legal institutions. The original enthusiasm, evident in October 1918, turned into insecurity and fear of the future.

It was under these conditions that the state organs and local governments were formed in Slovakia. For the first time members of the Slovak intelligentsia were called upon to take up positions as ministers of government, and were posted as the heads of districts and regions, as well as heads of banks, government-owned enterprises and schools. Bratislava became the capital and the site for not only government offices, but also the headquarters of the resuscitated and newly established political parties, together with their newspapers. At the same time the national university was founded, along with a host of other cultural, social and educational institutions. In spite of all the problems, normal, peaceful life began to be resumed throughout Slovakia.

As far as the formation of the administrative bodies and local government is concerned, it can be stated that one of the most positive outcomes of the 1918 changeover was the demarcation of the Slovak territory. The foremost condition, striven for by generations of campaigners for national independence, was thus realized: the formal recognition of the Slovak region. The celebrated days of October 1918 could not, however, solve all problems. The road to modern European nationhood and statehood was just beginning to unfold ahead of the Slovak nation. The Martin Declaration was only the first part of a very important chapter of Slovak history. Unfortunately, the twenty-year period which followed was far too short to bring to fruition many of the aims of the manifesto with which the enthusiastic leaders of both nations of Czechoslovakia had started. These were times of learning, of growth, reaching maturity, mutual tolerance and acceptance, and of the search for solutions to the problems of existence of a small nation within the crowded quarters of the region, with some friendly and some less friendly neighbours. For Slovakia, Prague became the source of currents of Western thought (although these were somewhat filtered and transfigured by Czech interpretation), and of the latest economic theories and the fruits of modern artistic endeavour. Slovakia became part of a centrally governed multinational state, with numerically significant ethnic minorities from the former ruling nations who were much more politically aware, better organized and more mature in every respect. This situation became the source of many serious and difficult internal problems. Considerations of the pervasive restlessness, unhappiness and ever-growing demands of these minorities frequently clouded the mutual understanding between the two closest partners – the Czechs and the Slovaks.

The Slovak National Council empowered one of its members, V. Šrobár, to represent its interests at the creation of the new administrative organs, and requested that he should promptly and objectively report on all important developments in the political scene in Prague.[17] Šrobár became the sole representative of the Slovaks on the Czechoslovak National Council, which fulfilled the role of a temporary government before the first sitting of the Czechoslovak National Assembly. He was appointed as vice-chairman and Minister for Health, and also had a deciding influence on the selection of originally 40, and later 54, Slovak MPs who formed the Slovak parliamentary caucus in the 370-strong Revolutionary National Assembly.

The Slovak National Council was trying to organize political and economic life in Slovakia by forming local councils, for which a procedural administrative manual was prepared. Through the press, the Slovak National Council published their programme, informed the population of Slovakia about the takeover of power from the empire and about their own objectives, policies and initiatives: 'Among other things, we have learned from the world war that small nations do not have a chance in the big league ... We Slovaks have a powerful brother in the Czech nation, whose language is similar to ours, whose life and fate are parallel to ours, and it is for these reasons that the siblings are embracing each other, so that together they may better defend their freedom and their right to self-determination in the future.'[18]

The first real attempt to organize the takeover of state administration was signalled by the arrival in Slovakia of a temporary Slovak government, headed by Šrobár, on 6 November 1918. Its effectiveness was marred from the outset by a lack of finances and of military backing. The Slovak politicians who arrived with Šrobár were at the same time MPs in the Czechoslovak National Assembly and their recall to Prague for the first session of the parliament, scheduled to commence on 14 November 1918, terminated the activities of this short-lived temporary Slovak government. Šrobár returned to Slovakia shortly afterwards (in December 1918) in his new role as a plenipotentiary representative and minister of the Czechoslovak government responsible for the administration of Slovakia. His first task was to dismantle the old Hungarian administrative and court systems, and replace them with a new administration, loyal to the new regime in Prague. This time Šrobár had strong backing, not only through parliamentary decrees and wide powers, but also by the presence of units of the Czechoslovak legionnaires under the command of allied officers. During his administration (December 1918 to May 1920) he reorganized local government, installed new administrators in 18 districts and issued 214 decrees.

One of the first of these decrees (of 8 January 1919) effected the dissolution of the Slovak National Council and of all the local councils which were formed by it in numerous villages and towns. This move by Šrobár was received in Slovakia with mixed feelings. The majority of Slovak politicians and intelligentsia saw it as an important step towards centralism, which had not been popular in Slovakia in the times of the Hungarian overlords, and was equally resented under the Czech administration. As early as 1919, some departments of the Ministry for the Administration of Slovakia were dismantled, and their tasks were taken over by the Bratislava regional offices of the central ministries. After the first parliamentary elections, the Slovak caucus was dissolved (in April 1920) and the powers of the 'Ministry for Slovakia' were further eroded. These events contributed to increasing tension in Slovakia, which was further aggravated by the intolerant stances taken by several eminent personages in the government towards some religious groups. All these problems were reflected in the programmes of most Slovak political parties in the years 1918–22.

Between 16 and 29 political parties and movements participated in the parliamentary elections of 1920, 1925, 1929 and 1935. The spectrum of political opinions represented was much more varied in the first decade after the First World War than in the following decade, when wide-scale political takeovers occurred and the formation of voluntary blocks and groupings increased. During the whole period 1918–38 the leading position was held by a group of parties which traced their parentage to the prewar factions of the Slovak National Party. Among the main points in the programmes of the many political parties which were active in Slovakia[19] were proposals as to how to resolve the sharing of power between the two main nations within the institutions. The agenda also included the effective decentralization of government, and the definition of the responsibilities and powers of the proposed individual tiers of government. The evolution of state, regional and local levels of government, including the legislative and court systems, was influenced and shaped by the following: the central government, in particular the Ministry for the Reform of Local Government and By-Laws; political parties; professional and scientific associations; and influences from abroad, in particular in the late 1930s, when such pressures easily permeated bureaucratic and administrative bodies.

Even though the Slovak parliamentary caucus voted unanimously for the constitution of the Czechoslovak Republic and for the first statute, which regulated the structure of local government in Slovakia (the District

Act, signed on 29 February 1920), this consent was not dictated by an internal unity of the political parties within the caucus, but was actually determined by the unstable and exceptional political circumstances of those times. As early as 1919, there were voices at the internal and public meetings of individual political parties which criticized the division of power between the two nations, and the structure and lack of legislative independence of the regional and local authorities. On the surface, these critical voices were aimed at the 'Ministry for Slovakia', but the roots of their complaints went much deeper. What was visibly surfacing was the absence of a workable agreement between two nations which were attempting to coexist in a united country, and to share power and political representation in the national government. Centralist tendencies brought about painful reminders of the former Hungarian administration, in which Slovakia had been totally subservient and had been denied its rightful share of power and influence.

From the very first weeks of the existence of the new state, there were calls in Slovakia for the decentralization of state powers, and of executive and administrative functions. This is not to say that there were no followers of a strong centralized system in Slovakia, but they were an insignificant minority. As an alternative to the nascent political and administrative system, a proposal for the autonomy of Slovakia was repeatedly presented by individuals and political parties. This concept of autonomy was strictly seen and thought of as only one of several possible internal arrangements within the context of a united Czechoslovak state. There were many protagonists who strongly preferred this proposal, although their conceptual visions frequently changed.

The struggle for autonomy went on until the very end of the interwar period and influenced both the parliamentary discussions and the dealings of the executive organs of government. It must be said that the anti-centralist forces in Czechoslovakia were in no way unique in the European context. For example, there were strong decentralizing tendencies in France, which was also ruled by a strong government, but the difference was that Czechoslovakia consisted of two main nations and the fight for local government autonomy was increasingly transforming into a power struggle between two distinct nationalities. Considering that before 1914 the main aim of Czech political representatives had been the regional independence of what were then parts of the Habsburg empire, it becomes clear that these ideas had been revived by autonomist political currents in Slovakia. A contemporary attempt to explain why the Czechs ceased to be interested in regional decentralization was offered by Stodola, who said: 'It is no surprise that the Czechs, who were in the past the greatest proponents of autonomy, are not interested in this issue any more – the reasons are obvious. Now they themselves are at the heart of the country, they control the central institutions and have almost the entire legislative and executive power in their hands.'[20] Proof that Stodola was right can be seen in the fact that the most frequent demand of the autonomists in Slovakia was the parity of representation of Czechs and Slovaks in the central administration and in the organs of the government in Prague. At the beginning of the existence of the new state, such demands were quite whimsical, because Slovakia simply did not have sufficient educated and politically acceptable people (i.e. those not loyal to the Hungarian system) to assure fair representation. But this was quite possible and realistic in the second decade of the republic, by which time the Slovak education system had produced large numbers of capable young professionals, who persistently, but with little success, applied for positions in the central administration. The situation had become so acute that it was discussed in the pages of a serious, non-sectarian yet pro-government journal, *Politika*, and even Hodža, upon becoming Prime Minister in 1935, asked for a complete list of all civil servants of Slovak nationality in the central administration. The statistics spoke for themselves when, even as late as 1938, the head count of all those employed in the ministries, together with the office of the president and the executive council, totalled 10,825, yet only 123 of these positions were occupied by Slovak nationals.[21]

A constantly recurring request for parity of representation (corresponding to the ratio of the population) in the civil service existed in the political programmes of the various groups campaigning for Slovak autonomy, but it seldom headed their agenda. At the same time, no one was in doubt of the importance of the civil service. Even children's and young people's magazines jokingly observed how the elected ministers came and went. Very few of them lasted long enough to understand the fine points of their portfolios in the same way as the permanent heads of departments, who were the bastions of continuity in the administration. It was the bureaucrat's responsibility to explain and apply the rules and regulations, thus enabling him almost at will to speed up or impede the realization of economic plans and reforms, as well as changes in the educational, cultural and social spheres.

The first point on the agenda of the proponents of autonomy was the demand for an elected regional parliament in Slovakia which would be the base of a Slovak state government. An impetus for these demands was provided by the way Transcarpathia (officially named in those days 'Sub-Carpathian Russia') was treated when it was annexed into Czechoslovak territory. The peace treaty of Saint-Germain-en-Laye, signed on 10 September 1919 (and ratified on 16 July 1920), promised autonomy for this easternmost part of Czechoslovakia, with an elected parliament and independence of legislative and policy-making powers in several areas. Upon learning of the contents of the treaty, a delegation of Slovak autonomists instantly left for Paris (in August 1919) to intervene in the negotiations and implore the signatories to grant similar privileges to Slovakia. Their request was not even put on the agenda, partly because the negotiations were reaching the final stage, but also because they were not recognized as officially representing a constituency. The mere fact that such a delegation travelled to Paris is sufficient proof that the political situation in Slovakia was complicated from the very outset. The international and legal guarantees under which the Transcarpathian parliament operated were regularly used in the arguments of the followers of the autonomy option, even though the realization of the guarantees was not at all smooth.

Along with the group which was campaigning for political autonomy in Slovakia was another which preferred administrative rather than political autonomy, which meant giving more power to the current administrative divisions governing Slovakia, above all to the 'Ministry for Slovakia', or creating new and more appropriate administrative structures. Hodža, Stodola and finally, in the 1930s, the majority of the young Slovak intelligentsia who were favourably disposed towards the Prague government all belonged to this group.

The reorganization of local government carried out by the civil service at the end of the 1920s brought brief hope for the autonomists. The main achievement of this process was the end of the dual system of local administration. The old district scheme (*župas*), which existed only in Slovakia, was replaced by a regional system. As mentioned earlier, there were 20 districts in the territory of Slovakia, which were now replaced by one regional administration. For the first time, Slovakia became not only the object but also a source of political power. At the head of the regional administrative departments was the regional president selected by the Minister of the Interior.

Part of this reform was also the rise of the elected regional assembly, which was a peculiar mix consisting of two-thirds universally elected representatives (political parties selected the candidates) and one-third directly chosen by the civil service. It was intended that the latter group should consist of impartial professional advisers, in particular in the sphere of the economy and superstructure, but in reality this was not the case. As a rule, the civil service nominated representatives who were in favour of central administration, and thus assured that a majority vote on the most important issues was in line with the policies of the central government. The reorganization had, like most similar reforms, positive and negative sides. One disadvantage of this system was that the total budget of the regional administration was smaller than the total amount spent on the old districts. However, the advantages were probably more important – many decisions were speedily facilitated by the new central regional administration, whereas in the past the old districts had been incapable of reaching agreements.

Among the most important decisions was the reform of railway tariffs. In Bohemia, the great majority of railways had already been nationalized by 1925. In Slovakia, even at the beginning of the 1930s, almost 50 per cent of railways were in private hands and charges for the transport of raw materials and consumer goods were much higher on private lines than on state-owned lines. Slovak enterprises had to add these overheads to their overall costs, with the resulting increase in the prices charged for raw materials or products, and were obviously at a competitive disadvantage when they tried to export to Bohemia and abroad. In 1932, the Slovak railways finally passed into full state ownership. Between 1918 and 1932 the Slovak economy had paid 600 million crowns more than their Czech counterparts in tariffs. Additionally, a tax reform was carried out in the 1930s, assuring that Slovak taxpayers and enterprises were finally operating on an equal level. The banking interest rates in Bohemia and Slovakia were also made equal. Slovak technical and engineering professionals were given the opportunity to prove themselves on large-scale infrastructure projects, such as a system of dams and associated hydroelectric works on the River Váh.

The regional administration in Slovakia established an important advisory institution – the Institute for National Economic Infrastructure, whose sphere of influence spread over the Slovak borders and became important for the whole country. It seems that there was a strong movement among the Czechs in support of the regionalization of administration, and the Slovak regional offices were used to achieve the objectives of this group for the entire republic. Ultimately, this movement was responsible for many initiatives of national importance which were addressed above the party political level. Initially, the institute mapped and analysed all regions, recording their problems, later prioritizing and implementing solutions. It not only dealt with economic issues, but also built schools, hospitals, cultural clubs and institutions, and other projects of public importance.

In spite of the existence of the regional departments, the work on administrative reforms did not cease. Both the civil service and the political parties were responsible for keeping the momentum going. The rise of the political representation of ethnic minorities and their increased calls for recognition in the late 1930s also led to an acceleration of reforms. The government formed a commission which had representatives from all coalition parties prepare a so-called Statute of Nationalities. A part of this was also a statute of national autonomy, which was to be implemented within the framework of the further decentralization of government. The preliminary work of this commission culminated in the summer of 1938, when, in agreement with the president, Edvard Beneš, the government agreed on the definitive text of the document outlining the administrative reforms. Part of the reforms were to include fully democratically elected regional assemblies. Unfortunately, due to the overwhelming international events of that year, the National Assembly did not have the opportunity to discuss these plans.

Conclusions

The concept of the Slovak and Czech political representatives regarding self-determination and self-government underwent radical changes over several discrete periods. Perhaps the most important among these was the time between the world wars, which was the period of a united republic embracing both nations. During this period, various visions of administrative models and competencies of the individual tiers of government were formed. The questions of central versus local government and their solutions were further complicated because of the ever-present tension created by the lack of power-sharing arrangements between the two major ethnic groups, who through the wisdom and geopolitical sensitivity of such remarkable politicians as T.G. Masaryk and M.R. Štefánik had been brought together in a shared state. It is apparent that the reasons which led to their decision to create a joint Czechoslovakia are just as valid at the end of the twentieth century. This can be said despite the misunderstandings and outright blunders that marred their period of shared history. It is possible that future generations will be less petty and more able to overcome the shortcomings of the past with equanimity, generosity and mutual good will. It is a historical reality that small nations depend on the friendly disposition of their more populous and more powerful neighbours, and that those small nations who can act in accord with each other will win more respect.

Analyses presented in several past studies have dealt with the desire of the Slovaks (or at least a significant part of the Slovak nation) for autonomy and with the reasons why this desire was not fulfilled in the interwar period. Such a desire must be seen as a natural evolutionary stage of a developed nation, which craves a fair share of political power. It was a fatal mistake that the concept of the fair sharing of political power was allowed to be pioneered by the representatives of religious and national socialist movements, among whom were active sworn enemies of the joint state, and by those representing the interests of other countries. This deterred many otherwise politically sympathetic personages from supporting the drive for autonomy. A further reality was the presence of a politically and economically strong German minority on Czechoslovak territory, which, if the Slovaks had gained full autonomy, would have sought similar status, in particular because their numbers may actually have exceeded the Slovaks. One of the reasons why the Slovaks were not fairly represented in the administration was the fact that positions were given to relatively young applicants soon after the First World War, when Slovakia did not have suitably qualified personnel, and that there was little natural attrition among these experienced and hard-working civil servants in the twenty years that followed. But this was difficult to explain later to the well-educated and eager young Slovaks looking for work, who perceived the imbalance as a gross injustice. They were the first generation educated in the new school system and they entered the fray of the middle-management job market in the most inhospitable of times – during the depression and at a time when Europe had started to feel great political tension. But they had no say in the timing of their maturation process. Their problems demanded a sensitive and responsible approach by the authorities, who failed to find the right way of dealing with the disillusionment of a whole generation.

The key reason for most of the misunderstandings and much of the animosity between the Czechs and the Slovaks can be found in the fact that both nations did not insist on a clear agreement on a method of mutual coexistence, or at least on a firm timetable and definitive agenda for dealing with such problems in the period between the world wars. In retrospect, the first period of their cohabitation was influenced by economic shifts and power struggles of worldwide significance, where many former friends suddenly fought bitterly over the same markets for their produce. It is clear that such a magnitude of underlying external tensions did not contribute to the political tolerance and generosity of both Czechs and Slovaks in their attempts at internal problem-solving. Is it at all possible that future generations will learn from these problems and avoid their repetition?

178   *Alena Bartlová*

Notes

1 The full text of the first sentence reads: 'When, in the course of human events, it becomes necessary for one people to dissolve the political bands which have connected them with another, and to assume among the powers of the earth the separate and equal station to which the Laws of Nature and of Nature's God entitle them, a decent respect to the opinions of mankind requires that they should declare the causes which impel them to the separation.' Quoted in R. Birley, *Speeches and Documents from American History*, vol. 1 (1943).
2 V. Lacina, *Formování československé ekonomiky 1918–23* ('Evolution of the Czechoslovak Economy, 1918–23'), Prague: 1990, p. 25.
3 K. Malý and F. Sivák, *Dějiny státu a práva Československa do r. 1918* ('History of the State and Laws of Czechoslovakia to 1918'), Prague: 1988, p. 454.
4 J. Mesaros, 'Státoprávné snahy Slovákov po buržoaznej revolucii' ('Statehood Aspirations of the Slovaks after the Bourgeois Revolution'), in *Slováci a ich národný vývin* ('Slovaks and their National Development'), Bratislava: 1966, p. 213.
5 P. Vošahlíková, 'Vzájemné vztahy Čechů a Slováků na přelomu 19. a 20. století v zrcadle dobové publicistiky' ('Mutual Relations of Czechs and Slovaks at the Turn of the Nineteenth and Twentieth Centuries through the Mirror of Contemporary Publishing'), in *Sborník k dějinám 19. a 20. století* ('Compendium to the History of the Nineteenth and Twentieth Centuries'), Prague: 1993, pp. 47†68.
6 *Vyklad programu Slovenskej národnej strany* (Declaration of the programme of the Slovak National Party), Martin: 1914.
7 K. Rebro, *Cesta národa* ('The National Road'), Bratislava: 1969, p. 27.
8 E. Stodola, *Přelom* ('The Breakthrough'), Prague: 1933, p. 137.
9 F. Soukup, *28. říjen 1918* ('28 October 1918'), vol. 2, Prague: 1928, p. 1101.
10 V. Fajnor, 'Práca slovenských právnikov pred prevratom a v prvom desatročí Republiky' ('The Activities of Slovak Lawyers before the Revolution and in the First Decade of the Republic'), in *Právny obzor*, 11, 1928, p. 708.
11 M. Hodža, *Články, řeči, studie* ('Papers, Speeches, Studies'), vol. 7, Bratislava: 1934, p. 9.
12 *Dějiny státu a práva: 1848–1945* ('History of the State and Law 1848–1945'), Bratislava: 1973, p. 52.
13 The minutes of the meeting of the Executive of the Slovak National Council are deposited in the Slovak National Archive, collection of the Slovak National Council, box 1, file 2.
14 ibid.
15 *Dějiny státu a práva*, op. cit., p. 50.
16 V. Kalousek, 'O vojnové diktature na Slovensku a Podkarpatské Rusi v letech 1919–22' ('On the Military Dictatorship in Slovakia and Sub-Carpathian Russia in the Years 1919–22), in *Právny obzor*, 11, 1928, pp. 281–91.
17 Slovak National Archive, collection of V. Šrobár, box 5, file 34.

18   'Čo chceme? Slovenskú reč, slovenskú zem' ('What do we want? The Slovak Language and Slovak Soil'), Martin: 1918, p. 14.
19   It is necessary to avoid here the form 'Slovak parties' because some of the political parties represented national minorities and some were statewide, drawing their membership and support from all regions of Czechoslovakia, and had their headquarters in Prague.
20   E. Stodola, op. cit., p. 145.
21   K. Čulen, *Češi a Slováci v štátnych službách* ('Czechs and Slovaks in Public Service'), Bratislava: 1944, p. 99. Here a table is given with statistics of employees of the individual central organs and their salary categories.

10 From Autonomy to Federation, 1938–68

JAN RYCHLÍK

I

In 1938 the programme for the political autonomy of Slovakia which had been drawn up by Hlinka's Slovak People's Party (the HSPP or the so-called 'Ľudáks')[1] nineteen years previously, finally became reality. Taking advantage of the Munich Agreement, which had weakened the Czechoslovak Republic, the party, at its Executive Committee meeting in Žilina on 6 October, presented an ultimatum to the Czechoslovak government and forced it to transfer power into the hands of the newly established autonomous Slovak authorities.[2] It was made clear to the representatives of other political parties (except those of the Communist Party and the Social Democrat Party, with which the Ľudáks had refused to communicate) that they had to support the autonomy project or be swept off the political scene. The Prime Minister, General Jan Syrový, who was acting as president (instead of Edvard Beneš, who had resigned), capitulated and appointed the vice-chairman of the HSPP, the Catholic priest, Jozef Tiso, firstly Minister for Slovakia and later – after the installation of other ministers – Prime Minister of the autonomous Slovak government.

The request for autonomy was the consequence of the failure of the concept of a coherent Czechoslovak political nation. During the twenty years of Czechoslovakia's existence the Slovak nation had matured culturally and socially, and had acquired a different awareness from that of the Czechs. Consequently the Slovaks required separate and independent political representation. However, it was a tragedy for the development of Slovakia that the leading force in this process was the HSPP, because since 1936 this party had rejected democracy and oriented itself towards authoritarian regimes. There were two wings within the HSPP. The moderate wing, led by Jozef Tiso, wanted to model Slovakia on the Austrian corporatist 'estate

state', fascist Italy, Salazar's Portugal or Franco's Spain. The radicals, represented by Alexander Mach, Vojtech Tuka and Ferdinand Ďurčanský, were adherents of Nazi Germany. Regardless of which wing held sway, the consequences of the rise of the HSPP were to be catastrophic in the long term. Autonomy under the leadership of the Ľudáks meant the introduction of a totalitarian regime in Slovakia and, owing to the international and political situation after Munich, entailed its absolute dependence on Nazi Germany.

On coming to power, the Slovak government immediately started to impose a totalitarian regime. The Communist Party was prohibited and the Social Democrat Party was dissolved. Other parties were merged with the HSPP, which was temporarily renamed 'HSPP – the Party of Slovak National Unity'. Except for the HSPP, only two parties representing ethnic minorities – one representing the Hungarians and one representing the Germans – were allowed. Even these could not run independently in the elections for the new Slovak parliament which took place on 18 December 1938. Their candidates had to join those of the HSPP on a single list of candidates which was then presented to the electorate. As there was no opposition the HSPP 'won' the elections with an 'overwhelming majority' of 98 per cent.[3] Trade unions, social and sport organizations were also forced into conformity. All were subordinated to the HSPP.

From its very beginning, the Ľudák regime was anti-Czech and anti-Jewish. The so-called 'national committees', i.e. the local action groups of the new regime, together with paramilitary organizations called Hlinka's Guard, started campaigns against Jews and Czechs, trying to expel them from Slovakia.

Although Slovakia obtained autonomy on 6 October, the formal legal approval of the new state of affairs did not take place until November. Between 18 and 22 November both chambers of the National Assembly (the Czechoslovak parliament) approved the constitutional law on Slovak autonomy.[4] This law stated that Slovakia was 'an autonomous part of the Czecho-Slovak Republic' (the new official spelling of the name of the state). In fact Czecho-Slovakia now became a loose federation with strong confederative elements. The same status was given to Ruthenia, the easternmost part of the Czecho-Slovak Republic. The central legislative body was the National Assembly, which worked as a Czech parliament if only Czech problems were on the agenda. In such cases the Slovak and Ruthenian MPs were not present. The same National Assembly had legislative authority in twelve spheres concerning the whole country (among them foreign policy, defence and finance) if the Slovak and Ruthenian MPs participated. In such cases, however, the draft was approved only if it also obtained the majority of the votes of Slovak and Ruthenian members of parliament. All other matters, apart from the previously mentioned joint matters, were under the jurisdiction of the Slovak and Ruthenian governments. In practice, however, this complicated parliamentary system never came into existence. On 15 December the National Assembly authorized all three regional governments to issue decrees with the validity of laws.[5] By this act the parliamentary process was to have no future of any importance in prewar Czecho-Slovakia.

However, the main influence in the process of the disintegration of Czecho-Slovakia came from Berlin. By autumn 1938 Hitler had decided to 'finish with' the rest of post-Munich Czecho-Slovakia. The leaders of the radical wing of the HSPP (Mach, Tuka and Ďurčanský) were to serve for this purpose. The German tactic was to widen the gap between the central government in Prague and the Slovak government in Bratislava. On the one hand Berlin warned the government in Prague that it held responsibility for events in Slovakia and made it clear that the new borders would be guaranteed only after the consolidation of Czecho-Slovakia, but at the same time it urged Bratislava to break away, promising economic and political support.

While the radicals in the HSPP wanted to establish an independent Slovakia immediately with the help of Germany, the moderates, led by Tiso, demanded a gradual loosening of ties with the Czechs and envisaged that Slovakia would proclaim independence later, after becoming economically self-sufficient. In reality, this meant the gradual construction of Slovakia's independence, paid for by Czech taxpayers, a move which brought no advantage whatsoever to the Czech side. Consequently, the Czech part of the central government, instead of being witness to a gradual disintegration, gave priority to military intervention in Slovakia, running the risk that Germany would take this as a pretext for a direct invasion of Czecho-Slovakia. In this case, the Czechs believed, the world would clearly see that the republic had ceased to exist as a result of aggression and this would facilitate its restoration in the future. The Czech ministers also lost confidence in Tiso, and decided to remove him from office and to install a new, more cooperative government which would try to keep Slovakia in Czecho-Slovakia.

The new Ľudák demands only speeded up the decision of Prague to intervene. On 9 March 1939 Emil Hácha, the Czecho-Slovak president, suspended Tiso's government and placed Slovakia under martial law. Some Ľudák leaders were arrested, others fled to Vienna from where they tried to organize an anti-Czech uprising. President Hácha appointed a new Slovak government, headed at first by Jozef Sivák and later by Karol Sidor.

German representatives arrived in Bratislava and tried to force Sidor to proclaim the independence of Slovakia. When Sidor refused to do so, they contacted Jozef Tiso with an invitation to Berlin from Hitler. Tiso arrived there on 13 March and was confronted with an ultimatum: either Slovakia proclaimed independence or Germany would give free reign to Hungary against Slovakia. After his return to Bratislava, Tiso addressed the Slovak parliament on 14 March and explained the latest developments. Subsequently the parliament passed a law proclaiming Slovakia an independent state.[6] A day later the German army occupied the rest of the country and annexed it as the so-called Protectorate of Bohemia and Moravia. Czecho-Slovakia had ceased to exist.

II

The Slovak state came into existence unexpectedly and, at the time, even had to face the opposition or the apathy of its citizens. In addition, the conditions under which Slovakia obtained independence condemned it to absolute dependence on Nazi Germany. In occupying the Czech Lands, the German army penetrated into Slovakia as far as the River Váh. It became clear that the Germans wanted to incorporate this part of the country into the Reich and to establish some kind of protectorate in the rest of Slovakia. At the same time Slovakia was attacked by Hungary. The Hungarian army annexed Ruthenia (15–18 March 1939) and parts of eastern Slovakia. Consequently – together with southern Slovakia, which had already been occupied by Hungary in November 1938 – Slovakia lost one-third of its territory. Germany finally abandoned the plan for a protectorate over Slovakia but forced Tiso to sign the special 'Treaty of Protection' (*Schutzvertrag*) on 18 March, which was then ratified on 23 March in Berlin, according to which Slovakia had to subordinate its army and foreign policy to the Reich.[7] A secret protocol put the Slovak economy under German control.

The character of the Slovak Ľudák state cannot easily be defined. According to the constitution of 21 July,[8] it was a republic headed by a president; legislative power was in the hands of the parliament consisting of 80 MPs, and executive power was in the hands of the government. But the HSPP had a political monopoly secured by the constitution (paragraph 58) and the government could rule even without the parliament (paragraph 44). There were no elections during the whole period of the Slovak Ľudák republic. The parliament existed practically in the same form as it had been in when it was 'elected' on 18 December 1938.

When the mandates expired in December 1943, MPs passed a special constitutional law by which their term of office was 'extended' until 31 December 1946.[9] Human rights, technically guaranteed by the constitution, were 'temporarily' suspended from the beginning to the end of the Ľudák state.[10] The constitution also included some elements of Austrian and Italian fascist institutions, such as the estates and the State Council.

Despite these developments, life in Slovakia was much easier compared with conditions in the Protectorate of Bohemia and Moravia. While open terror dominated in the protectorate and the German presence was clearly visible, conditions in Slovakia were relatively mild, at least according to the standards of totalitarian systems. Although even the Slovak regime had its concentration camp in Ilava, no political death sentence was carried out in the country until the beginning of the Slovak National Uprising in 1944. Except for the short campaign against Poland in September 1939, Slovakia was not involved in the war until 1941. It took advantage of the war prosperity which improved the living conditions of wide strata of the population. Tiso, who became president on 26 October 1939, was relatively successful in avoiding direct German intervention in Slovakia's affairs and in controlling the radicals. But in July 1940 Germany did intervene when the Foreign Minister and Minister of the Interior, Ferdinand Ďurčanský, tried to contact the British government through the Slovak envoy in Rome, asking for recognition of Slovak neutrality. Ďurčanský was replaced as Minister for Foreign Affairs by Vojtech Tuka, who had been Prime Minister since 27 October 1939, and Alexander Mach succeeded him as Minister of the Interior. This new government started to introduce so-called Slovak national socialism, although total nazification did not occur. However, the regime did pursue an anti-Semitic policy. Jewish citizens' property was confiscated and in 1942 the Jews were handed over to the German authorities, who killed most of them in the extermination camps.[11] Despite these measures, the regime was more or less accepted by the majority of Slovak inhabitants.

The Slovak question also had a foreign political dimension. The problem of whether there were to be two separate states after the war, or whether Czechoslovakia was to be renewed in some form was not clear in the period of 1939–40. The Slovak problem had already gained an extra dimension after 14 March 1939, because in three of the five states looked upon as potential enemies of Germany (Poland, the USSR, Great Britain, France and the USA), the Czecho-Slovak envoys were Slovaks: Juraj Slávik in Poland, Štefan Osuský in Paris and Vladimír Hurban in Washington. All of them refused to surrender their legations to the Germans or to put them under Bratislava's control. In this way they let the whole world know about the formation of an independent Slovakia. Both France and Britain were rather reserved regarding establishing diplomatic relations with Slovakia. Poland recognized Slovakia *de jure* immediately after 14 March, whereas Great Britain and France recognized it only *de facto* on 4 May and 14 July

1939 respectively. However, all three states allowed the Czechoslovak diplomatic missions to continue functioning. After the start of the war, the situation became even more complicated. The Slovak minister to Warsaw, Ladislav Szatmáry, and the Slovak consul in London, Milan Harminc, refused to accept the authority of Bratislava and joined the resistance movement of Edvard Beneš, whose goal was the restoration of Czechoslovakia. As there was no consul in Paris, and the British and French governments had recalled their consuls from Bratislava, diplomatic relations between Slovakia and the Allies were broken off. On 13 November 1939 France recognized the Czechoslovak National Committee of Edvard Beneš, and Great Britain followed on 20 December. As early as 2 October Štefan Osuský, on behalf of the still nonexistent provisional Czechoslovak government, had signed a treaty with the French Prime Minister, Edouard Daladier, which allowed the formation of a Czechoslovak army in France. But even at that time Great Britain and France did not consider the restoration of Czechoslovakia to be the only possible alternative. Instead of a united Czechoslovakia they preferred a broader federation or confederation in central Europe including the Czech Lands, Slovakia, Poland, Hungary, Austria and possibly other states. For this reason the French government did not support Edvard Beneš, but gave priority to Štefan Osuský. The idea of a broader federation or confederation had support even among some Ľudáks, mainly the group around Karol Sidor, the Slovak envoy to the Vatican.

At the same time the French government tolerated the activities of Beneš's opponents. On 22 November 1939 Milan Hodža, the former Czechoslovak Prime Minister, together with a Slovak autonomist, Peter Prídavok, founded the Slovak National Council.[12] On 14 January 1940 the Slovak National Council joined a group of anti-Beneš Czech emigrants (including the deputy of the National Democrats, F. Schwarz; the editor V. Ležák-Borin; and Generals Prchala and Šnejdárek) which called themselves the Preparatory Committee of the Czech National Council. Combined, these groups formed a new organization called the Czecho-Slovak National Council, which came into existence on 28 January 1940. The programme of the Czecho-Slovak National Council was the restoration of Czecho-Slovakia on federative principles.[13]

Beneš's National Committee[14] refused to acknowledge the Czecho-Slovak National Council. Beneš also categorically rejected any idea of the restoration of only a Czech state, as was advocated by some domestic Czech political circles, and refused to give any guarantees about the future status of Slovakia within Czechoslovakia. Among the Czech domestic resistance Slovak autonomy was considered to be one of the reasons for Czechoslovakia's disintegration. This resulted in the conclusion that Czechoslovakia should be decentralized administratively, but that the dualistic model that had existed in the post-Munich republic was not to be renewed.[15]

The capitulation of France (22 June 1940) brought a major change: Britain no longer had to consider the negative attitude of France towards Beneš. The British now had no other allies except the governments in exile and the resistance movements in the occupied countries. For the new British government of Winston Churchill it was not important whether Beneš had support in Slovakia or not; what was important was whether he could somehow contribute to the British war effort. As Beneš could contribute with an efficient network of secret service operations in central Europe,[16] he was certainly more useful to the British than Hodža. On 21 July 1940 the British recognized Beneš's National Committee as the provisional Czechoslovak government in exile. Hodža's Czecho-Slovak National Council was practically liquidated and he accepted the post of vice-chairman of the State Council, a body which, in exile, was to substitute the parliament.

Nevertheless, from the point of view of postwar developments, the attitude of the USSR was decisive, since both Czechs and Slovaks were to fall under the political influence of Moscow. The Soviet government refused to recognize Slovakia's independence until as late as 16 September 1939, when it did so as a result of the Nazi-Soviet Pact concluded on 23 August 1939. At the end of that year the Czechoslovak mission in Moscow was officially closed. During the short period 1939–41 Slovak-Soviet relations were quite intensive. However, on 22 July 1941 Slovakia joined Germany in the war against the USSR and the Slovak army was sent to the eastern front. On 12 December of the same year Vojtech Tuka, the Prime Minister of Slovakia, formally declared war on the USA and Great Britain.[17] The result of this was that the USSR and Great Britain – and later the United States – recognized the Czechoslovak emigré government in London and Beneš as its head. Consequently Slovakia was not to be treated as a state but as an integral part of Czechoslovakia.[18]

Meanwhile Tiso's regime was quickly losing popularity. The war was unpopular in Slovakia, Slovak soldiers saw no reason to fight the Russians, a Slavic people like themselves, and whole military units started to desert, crossing over to the Soviet army. The soldiers who had deserted or been captured were sent to Buzuluk, where a Czechoslovak army was being organized under the command of Colonel Ludvík Svoboda. On 12 December 1943 a new Czechoslovak-Soviet treaty was signed in Moscow.[19] Thus the future existence of independent Slovakia in whatever form depended on the result of the war: the victory of the democratic and anti-Hitler forces would mean its liquidation. More and more people in Slovakia realized that the regime which had discredited itself by the deportation of Jews and by fighting on the side of Nazi Germany would not be acceptable to the anti-Hitler coalition. From 1943 on it became clear that the Ľudák state would not outlive the end of the war. The regime fell into a deep crisis, resulting in the almost total paralysation of the state and police authorities.

Opposition to the regime had existed in Slovakia ever since the state had been established. This opposition, however, did not necessarily intend to bring about the restoration of Czechoslovakia. The communists, for example, to some extent preferred either an independent socialist Slovakia or incorporation into the USSR as another Soviet republic, and only in 1943 – partly under instructions from Moscow – did they accept the idea of the restoration of Czechoslovakia. On the other hand, the so-called Civic Bloc, consisting mainly of the former Agrarians (i.e. Hodža's party), advocated a united Czechoslovakia in some form from the very beginning. The international situation proved that this orientation was the only realistic option.

In 1943 the Civic Bloc, together with the communists, formed a resistance organization which again went under the name of the Slovak National Council (SNC). The clandestine SNC had six members: three (Ján Ursíny, Jozef Lettrich and Matej Josko) representing the non-communists and three (Gustáv Husák, Ladislav Novomeský and Karol Šmidke) from the Slovak Communist Party. The programme of the SNC, known as the 'Christmas Agreement', called for the restoration of Czechoslovakia on the principle of 'equal with equal',[20] which in fact meant a federation. The Slovak adherents of pre-Munich Czechoslovakia, led by Vavro Šrobár, were not represented in the SNC. These groups of 'centralists', linked with Beneš's Czechoslovak Intelligence Service, operated in coordination with the SNC but were not successful in penetrating the Slovak army; the SNC, on the other hand, was. With the help of democratically and pro-Czechoslovakia oriented officers led by Lieutenant-Colonel Ján Golian, it prepared an insurrection to overthrow the Ľudák regime and to restore Czechoslovakia. However, the preparations for the uprising were affected by the actions of Soviet partisans. These were dropped from Soviet planes in the spring and summer of 1944 with the object of sabotaging rail and road transport, and military objects. They were partly supported by the local population, while the already paralysed Slovak army and police took no action. When German troops entered Slovakia on 29 August 1944, the signal was given for a military insurrection – the Slovak National Uprising.

III

At the outbreak of the Slovak National Uprising, the government in Bratislava claimed that it was not a national uprising but only a 'Czech-Jewish-Bolshevik coup', with which the Slovak nation had nothing in common. Ever since this time this theory has been repeated by pro-Ľudák historians and journalists, who argue that no nation can possibly rise up in arms against its own state.[21] Nevertheless it must be said that the insurrection was not a rebellion against the Slovak state but only a revolt against the Ľudák regime which, by its alliance with Germany, had dragged Slovakia into catastrophe. It is true that Edvard Beneš, as well as the Czech population in the protectorate and some resistance groups in Slovakia linked with London, imagined the restoration of Czechoslovakia simply as a return to the conditions before Munich. However, the reality was different.

The most important pro-Beneš group was the group around Vavro Šrobár. Despite the existence of the Slovak National Council, Šrobár had founded his own national committees. On 1 September 1944 the representatives of these committees assembled in Banská Bystrica and established an umbrella organization, the Revolutionary National Council. Although not invited, Gustáv Husák and other members of the SNC came to the meeting and put a stop to Šrobár's further activities by appointing him a co-chairman of the SNC together with the communist Karol Šmidke. The SNC coopted more members and formed its own presidium and executive bodies. It took over the existing state authorities, the army and police forces, as well as the local national committees. The SNC declared the restoration of the Czechoslovak Republic and at the same time declared itself to be 'the bearer of all legislative, executive and governmental power in Slovakia'.[22] This declaration could be interpreted in two ways: either the SNC was temporarily exercising the power of the Czechoslovak government, as the latter was not able to do so from London, or the Slovak National Council was exercising it absolutely. The second possibility meant that only after an agreement with the Czechoslovak government would the SNC decide whether it would hand over part of its jurisdiction to the joint Czechoslovak authorities.

Naturally President Beneš, his government in London and the majority of the Czech population in the protectorate understood the declaration of the SNC to be a temporary exercising of power. On 24 September the émigré government sent a message to Banská Bystrica, the permanent seat of the SNC, according to which the Slovak National Council was to be recognized as a regional national committee subordinated to Beneš through a special delegate. This delegate was František Němec, who had been waiting with his staff in Moscow since 25 August. Both Beneš and Němec had been informed about the existence of the SNC, but expected the uprising to be led by Šrobár. When Němec arrived in Banská Bystrica the SNC refused to hand over power. A special delegation was to be sent to London to negotiate with Beneš about the future status of Slovakia within a restored Czechoslovakia. Coincidentally, this delegation – consisting of Ján Ursíny, Ladislav Novomeský and Lieutenant-Colonel Mirko Vesel – flew to London on the same day (7 October) as Němec's arrival in Banská Bystrica.

Ursíny, Novomeský and Vesel did not manage to contact Beneš until 25 October. They presented him with the requirements of the SNC to be recognized as the permanent legislative and administrative body in Slovakia, a demand which in fact meant broad autonomy. The Czechoslovak government discussed the matter on 23 October. Since the SNC held real power, Beneš had to accept its demands. The military developments in Slovakia, however, changed the situation. Until the middle of October the insurgent army had been more or less successful in defending liberated Slovak territory. After the ultra-fascist coup of Ferenc Szálasi in Hungary (15 October) the German army opened a new front in the south and on 27 October Banská Bystrica fell into their hands. Thus Slovakia was occupied by the Germans – though guerilla fighting continued – and the SNC was removed from power. It was then reinstated by the Soviet army, which gradually liberated the country from the east. However, the Soviet authorities did not hand over power directly, but through the office of Beneš's delegate, Němec, according to the Czechoslovak-Soviet treaty on the administration of the liberated territories.[23] This meant a weakening of the SNC's position.

At first it seemed that the SNC would try to defend its position. After the German invasion, its members had dispersed into the mountains, while some of them had made contact with the Delegation of the SNC for the Liberated Territory. They assembled first in Trebišov (21 January 1945) and then in Košice (30 January), where the delegacy officially started its activities on 1 February 1945. This 'rump' of the SNC appointed a collective executive body called the Board of Commissioners, which in fact acted as the Slovak government. On 2 March the SNC passed a resolution known as the Standpoint and Requirements of the Slovak Nation. According to this, Czechoslovakia was to be a very loose federation. Only three matters – foreign affairs, foreign trade and defence – were to be under the jurisdiction of the central government and even in these matters 'Slovakia was to have appropriate influence and Slovak standpoints were to be respected'. Railways, post and telecommunications, finance, and the question of postwar reconstruction were to be under the joint jurisdiction of the central and the Slovak authorities, while all other matters were to be decided exclusively by the SNC. Slovak conscripts were to serve in Slovak military units. Temporarily, Slovakia was even to be a separate customs and currency territory.[24]

The negotiations between the representatives of the SNC and the Czechoslovak government took place in Moscow on 22–29 March 1945. Beneš was present but did not take direct part in the negotiations. These dealt not only with the Slovak question but also with the new political orientation of postwar Czechoslovakia, and were very intricate. Ultimately a compromise was reached which generally met all the main Slovak requirements. These were included in the government programme which was announced on 5 April in Košice. The Czechoslovak government promised to guarantee the status of Slovakia in a new constitution.[25] Clarification of the division of jurisdiction between the central government and Slovak bodies was to be resolved later.

The SNC originally expected a similar body to be created on the Czech side. Indeed the Czech National Council (CNC) was formed to lead an uprising against the Germans in the protectorate. The uprising against the German occupation broke out on 5 May and swept away the protectorate government of President Emil Hácha, which had collaborated with the occupants. But the CNC had no aims of maintaining power, unlike its Slovak counterpart, and accepted Beneš's leadership. In addition, the Soviet military authorities had no confidence in the CNC because it was not dominated by communists. Consequently, the CNC was dissolved. Thus, as in 1938–9, an asymmetrical model was established. The central government, consisting of Czech and Slovak ministers,[26] served either as a government for the whole of Czechoslovakia if common affairs were on the agenda, or as a Czech government if other matters were to be resolved. The same applied to the parliament. In Slovakia, however, all non-Czechoslovak matters were under the jurisdiction of the SNC and the Board of Commissioners, and the central authorities could not interfere.

IV

The Slovaks entered the renewed Czechoslovak Republic of 1945 under totally different conditions from those of 1918. Initially Slovakia was a semi-independent state ruled from Bratislava, to where the SNC and Board of Commissioners had moved. As the Košice governmental programme had not clarified the division of jurisdiction, and existing provisions were not sufficient, new negotiations between the representatives of the SNC and the Prague government took place (31 May to 1 June 1945), resulting in the First Prague Agreement, which was signed on 2 June 1945. There were twenty common areas which were temporarily to be governed by presidential decrees. These had to be approved by both central government and the SNC, which in fact meant that Czechoslovakia functioned on a confederative principle.[27]

On 28 October 1945 the provisional National Assembly convened. It consisted of 300 MPs, out of which 100 were from Slovakia. The body was not in fact elected by the citizens but by the assemblies of delegates of the national committees (the Slovak National Council was elected in the same way on 28 August). The provisional National Assembly put an end to the 'confederative principle': decisions in all twenty common areas were henceforth to be made by a simple majority. In matters dealing with Slovakia's status, however, approval had to be obtained from a majority of its representatives in the assembly, who thus had the power of veto on these questions.[28]

The system introduced in 1945, though clumsy, nevertheless worked. The compromise reached by the First Prague Agreement was hardly permanent but could have worked for a fairly long time. But it did not: the central Czechoslovak authorities struggled to renew at least a part of their influence over Slovakia. In this respect they had the support of all Czech parties including the Communist Party of Czechoslovakia (CPC) which was really only a Czech party, regardless of its name. The Communist Party of Slovakia (CPS) was formally independent, but was in fact subordinated to the CPC, which forced the Slovak communists gradually to abandon their national programme in favour of 'class struggle' and the 'socialist revolution'.[29]

The first opportunity to limit the influence of the Slovak authorities came in spring 1946 with the preparations for the elections to the Constitutive National Assembly, which was to draw up and pass the new constitution. Czech parties[30] demanded the subordination of Slovak commissioners to the ministers of the central government in matters of joint jurisdiction. In addition, the prerogatives of the president (the right to pardon convicts, to appoint professors to the universities, etc.) were also to be extended to Slovakia, where until then they had been in the hands of the SNC. Both existing Slovak parties – i.e. the CPS and the Democratic Party, the former Civic Bloc – rejected the first proposal but, after some hesitation, accepted the second one. This compromise was set down in the Second Prague Agreement of 11 April 1946. The basic principles of this agreement were included as an appendix to the law on the Constitutive Assembly which was approved on the same day. The right of veto of the Slovak MPs in matters dealing with the status of Slovakia was maintained.[31]

Nevertheless the turnabout came only after the elections to the Constitutive Assembly on 26 May 1946. While in the Czech Lands the communists came top (40.17 per cent), in Slovakia they suffered a defeat (30.37 per cent). The outright winner was the Democratic Party (62 per cent) which, by a secret agreement with former moderate Ľudáks, had obtained the votes of the Catholic electorate. In this situation the Slovak communists were ready to agree to a temporary limitation (or rather suspension) of Slovak powers and to a strengthening of the central government. Naturally, all the Czech parties also took advantage of this opportunity. The Democratic Party thus remained the only party defending the rights of the Slovak authorities, but ultimately it too had to capitulate. On 28 June 1946 all political parties signed the Third Prague Agreement, by which the jurisdiction of the Slovak authorities was severely restricted: the Board of Commissioners was subordinated to the Prague government; the SNC had to present the drafts of its laws to the central government, which was to decide whether the matter came under Slovak or joint jurisdiction; and the particular commissioners were also to function as the executive personnel of the Prague ministers in joint affairs.[32]

The Slovak parties understood the Third Prague Agreement as a temporary solution, while the Czech parties wanted to make it a permanent basis of Czech-Slovak coexistence. The final definition of Slovakia's status was to be set down in the constitution which was being prepared by the Constitutional Committee of the new Assembly. Czech parties and both Czech and Slovak communists advocated a strong central authority. To support this they used the events connected with the trial of Jozef Tiso (2 December 1946 to 15 April 1947), who was sentenced as a war criminal and executed. Several demonstrations supporting Tiso and an activization of the remains of the HSPP supported by Slovak Ľudák émigrés were a welcome pretext. In autumn 1947 the State Security Police, already under strong communist influence, discovered an alleged Ľudák conspiracy and claimed the centre of it to be in the Democratic Party. This 'conspiracy', which later proved to be a mere fabrication, was used by the Slovak communists to discredit the democrats. This resulted in a governmental crisis in Slovakia where, in the autumn of 1947, the Democratic Party lost its majority on the Board of Commissioners.

Although the Slovak communists still supported Prague centralism, they retained the naive idea that after the 'final victory of the working class' Slovakia would regain all jurisdiction. How naïve these dreams were became clear after the communist coup on 25 February 1948. The Constitutional Committee, now fully in the hands of the CPC, rejected the proposals of the Slovak communists. Prime Minister Klement Gottwald, chairman of the CPC, who was soon to succeed Edvard Beneš as president, fully adopted the idea of the Czech communists that it was necessary to keep a permanent and strong Czech influence over Slovakia. The Constitutive Assembly, purged of 'reactionary elements', first abolished the Slovak right to veto in Slovak affairs (16 April) and on 9 May 1948 it approved the new constitution, which left the Slovak authorities with even less jurisdiction than the Third Prague Agreement had done. The central authorities were now allowed to decide on all matters, whereas the SNC could handle only matters of 'regional and national character' where they were 'not regulated by a central law'.[33] In the new situation, however, the constitutional status of Slovakia was of little importance because real power was transferred from the parliament and government to the Presidium of the Central Committee of the CPC and later to its political secretariat. Of greater importance was the formal unification of the CPS and the CPC into one party (27–29 September 1948). From this time on the CPS was to be just a regional organization of the CPC. Centralization was even further strengthened by a reorganization of local government (1 January 1949) and the unification of criminal and civil law in 1950.

V

In the period 1948–68 there was an effort to gloss over the Slovak problem. The predominant idea at the time was that the problem would solve itself once Slovakia had reached the economic level of the Czech Lands. This corresponded with the official doctrine elaborated by Stalinists in the USSR that in a classless communist society nations would gradually merge together. Thus any even potential suggestions of specific national characteristics were denounced as a manifestation of so-called 'bourgeois nationalism'. Klement Gottwald purged the Communist Party of those Slovak communist intellectuals who had been demanding a special position for Slovakia or were even suspected of doing so. The campaign against 'bourgeois nationalism' resulted in several political trials based on fabricated accusations. In 1952 Vlado Clementis, Minister of Foreign Affairs, was sentenced to death and executed for alleged participation in 'Slánský's conspiratorial group'; two years later Gustáv Husák received a life sentence and Ladislav Novomeský was sentenced to ten years for the 'betrayal of the Slovak National Uprising'. The regime also cracked down on various churches, mainly on the Catholic Church, which was treated as a potential supporter of Ľudák emigration and thus a possible danger to the integrity of Czechoslovakia.

However, it has been said that the regime itself was not anti-Slovak. The regime crushed any of its opponents, real or potential, regardless of their nationality. On the other hand, Slovaks were present at all levels of the party and state apparatus, including the State Security Police, and persecuted their compatriots with equal cruelty.[34]

The idea of developing Slovakia's economy to a level equal to that of the Czech Lands, promoted by the Slovak communist Viliam Široký (who was prime minister from 1953), had a different effect from that intended. Objectively it helped Slovakia, as in around ten years it changed Slovakia from an agrarian to an industrial country.[35] However, the notion that this would solve the Slovak problem was completely mistaken: the standard of living of entire sections of the Slovak population increased and subsequently Slovak self-confidence increased too. Ultimately the Slovaks, including the local party bosses, grew to resent Prague centralism and tried to diminish their dependence on the central authorities. This problem, however, could hardly be resolved in the conditions of a communist state based on the principles of a centrally planned economy. In fact industrialization even served to strengthen centralism because – according to centralist planning – all new enterprises were organized by and subordinated to a particular ministry in Prague.

The question of Slovakia's status immediately emerged once political pressure had decreased. This happened after Stalin's death and mainly after Khrushchev's speech at the twentieth congress of the Communist Party of the USSR in 1956. Although in Czechoslovakia Khrushchev's denunciation of Stalin's crimes did not kindle a revolutionary movement as it did in Poland or Hungary, and did not even lead to the rehabilitation of Husák and other 'bourgeois nationalists', slight liberalization did occur, resulting in a change in the status of the SNC. After discussion among the leadership of the CPC on 31 July 1956, a new constitutional law was approved.[36] The SNC was again formally recognized as the bearer of state authority in Slovakia and its powers were slightly extended. What was more important was that from then on the Board of Commissioners was to be appointed by the Presidium of the SNC and not by the central government as had been prescribed by the constitution of 1948.

The law recognizing the authority of the SNC remained only on paper. In 1957 Antonín Novotný, who had been the secretary general of the CPC since 1953, was 'elected' president after the death of Antonín Zápotocký (president from 1953 to 1957). Novotný's negative attitude towards Slovaks was well-known, and under his regime centralism reached its peak. In 1960 the so-called 'Socialist Constitution' was approved, which abolished the Board of Commissioners (i.e. the Slovak government) and limited the jurisdiction of the SNC practically to cultural activities only.[37] The Slovak parliament thus lost all significance.

In his attitude to Slovakia Novotný concentrated – as Široký and Gottwald had done in the 1950s – on economic affairs. But, contrary to the situation in the 1950s, it was now no longer possible to balance the situation in Slovakia by economic growth, as the material resources had been exhausted. Stagnation in the economy deepened the political crisis in the whole country, but this crisis was felt differently in the Czech Lands and in Slovakia. As all economic and political decisions came from Prague, the Slovaks had the impression that Prague was damaging Slovakia both politically and economically. As a reaction, a reform movement was established in Slovakia, led by communist intellectuals linked with the Slovak National Uprising, and who had been sentenced in the 1950s as 'bourgeois nationalists'. Although all of them had been pardoned by 1960 or even earlier, in practice their rehabilitation was delayed practically until 1963.

Once Husák and others had been rehabilitated, the question of the revival of their ideas of Slovak-Czech relations came to the fore. Therefore the reform movement raised the question of the programme of federation as had been put forward by the SNC during the Slovak National Uprising and in 1945–6. The movement had a more democratic character, and also demanded a higher degree of liberty, though within the limits of the communist regime. The movement was supported by Alexander Dubček, secretary general of the Central Committee of the CPS from 1963, who, though he took no part in the movement, defended it in front of Novotný. The democratic aspect of the movement met with a positive response in the Czech Lands and Czech reformists supported it. Novotný's dictatorship was unable to react adequately to the new situation. Some changes were made in the government – Viliam Široký was removed as prime minister and was replaced by Jozef Lenárt in 1963, and the SNC got back certain powers. But this did not satisfy the Slovak emancipation process. In autumn 1967 a group of Slovak members of the Central Committee of the CPC, including Dubček, openly criticized Novotný and later demanded his resignation. Finally, on 5 January 1968, Notovný stepped down as secretary general of the CPC and was replaced by Dubček. On 22 March Novotný also resigned as president and eight days later the National Assembly elected as president General Ludvík Svoboda, commander of the Czechoslovak Army in the USSR during the war.

Surveying the events of 1968 in the light of the years 1989–92, the difference between the Czech Lands and Slovakia appears much more sharply. The Czech population considered the Czechoslovak Republic to be their state and, in general, had no objections to the centralized system. Czech demands were for democratization. The Slovaks, on the other hand, were not satisfied with a centralized Czechoslovakia. Although demands for more freedom and democracy also existed in Slovakia, the main aim of the population was the federalization of the state.

Officially the demand for federalization was presented by the SNC in its session of 14–15 March 1968. The Czech side accepted it. On 15 May a governmental committee was established, officially led by Prime Minister Oldřich Černík. This committee was to prepare the draft of the law on federalization. A special commission which was to solve practical problems was appointed under Gustáv Husák, who became deputy prime minister in Černík's government on 8 April.

The SNC prepared its own draft and presented it to the commission. According to its proposal, two semi-independent states – the Czech Republic and the Slovak Republic – were to be established. Practically all jurisdiction was left to the republics and the federation was to be just an 'umbrella construction' with minimal powers, necessary mainly for defence and the representation of Czechoslovakia abroad. The Czech side presented two different drafts. The first one, drawn up by J. Grospič and Z. Jičínský, was based on a 'strong' federation, i.e. relatively wide jurisdiction was to be kept by the federal authorities. The second draft, proposed by J. Boguszak, envisaged a very loose bond between the two republics. For the first time, the idea of dividing Czechoslovakia had also arisen on the Czech side, but was rejected by the Slovaks.[38]

As there was no counterpart to the SNC on the Czech side, it was first necessary to establish a Czech parliament – the Czech National Council (CNC). On 24 June 1968 the National Assembly approved the 'Constitutional Law on the Preparation of the Federation'.[39] This act founded the CNC, and the Slovak right of veto was reintroduced in matters dealing with Slovakia's status. The MPs of the CNC were not elected. The 'National Front'[40] presented a single list of candidates to the National Assembly, which subsequently approved their selection. The whole action was in fact a total negation of democracy. In addition, the majority of Czechs considered the CNC to be a totally useless body, as they considered the pan-state National Assembly as their parliament.

The final stage of Slovak-Czech relations was a compromise, which was nevertheless closer to a confederation than to a federation. The constitutional law transforming Czechoslovakia into a federation was approved by the National Assembly on 27 October 1968 and was signed by President Svoboda in Bratislava three days later. The Federation Law came into force on 1 January 1969 and remained in force, though with many amendments, until the disintegration of Czechoslovakia in 1992. According to this law Czechoslovakia consisted of two theoretically sovereign states – the Czech Republic and the Slovak Republic – which voluntarily relinquished part of their jurisdiction to the joint federal authorities. Foreign policy, defence, currency, federal material reserves and federal legislation were under the exclusive jurisdiction of the federation, and were to be governed by the federal authorities, namely the federal government, consisting of ministers and state secretaries, as the upper executive body, and the Federal Assembly as its legislative body. The Federal Assembly had two chambers: the House of the People and the House of Nations. While the first chamber was based on proportional representation, in the second one each republic had 75 deputies. In this chamber the Slovak right of veto was to be applied in some cases. Sixteen matters were under the joint jurisdiction of the federation and the republics. All others were under the jurisdiction of the republics. Each republic had its own parliament – the National Council – and its own government, which were to handle non-federal affairs.[41]

It is difficult to determine whether this system could have functioned had it not been established under the communist system. It could, at least for some time, have satisfied the emancipatory movement of the Slovaks. However, free and democratic conditions would have been necessary. From this point of view the military occupation of Czechoslovakia on 21 August 1968 by the Warsaw Pact armies under Soviet leadership was a decisive turning point in its history. The occupation interrupted the democratization process in Czechoslovakia and enabled the conservative forces within the CPC to regain power. The Federation Law of 1968 was based on divided sovereignty, in which power was transferred from below. The communist system, however, was pyramidal, based on so-called 'democratic centralism', i.e. the unconditional subordination of lower authorities to the higher ones. Thus, power came from above.

This meant that real federation and communism were incompatible. With the consolidation of the communist system after the Soviet occupation, federation became a mere fiction. Gustáv Husák, 'the father of the federation', who joined the pro-Soviet conservatives and replaced Dubček as secretary general of the CPC on 17 April 1969, soon lost any interest in the federative system. Thus the concept of federation degenerated during the period of so-called 'normalization'. In 1970 a new law was passed by which the position of the federal authorities was strengthened and the republics were subordinated to them.[42] The real centre of power remained in the hands of the CPC.

This is not to say, however, that federation, even in its normalized form, had no impact on the development of Slovak-Czech relations. From the Czech point of view it brought nothing but an excess of authorities and officials. In Slovakia, on the other hand, the feeling was that at least something had been gained in 1968. Many Slovaks were now employed in federal authorities, and Slovak ministries and other central bodies had been founded, thus strengthening the feeling of Slovak statehood. In this sense the federation laid the basis for Slovakia's future independence.

198   *Jan Rychlík*

Notes

1 Named after Andrej Hlinka (1864–1938), a Catholic priest and the first chairman of the party.
2 On 29 September 1938 in Munich, Great Britain, France, Italy and Germany forced Czechoslovakia to cede part of its territory to Nazi Germany. Subsequently other parts of its territory were annexed by Poland (1 October and 30 November) and Hungary (2 November).
3 K. Sidor, *Slovenská politika na pôde pražskeho snemu: II. diel* ('Slovak Politics in the Prague Parliament: Part II'), Bratislava: 1943, p. 309.
4 Constitutional Law No. 299/1938 Sb. (Sb. = Sbírka zákonů, i.e. the Collection of Laws).
5 Constitutional Law No. 330/1938 Sb.
6 Constitutional Law No. 1/1939 Sl.z. (Sl.z. = Slovenský zákonník, i.e. the Slovak Code).
7 The Germans were permitted the establishment of military garrisons in western Slovakia.
8 Constitutional Law No. 185/1939 Sl.z.
9 Constitutional Law No. 165/1943 Sl.z.
10 Decrees No. 9/1939 Sl.z., 141/1939 Sl.z. and 241/1939 Sl.z.
11 Between 25 March and 20 September 1942 about 57,000 Jews were deported from Slovakia. Subsequently deportations were suspended and about 30,000 remained in the country. Most of them were deported in 1944, when the Germans occupied Slovakia after the Slovak National Uprising. See I. Kamenec, *Po stopách tragédie* ('Reconstructing a Tragedy'), Bratislava: 1991; and L. Lipscher, *Židia v slovenskom štáte* ('Jews in the Slovak State'), Prague: 1992. See also Decree No. 198/1941 Sl.z. and the Constitutional Law No. 68/1942 Sl.z.
12 The Slovak National Council was originally a revolutionary body during the revolution of 1848. The same name was used for similar bodies in revolutionary movements in 1918 and in 1943–4, as well as in 1939. After 1945 the SNC served as the Slovak parliament. Today it is known as the National Council of the Slovak Republic.
13 See the respective documents in F. Vnuk, *Slovenská otázka na Západe v rokoch 1939–40* ('The Slovak Question in the West in the Years 1939–40'), Cleveland: 1974, pp. 175–9, 225–33.
14 Similar to the Slovak National Council (see note 12) the National Committee was a Czech revolutionary body during the revolution of 1848. The same name was used for a similar body in 1918. Local national committees were formed all over Czechoslovakia in 1918 and later in 1944–5. After 1945 these became local government authorities. They were abolished in 1990.
15 V. Vrabec, *Zmařené naděje: Antifašistický nekomunistický odboj* ('The Ruined Hopes: The Antifascist Noncommunist Resistance'), Prague: 1992, pp. 27–8.
16 Cf. J. Šold, *Podpalte Československo* ('Czechoslovakia Set on Fire'), vol. 1: *Operace Perun* ('Operation Perun'), Prague: 1991; vol. 2: *Akce Benjamin*

('Action Benjamin'), Prague: 1991.

17   J. Lettrich, *Dejiny novodobého Slovenska* (Bratislava: 1993), pp. 129–36. Available in English as *A History of Modern Slovakia* (1st edition, New York: 1955; 2nd edition London: 1956). Cf. also *Slovenská politika* (a Bratislava daily), 13 December 1941. On Soviet-Slovak relations see S. Glejdura, 'Slovak-Soviet Relations 1939–1971', in J.M. Kirschbaum (ed.), *Slovakia in the Nineteenth and Twentieth Centuries* (2nd edition, Toronto: 1978), pp. 347–50, and M. Ličko, 'The Development of Slovak-Soviet Relations During the Second World War', ibid., pp. 361–70.

18   L. Otáhalová and M. Červinková (eds.), *Dokumenty z historie československé politiky 1939L'1943* ('Documents from the History of Czechoslovak Politics 1939–1943'), vol. 1, Prague: 1966; document 203, pp. 247–8, document 204, pp. 248–9, document 214, p. 259.

19   E. Táborský, *Prezident Beneš mezi Východem a Západem* (Prague: 1993), pp. 196–7. Available in English as *President Beneš Between West and East* (Stanford: Stanford University Press, 1981).

20   V. Prečan (ed.), *Slovenské národné povstanie: Dokumenty* ('The Slovak National Uprising: Documents'), Bratislava: 1965; document 32, pp. 125–6.

21   Cf. F. Vnuk, *An Incredible Conspiracy* (Middletown, Pa: 1964). See also J. Hronský-Ciger, *Svet na Trasovisku* ('The World of Trasovisko'), 2nd edition, Martin: 1991, p. 249.

22   Decree of the Slovak National Council No. 1/1944 Zb.n. SNR, 1 September 1944 (Collection of Decrees of the Slovak National Council).

23   This treaty was signed on 8 May 1944. See Prečan (ed.), document 59, pp. 192–5.

24   See J. Měchýř, *Slovensko v Československu: Slovensko-české vztahy 1918–1991, Dokumenty, názory, komentáře* ('Slovakia in Czechoslovakia: Slovak-Czech Relations 1918–1991, Documents, Opinions, Commentaries'), Prague: 1991; document 7, pp. 44–50.

25   ibid., document 8, pp. 50–52.

26   In the new Czechoslovak government which was appointed by Beneš in Košice on 4 April and which was a coalition government of four Czech parties (the Communists, the Social Democrats, the People's Party and the National Socialists) and two Slovak Parties (the Slovak Communists and the Civic Bloc, which was later transformed into the Democratic Party), there were nine Slovaks out of 24 members. The system of state secretaries (if a minister was a Czech, the state secretary was a Slovak and vice versa), which had already existed in 1938–9, was reintroduced. The Slovak population, however, never trusted the central government, regardless of the number of Slovak ministers there. The same applied to the central parliament. This mistrust continued until the end of Czechoslovakia in 1992.

27   Měchýř, document 9, pp. 52–6.

28   Constitutional Decree No. 47/1945 Sb., article II/2.

29   The leaders of the Slovak Communist Party, Husák and Novomeský, were transferred to the Board of Trustees and replaced in top party functions by

Viliam Široký, a centralist under the authority of the chairman of the CPC in Prague, Klement Gottwald.

30 See note 26. There were four parties in the Czech Lands and two (later four) in Slovakia. These parties all formed a bloc called the National Front. No other parties were permitted after 1945.

31 Měchýř, document 10, pp. 56–60; Constitutional Law No. 65/1946 Sb., article 9; Decree No. 66/1946 Sb., appendix.

32 ibid., document 11, pp. 62–6. For further negotiations dealing with the status of Slovakia in the constitution, see K. Kaplan, *Příprava Ústavy ČSR v letech 1946–1948: Sborník dokumentů* ('Preparation of the Czech Constitution in the Years 1946–1948: Collection of Documents'), vol. 7, Prague: 1993.

33 Constitutional Law No. 74/1948 Sb. and the Constitution No. 150/1948 Sb., chapter 5, paragraphs 93–112.

34 This was true, for example, of Karol Bacílek, who was chairman of the Board of Trustees after Husák (from 1950) and later Minister of National Security (1952– 3), i.e. head of all police forces.

35 The industrial basis of Slovakia was, however, unbalanced. This was a result of the general orientation of Czechoslovak industry which was to serve mainly military purposes.

36 Constitutional Law No. 33/1956 Sb.

37 Constitutional Law No. 100/1960 Sb., 11 July 1960, articles 73–85.

38 Z. Jičínský, *Vznik České národní rady v době Pražského jara 1968 a její působení do podzimu 1969* ('The Formation of the Czech National Council during the Prague Spring of 1968 and its Functioning till Autumn 1969'), Prague: 1990, pp. 10–21. Cf. also the Slovak National Archives, Bratislava, Fund of the Central Committee of the CPS, information on the discussion in the governmental commission, Prague, 10 July 1968. The author wishes to thank Dr Žatkuliak for lending copies of these documents.

39 Constitutional Law No. 77/1968 Sb.

40 See note 30.

41 Constitutional Law No. 143/1968 Sb.

42 Constitutional Law No. 125/1970 Sb.

11 Towards a Shared Freedom, 1968–89

PETR PITHART

Public opinion polls in the Czech Republic and the Slovak Republic have revealed an unexpected fact (at least unexpected for the Czechs): the Slovaks considered the period of 'normalization' or 'consolidation', as the years 1968–89 were called by their proponents, to be the most successful and happiest period in their nation's history. What was so surprising for the Czechs was that it was precisely those twenty years which they looked upon as the least successful and most unhappy period, a period of general decline and dishonour.

This showed a striking change in attitudes on both sides. After all, the elections of May 1946 – the last free general elections before the communist takeover in February 1948 – had demonstrated that the European postwar shift to the left was much more striking in the Czech Lands (Bohemia and Moravia) than in Slovakia. In the Czech Lands, the Communist Party received over 40 per cent of the vote, and the Social Democrats 15 per cent; in Slovakia, the Communist Party, by then already merged with the Social Democrats, received only 30 per cent of the vote. This striking transformation will be the key to understanding what divided the two nations and their political representatives after November 1989.

One thing seems incontestable: the Czechs and Slovaks entered the post-communist period having had different, indeed even opposite, experiences of the years immediately preceding it. What was perhaps even more serious was that they were not aware of this fact. Communication between democratically oriented Czechs and Slovaks had been minimal in that period, as a result of deliberately placed obstacles.

What was remembered was the common experience of the August 1968 occupation and the weeks which followed. At that time, it had seemed that the two nations were not divided by anything. This is precisely the way things seemed again in the first days after 17 November 1989. Impressions gained from streets brimming with excited people are not, however, a reliable indicator.

Since the break-up of Czechoslovakia, we have once again been witnesses to a peculiar phenomenon in Czech-Slovak relations, which is difficult to name and even more difficult to interpret: the Czechs and the Slovaks, especially in critical periods, have passed each other by. The difference is not only in the emphasis which they place on individual values, aims and interests: on more than one occasion they have passed each other by while heading towards diametrically opposite goals.

Although they have come closer together in many ways which can be expressed in objective categories and which can be quantified (such as the degree of industrialization and urbanization, the social structure and standard of living), their subjective reactions are different, and in extreme situations or critical periods when it is necessary to hold elections, they generally distance themselves from each other. An element of mutual distrust and even suspicion, stemming also from a lack of information and knowledge, plays an important role here, but rather it appears that sometime long ago the Czechs and the Slovaks lost the common rhythm in their history – if, indeed, they ever had one. And it was, paradoxically, as if in the meantime each attempt at getting into rhythm led, as the result of a lack of trust, empathy and ultimately good will, to a reaffirmation of this being out of step. The break-up of the federation has distanced Czechs and Slovaks from each other once again, at least for a while, quite a while.

Or do these two nations actually live in different geopolitical and intellectual regions of the Eurasian continent, and is a common rhythm of history unattainable for them, as the fatalists claim?

These questions can be answered only with time, because, among other things, the twenty years of normalization have not yet been subjected to even preliminary study and examination in Slovakia. Despite systematic attempts, we have not found in Slovak journalism (let alone in the social sciences) in the post-November 1989 period a single attempt to describe the pre-November 1989 period in Slovakia as an individual, purely Slovak experience. After several years of political freedom, this fact is truly relevant: Slovak society either does not want to start in on this sort of examination, or it still does not see the problematic nature of the two apparently successful decades. Were it not for the individual and partial examination by Slovak dissidents in the period before November 1989, this entire chapter would have to be looked at entirely deductively, as an attempt at understanding the function of a 'black box' (in the cybernetic sense). It is true that the Czech experience of normalization has been evaluated mainly by dissidents and mainly in the pre-November 1989 period, out of the elementary need to define their situation of isolation, to attempt to understand it and, as much as possible, to overcome it. After November 1989, there has not been much interest within the Czech Lands in analysing how the normalization regime operated, especially since easy judgments on this period and its proponents are readily available.

It is true, therefore, that there is insufficient detachment for an evaluation of the normalization period, and not only in Slovakia; but to a certain degree the Czech experience has so far been stated predominantly by the dissident subculture, of which this author was once a part. An analysis of the everyday life of workers, farmers and bureaucrats, outside the arena of the confrontation with power, especially in small towns and rural areas, is almost unavailable. The limitations, of which this author is all too aware, follow from that.

The Prague and Bratislava Spring

If we follow the events in the late 1960s at the uppermost levels of power in the leading party, it is hard to avoid the temptation of concluding that the Prague Spring not only had a Slovak beginning but also a Slovak ending. The conflict within the leadership of the Czechoslovak Communist Party erupted in full force in the winter of 1967, when the Party's number one man, Antonín Novotný (a Czech), found himself in open conflict with his Slovak colleagues in the Party leadership, Alexander Dubček in particular. These men had resolved henceforth not to tolerate Novotný's condescension, which was only the tip of the iceberg of 'Prague centralism'. The self-esteem of the Slovak communists thus became, rather unconsciously, a factor in the pluralization of the Party's otherwise monolithic structure. Dubček, whom Novotný publicly called a nationalist, was unable to resist protesting – after all, this was the label used twelve years earlier when sentencing people, for example Gustáv Husák, to life imprisonment. This was the beginning.

And the end; or, perhaps, the beginning of the end? When the Extraordinary Congress of the Slovak Communist Party at the end of August 1968, under Husák's demagogic direction, rejected on formal grounds the political legitimacy of the Prague ('Vysočanský') Fourteenth Extraordinary Party Congress, which had immediately come out against the military occupation within days of its commencement, the finality of the defeat of the Prague Spring was decided. Husák argued in a formalist way at the time, by declaring that there had not been enough Slovak delegates at the congress. He was right – they had been unable to get to Prague in time, travelling across occupied territory for a congress which had been organized conspiratorially.

The reform movement which culminated in 1968 bore the distinct seal of the Czech *genius loci*. Slovakia left its mark in its emphasis on a greater degree of national self-determination, which could only mean a weakening of the democrats' position.

The Short Life of the Federation

The Slovak card was played – more in self-defence than as an offensive move – by the initiators of the Prague Spring (the reform communists), as well as by its liquidators (the occupiers and their lackeys, the anti-reform communists). The latter could not resist the temptation to use the classic techniques of weakening their opponents and breaking the resistance of the occupied country – divide and conquer.

That is why Brezhnev and his people allowed the realization of at least one project out of the entire programme of the Prague Spring (which they otherwise unanimously condemned in the protocols of the negotiations with the Czechoslovak communists), namely federalization. The federalization of the shared state of Czechs and Slovaks not only came late from the point of view of Czech-Slovak coexistence, but also came at an extremely inappropriate time from the point of view of the political chances of saving at least something of the plans of 1968. Indeed, as it turned out twenty years later, it came at an inappropriate time from the point of view of the development of Czech and Slovak relations.

The alternative of 'democratization or federalization', which reflected the difference in Czech and Slovak priorities, was of course a spurious one from the very beginning. On the whole, democratic relations are the condition for a feasible federalization, a fact which was underestimated or ignored in Slovakia. But given the concrete circumstances of the asymmetrically (and for Slovakia unfavourably) arranged Czechoslovakia, not even the reverse order of the strategy would have worked. The Czechs, though, rather dogmatically, did not understand this. Both nations, and above all their mutual relations, paid for the spuriousness of this alternative at the end of August 1968. It took, however, more than twenty years for this to manifest itself in all its seriousness.

The Czech reform communist leaders gained more than an opponent in the Slovak, Husák, who was a strong proponent of federalization. Moreover, the Czech public was disappointed, even disgusted, by the Slovaks' experience of having gained satisfaction with federalization; at best, it was seen as foolishness and at worst, as blind selfishness and even betrayal. That, of course, further weakened their not very great ability for resistance and intensified the overall psychological depression stemming from the occupation. The Husák-run Congress of Slovak Communists after the Warsaw Pact military intervention not only undermined the Czech communists, but also made one more demand, namely to speed up the preparation of the new administrative arrangement of the state so that the act of federation could be passed by the National Assembly on 28 October 1968 (the state holiday which commemorated the creation of the Czechoslovak Republic in 1918).

Although at the time it was not publicly mentioned to any great extent, it could not but occur to people with memories that the Slovaks had once before gained their problematic statehood, under the aegis of Hitler and at a time when the Czechs were on their knees, at the beginning of the German occupation in March 1939. Better informed sceptics would also recall the first Slovak revolutionary upsurge – also in the name of national interests – under the aegis of absolutist Vienna against the Magyar democrats in revolt, during the 'Springtime of Nations', 1848–9. These analogies had to occur to many people in Slovakia as well – a large part of the Slovak nation at the time was not too blind to see this. The pragmatic considerations of their national representatives, however, always confirmed that nothing more could be gained from the situation and that Slovakia rather identified with this position. The Czechs had lost everything, but it did not seem inappropriate to the Slovaks that they should get at least something.

For all these reasons, it cannot be discounted that the fact of federalization was not even properly taken note of by the Czechs, since it came about in such a depressing atmosphere. Still more probable – as was shown much later – was that the majority of them considered federalization to be essentially a Russian trick, a concomitant phenomenon of the occupation. It was, of course, a conclusion that was easy to come to (federalization had been in the making since the spring of 1968), whose consequences turned out to be very unpropitious. I would like to mention, merely as a hypothesis which would need proving, that even today there is in the Czech Lands an indefinite but firmly rooted impression that the federation was the work of 'communists'. Similarly, Slovaks continue to live in the belief that their postwar autonomy was taken from them by the communists (after the 1946 general elections, which the communists lost in Slovakia). Unlike the Czech impression, this one is based on reason. It is necessary to add, however, that after the war virtually all Czech political parties blindly identified with the communists in their anti-Slovak attitude. Moreover, the last remnants of autonomy were taken away only with the adoption of the 'socialist' constitution in 1960.

In 1968, by an act of the National Assembly, Slovakia attained statehood and the symbols and offices pertaining to it, all as part of federalization, of course. In the system of the 'leading role of the Party' and 'democratic centralism', however, this could be nothing more than a mere façade, and the expectations of the Slovak patriots had sooner or later to be left unmet. And, apart from a certain hangover felt by democratic Slovaks, there had to occur an even greater estrangement from the Czechs. The dysfunctional federation, despite having two Slovaks (Gustáv Husák and Vasil Biľak) at the head of the 'State Party' (Husák was said to have attached the Czech Lands onto Slovakia), was attributed by many disappointed people in Slovakia not to these two Party men, but to Prague and the Czechs, in whom they saw the traditional proponents of centralism. Thus, as in all of Czechoslovakia's history, in Slovakia this time all trends of development (though mostly the negative ones) were connected with Prague and the central authorities. This, even in the microcosm of Slovak society, could only provide support for the historically reproduced defensive strategy of 'survival', typical of Slovak society since the time of the nineteenth-century National Revival.

On the other hand, in the Czech Lands there was an increasingly obvious disgust for the regime and for the Slovaks, as the ones through whom normalization was allegedly introduced and carried out. No matter how much an exaggeration this was, the Slovaks functioned reliably as the lightning rod and substitute target of verbal aggression directed at the regime. For the latter, it was the least dangerous channelling of the resistance it faced – nevertheless, in recent years, the word 'Slovak' could not be used in an official context, because it seemed to be an obvious jab at the regime.

One can, then, preliminarily conclude that federalization did not bring anybody – apart from the occupying forces and their local lackeys – anything good. Realistically, though, it must be added that it more than met the requirements of the wildly mushrooming Slovak bureaucracy.

The question of whose powers in a federation are primary and whose are derived and secondary can easily be answered in cases where it can be formulated as a question of which political unit came first and which followed, such cases being those where the individual states originally decided to create a common state, a federation. When an initially unitary state such as Czechoslovakia divides, however, it does not follow that the federation is the primary, 'original' and in that sense 'higher' element, endowed with sovereignty, and that it devolves to its constituent parts a sovereignty of only the second order (understandably, it is always sovereignty which is divided one way or another).

The federalization of unitary Czechoslovakia in 1968 was in the end conceived on the basis of a proposal by the Slovak National Council (that republic's legislative body) in such a way as to place the centre of power (i.e. that primary, original power) in what were to be the constituent, Czech and Slovak, republics. The sovereignty of these constituent republics was original – the federation and its organs exercised only those powers which the republics devolved to it. The expression of original sovereignty of the republics according to the act meant primarily that each of the republics would have its own constitution (during the next twenty years, work on the constitutions was, however, never even begun). The republics were represented by their representative organs, i.e. the national councils (parliaments), and formed a complex state mechanism, i.e. a constitutional court of the federal republic, a federal government, ministries and other central organs of the state administration, such as a supreme court and an office of public prosecutions. The basic law (constitution) of the federation provided organs of the executive with far-reaching powers. The Czech and Slovak organs then delegated part of their sovereignty to the joint organs, the organs of the federation.

The Czech side's original objections to the relative weakness of the federal government were not accepted. Seen from a historical perspective, the Czechs had too bad a conscience to argue their own cause at any cost; mainly, though, the initiative was clearly on the Slovak side after the Soviet occupation. That does not mean that this loose federation in and of itself was conceived as basically bad or dysfunctional. Rather, it is fair to say that a situation never arose when this functionality could have been tested. It is remarkable that the basic objection, namely that the leading role of the Party (guaranteed in the constitution and based on 'democratic centralism') was incompatible with any conception of federation, was never raised, not even by the Slovak side. It is in keeping with the lack of thoroughness of reform communism and with the immaturity of Slovak policy, that before August 1968 it was only hoped that this same Communist Party would go through some kind of 'internal transformation' and that this conflict would thus disappear by itself. After August, it did not really matter one way or another.

The fact is that doubts about the functionality of the federation could neither be unanimously confirmed or rebutted. As early as December 1970, an act was passed by which the function of the organs of the federation was strengthened. Of those parts of the constitution which dealt with the devolution of powers to the federation and the republics, only six of them remained untouched. When the Czechoslovak federation was created in 1969, the Czechoslovak economy was defined as 'the link between the two economies of the republics', but one year later an amendment stated that the 'economy of the Czechoslovak Socialist Republic (ČSSR) is unified'. Article 4(2) of the constitution originally read: 'the Czech nation and Slovak nation are economically independent'. As of the beginning of 1971, the federal government had the right to 'veto or even quash measures of the governments of the republics, if they are in conflict with measures of the government of the ČSSR'. The governments of the republics thus entered a relationship of subordination *vis-à-vis* the federal government.

Independent legislative activity by the parliaments was also abandoned after amendment of the constitution. From that time on, the laws of the national councils were unified and the different statutes in the Czech and Slovak legal codes dating from the time of the Prague Spring were revoked at this phase in consolidation (including, for example, an important act of the Slovak National Council, which had created a different local govern-ment structure from that in the Czech Lands). With the exception of a few minor laws which dealt only with insignificant, specific matters of one of the republics (e.g. the act of the Slovak National Council on 'the develop-ment of the Tokaj wine region'), all the laws of the two National Councils were identical – differing only in language (Czech or Slovak), place names and the names of those who had signed them. The ČSSR was from the beginning of normalization a federation in name only.

If Husák deserves the credit for gaining the support of the sceptical, more nationalistically oriented Slovaks for the federalization just after the occupation, by the time the process of normalization was well underway (i.e. with centralization and the jettisoning of those elements of democracy and human rights which had come with the year 1968) this dexterous technician of manipulation helped in Czechoslovakia's defederalization. In both cases, the aim was to firm up the position of the normalizers and Husák's own personal power.

The whittling down of the federation was carried out in a situation of overall tranquillization and resignation, and it is, therefore, fair to assume that if federalization was not lodged in the memories of many Czechs at the time, then it is all the more likely that defederalization also escaped their attention. It turned out later that this was of significance. The new group of politicians and bureaucrats in the governments and parliaments of the republics could not accept this willingly, but it was in keeping with the situation that they did not make that fact known: in an atmosphere of general purges they could be happy that they had a seat to sit in, albeit without any actual influence.

*   *   *

Extempore: Summer 1990. At this point it is not possible to avoid running ahead of historical time and recalling the atmosphere which existed in the Czech Republic after the commencement of negotiations on the devolu-tion of powers to the governments at the federal and republic levels in Trenčianské Teplice in the summer of 1990.

The negotiations were formally initiated by the federal government, in actual fact by Slovak Premier Vladimir Mečiar (the Slovak governing party put themselves behind him, as well), and no matter how excessive some of his original ideas on a redistribution of powers were (in that they would have made the federation unnecessary and untenable), they were in principle moving in a legitimate direction: they tried to return the division of powers between the federation and the republics to its original, pre-normalization state (i.e. prior to December 1970). Husák's normalization correction – the whittling down of the federation – was either forgotten in the Czech Republic or, as has already been mentioned, had never been seriously noticed. It is also entirely possible that Czech public opinion at the time actually tacitly identified with it. These are serious questions, to which we do not have, and will probably never have, a provable answer.

The idea of returning to the original project of the federation, of renewal from below (i.e. at the level of the republics and their parliaments) appeared, however, at that time in Czech politics as a thoroughly unacceptable act of appeasement of the Slovak side or, at best, as an excessively high risk from the point of view of the will to preserve the shared state according to the Czechs' idea of it.

And so the negotiations themselves were already being completely condemned in the Czech part of the federation, and their actors were under fire from critics in the public and the mass media as allegedly the grave diggers of the shared state. To have refused these negotiations, however, would have actually meant also denying the way in which the federation had originally been created, and, what's more, it would have meant coming down on the side of Husák at the beginning of the period of normalization.

More than twenty years on, it turned out indirectly that the Czech public had perceived federalization in 1968 in an oversimplified way, through the prism of the occupation. That, however, occurred after the project of the federation had been assessed and more or less prepared through available democratic means. It seems, however, that its promulgation at the end of October (the Federation Act became effective as of 1 January 1969) enabled the unitarily oriented Czech public to perceive this basic transformation of the constitutional arrangement of the relations between the Czechs and the Slovaks as merely a part of the gradual disassembling of the achievements of reform. This sort of disassembling did not occur, however, until its actual restriction in December 1970 and the years which followed.

The shock of the military intervention followed by more than twenty years of atomization of the two non-communist national societies, together with both managed and spontaneous forgetting, brought wrack and ruin.

*   *   *

If we go back, then, to the early Seventies, we can only say that federalization did not bring the Czechs and the Slovaks even their long-desired equality, although it would have been equality in the depressed, undemocratic conditions of an occupied country. The asymmetric solution in the period from the end of the war up to federalization had intentionally disadvantaged the not entirely reliable Slovaks (recall the bugbear of the 1946 elections!), even though its intention was to give the opposite impression: the Slovak constitutional and Party organs had no parallel on the Czech side, which had the paradoxical effect, however, that the term 'statewide' (*celostátní*) – i.e. based in Prague – was perceived by both the Czechs and the Slovaks as meaning 'Czech'. Similarly, the asymmetric solution (in the conditions of the federation this could now apply only to the internal structure of the Czechoslovak Communist Party) was implemented after the occupation. The motivation at the time was the reverse: it was a matter of disadvantaging the Czechs and the Czech Lands. Out of a desire to prevent other Czech communists being infected by the spread of the virus of reformism, none of the initially planned Party organs at the republic level was ever established in the Czech Republic. In other words, the Party, the 'leading party', was not federalized. And, because Slovaks were at the time in the highest Party offices, asymmetry operated clearly to the disadvantage of the Czech side.

A double standard in the purges? The Czech part of the federal republic suffered from a much greater shock than did the Slovak part during the normalization period. In the Czech Republic, hundreds of thousands of people had become politically active in favour of a democracy which ended up being spectacularly defeated, and the vanquished had to be commensurately punished. In the Slovak Republic, people became politically active towards the national cause, Slovak statehood and the federation which had apparently triumphed.

The Czechs, more sceptical, knew that a federation without democracy was only an empty shell, and they dismissed it as such. From the Czech point of view everything appeared quite different than from the Slovak. For example, the nationwide Slovak movement for the building of a prestigious *Alweg*, a mountain railway in the High Tatras, at a time when the last remnants of sovereignty were at issue, was considered by the Czechs to be absolutely preposterous. The Czechs had with similar hope and self-sacrifice once raised funds for their National Theatre, but that had been more than a century ago. Even though the Slovaks did not in the end build their *Alweg*, they still did not suffer the same feeling of defeat after August 1968 as the Czechs did. Some of them might even have had a feeling of victory.

And most probably, therefore, the purges in the Czech Lands were carried out completely differently than in Slovakia. It was a matter of 'vetting' within the Communist Party of Czechoslovakia and the Communist Party of Slovakia, as well as in other quasi-independent parties on the one hand, and a matter of evaluating the political reliability of employees in enterprises on the other hand – the state, after all, had the monopoly on employment. In the Czech Republic some low-profile sinners/Party members could save their skin by expressing agreement with the military intervention, while the most important people were condemned in advance for having 'written their cadre assessments themselves', as one turn of phrase from those days put it. Non-Party members (remember that at the time of the purges the Party had 1.7 million members) were presented with noticeably milder demands, and capable and decent people were not entirely without a chance of holding on to their jobs, so long as their colleagues and superiors were not fanatics. It is safe to say that individuals could even – insofar as possible at the time – pursue meaningful goals and push for relatively reasonable solutions to problems in the heavily politicized situation. Nevertheless, more than 1.5 million people were directly and indirectly affected in their efforts to earn a living, or their careers progressed only up to the low ceiling set by nomenklatura rules. The limitations applied to the children of people who were affected in this way (they were the regime's hostages, in the true sense of the word); this concerned in particular their limited chances of getting education commensurate to their abilities. In addition, thousands of books were taken off the shelves of every kind of library, not so much because of their tainted contents, but because of the names of their authors or translators, who had refused to submit themselves to the humiliation of acknowledging the legitimacy of the occupation. These authors were then unable to publish even fairy tales. This applied across the board to theatre, film, fine arts and science, including the natural sciences and technology. Within a few years Czech society was intellectually and culturally decimated. Unexpected career opportunities were, however, presented to people who were absolutely below average and, above all, morally cynical. In the Czech Lands one could, without much exaggeration, say that there was a cold civil war going on.

In Slovakia all this was happening as well, but to a much lesser extent and, above all, with much less serious consequences. In the Czech Lands, the Husáks, Biľaks and other normalizers 'liked it hot'; in Slovakia, they let it cool off quietly. The vetting in Slovakia, in comparison with the vetting in the Czech Lands, gave the impression of formality and especially leniency – as if there were a tacit agreement which said that: 'We are all Slovaks, aren't we, and we know what this is about, so we aren't going to do ourselves in for no reason. Anyway, it was the Czechs who came along with democracy and the utopia of "socialism with a human face", when we were concerned only with the legitimate cause of national interests, the federation, which is what we finally have.' This attractive and understandably more implicit than explicit philosophy of the preservation of the nation truly worked, and something was actually saved. It turned out later that the price of this preservation was not, and for some time to come would not be, small. But many capable and decent people in Slovakia remained at their jobs, and those who did not stayed at least within the same enterprise; getting back their jobs, even for big sinners, was not unusual, and cultural activity did not, by any stretch of the imagination, suffer from gaps as in the Czech Lands. And not only cultural activity: in Slovakia everything functioned noticeably better that in the Czech Lands; there was less fear and less hate in Slovakia.

Then, as in the past, the 'family model' was implemented in Slovakia, asking the Slovak community not to get into any basic confrontations with the omnipresent state authorities. Anyway, the broad meaning of the concept of family and the imperative of family solidarity, as well as solidarity between people from the region (*rodáci*) further mitigated the course and consequences of the purges.

Slovakia paid no small price for that: satisfied by federalization and by the fact that things had not turned out as badly as in the Czech Lands, it gave up on its potentially nonconformist minorities. Democracy remained a fiction, an impractical, unattainable goal, about which almost no one was then able to speak. The nation and national interests, therefore, remained the highest value which could not be made relative to anything. The Czechs could then, in the light of this self-flattering Slovak national-defender philosophy, easily be seen as irresponsible adventurers or, at best, as unrealistic dreamers, utopians, who moved from one extreme to another and threatened to pull healthy, conservative, traditionalist, Catholic Slovaks down into the chasm of their defeats.

Since November 1989, it has become clear that Slovakia paid the most for the relatively peaceful repression, by the fact that it lacked the motivation for a more thorough self-examination. This sort of motivation is usually the experience of defeat. At the end of the twenty years of normalization, despite numerous signs of economic, environmental and moral crisis, despite the intensifying backwardness in terms of its civilization, technological decline and the growing political gap between it and the rest of Europe, there was in Slovakia little awareness of the fundamental political crisis and the unfeasibility and unreformability of the communist regime. After November 1989, there has been nothing so important as that awareness, the ability for sober-minded self-examination which asks: Who are we? Where did we come from? Where are we going? Not that there is a surplus of this sort of thinking in Czech society, but it was and is absent in Slovak society and will be for some time.

It was not so much a matter of a 'double standard' in the purges as a matter of two quite different stories which might both have begun in 1968 and are, to all outward appearances, similar to one another but which, in fact, confirm that Czech and Slovak history are out of step with each other. During the twenty years from 1969 to 1989, the Czechs were most probably paying an unfairly (that's geopolitics, though!) high price for their past groping and fumbling about and found themselves under direct threat of losing their identity, but the democratic élites had more or less reflected on, and articulated, all of this. Although they were unprepared to assume direct political responsibility, they could basically find their bearings in the new situation which followed after November 1989, and they at least knew what it was that they did not want. In Slovakia, in the same period, they may have completed the process of modernization of society and the related homogenization of the nation, but it was done only in terms of objective reality, without the commensurate examination and articulation. Slovak identity, which henceforth was no longer an unrealistic dream, now became the commodity most in demand. *Objectively*, Slovakia had the wherewithal for it, *subjectively*, under the normalization regime, it dared not try it. This was the ideal opportunity for nationalists or 'mere' populists with nation-alistic rhetoric, who were waiting for their chance.

The Czech Dissident Movement and Slovak Dissidents

Creative, democratically oriented people in the Czech Lands, who found themselves at rock bottom and employed as stokers, night-watchmen and low-ranking bureaucrats, were finally left with no other choice but to use the circumstances to take a basic, critical look at the Czech situation in the modern age. They were thus more prepared for what was to come, unexpectedly, in November 1989, and thanks to the dissidents and the people who helped them, they were more 'persuasive' than their colleagues (of more or less the same orientation) in Slovakia. With the wide dispersion of the essentially weaker Slovak opposition, it made it possible, for example, that some of the key actors of post-November politics in Bratislava first met with the main leaders of Public Against Violence only during the formation of the leadership of that movement – something like that could never have happened in the Czech Lands. With only rare exceptions, it is fair to say that these people in Slovakia may have been uncomfortable, but they survived, indeed some of them were not even entirely cut off from official politics (especially in the area of the arts). They were not, in short, put under the sort of pressure which comes from difficulties in trying to earn a living or faced with existentialist worries, and the situation did not force them to have too much at stake.

The number of Czech dissidents, and their interconnectedness, was mainly an unwanted consequence of increased police and political pressure. Being a dissident in the Czech Lands was not always a matter of a supreme, a priori moral choice, despite the way legend would have it. Many, possibly the majority, of the more recent dissidents first found themselves in a situation where there was almost nothing left to lose, and only then did they opt for the life of a dissident. The regime, specifically the personnel department at the workplace, to which the secret police (StB) kindly provided 'suggestions', put them in a situation where it was possible, even advantageous, to calculate whether to remain isolated, in anonymity, in a low-ranking job with above-average pay, or to 'come out into the open', sign a petition or charter and thereby join an inspiring milieu of free-thinking and creative people, gain access to banned literature and have the opportunity of publishing in samizdat and abroad. Connected to all of that was a certain protection provided by public opinion in the West. Some people found themselves among the dissidents, because with the relatively intensive communication, especially in Prague and Brno (with the circulation of banned literature, modern music concerts and lectures in people's homes, all organized without the consent of the authorities), the police got them into their nets and then it was better to sign, say Charter 77, than not to. The word 'calculation' is not intended to minimize the value of the dissidents' attitudes and activities in the Czech Lands; they were always connected with significant but not always predictable risks. It only makes them sociologically and socio-psychologically more explainable – for example, in regard to the Slovak situation, where there actually was no dissident movement, just a few dissidents.

In Slovakia, a sober term which aimed at avoiding pathos gained currency for describing groups of nonconformist individuals: 'little islands of positive deviation'. The insufficient awareness of the political crisis in society, the relatively closed-off nature of the Slovak opposition *vis-à-vis* the Czech Lands and dissidents abroad (in Poland and Hungary), led to that island existence of civic dissent, to the Christian community (including the underground Church), independent culture and environmentalist activity.

Charter 77, which had over one thousand signatories in Bohemia, Moravia and Silesia, of whom several hundred were active, did not manage to get even ten important cultural figures in Slovakia who had intensive contact with the Czech milieu, Czech friends and colleagues. A Slovak historian, living in Prague, recalls how Václav Havel had hoped that the Slovaks would be the first to sign the Charter immediately after the introductory declaration, in order to show that there was no desire to make the whole project a Czech undertaking. In fact, it ended up demonstrating the reverse, since hardly any other Slovak signatures were added to the list, and the impression that it was indeed a Czech enterprise was the one which came to predominate abroad and in Slovakia.

Today, when the Czech side is building a guardable, physical frontier along an area where for 466 years there were only symbolic markers, one has to recall that this frontier was in a certain sense preceded by a frontier for dissidents: the Czech and Slovak police (the latter with noticeably more zeal), tried to isolate dissidents from both sides and disrupt their contacts. Many times it happened that the dissidents were forced as soon as they arrived at the railway station of their destination to board a train under escort and return straight to Prague, Brno or Bratislava, at their own expense: the Slovak police seldom resisted giving the Czech dissidents the advice that they 'Go and do that at home in the Czech Lands, but don't come here to do it!' This was to be understood as: 'Don't come here spreading the virus of upheaval in our orderly, developing and basically satisfied Slovakia!'

It has to be stated that the Slovak dissidents were superb in every way, but there were so few of them that it could only increase doubts as to whether or not the Czechs and Slovaks had anything of importance in common and were living through one and the same period in history.

The Czech dissident movement consisted of many social strata (even though far from proportionally represented), all political orientations and all levels of expertise. It was active for more than twenty years, published hundreds of collectively edited reports (called *dokumenty*), monitored almost without a pause the repressive activity of the authorities, and created the space for numerous publishing activities. Slovak dissidents were predominantly recruited from Catholic and environmentalist circles. The Catholic pilgrimages in Slovakia (and Moravia), in which hundreds of thousands of people participated during the last few years prior to the end of the communist regime, were the result of more than just Slovak piety; Catholic samizdat literature had begun to spread in the years before November 1989, and Slovak Catholics dared to take to the streets in March 1988. Slovak environmental activists had maintained a continuity with the Sixties; the putting-together and publishing of the occasional volumes of the journal, *Bratislava nahlas* ('Bratislava out loud'), meant not only the culmination of their activity, but above all the express politicization of the environmental movement.

For the nascent and only gradually uniting and weakly communicating Slovak opposition, November 1989 came, paradoxically, too soon. If it had come later, however, reform communist forces would probably have already been activated within the organs of power and could have taken over the leadership of the political struggle that was underway. In the Czech part of the federation, such forces of reform within the organs of power did not – as a consequence of the much more thorough purges there – exist even in embryo. They existed only outside the circles of power and as a minor part of the opposition movements.

A coming together or a moving apart? The difference in emphasis within the reform movement in the late Sixties, the different ways in which the authorities came to terms with the vanquished, and the different extent and orientation of the nonconformist, opposition activity, all seem to testify to the fact that the Czech Lands and Slovakia were moving apart from each other. In fact, it has been possible to say this with certainty only since the division of the common state, in early 1993.

During the twenty years of normalization, the objective economic, demographic and sociological indices on the state of the Czech Lands and Slovakia and the trends in their development had come closer together than ever before. Nevertheless, a single society did not come into being. These objective processes were clearly experienced in different ways, because they were experienced at a different subjective time of national history and, above all, the difference had not been articulated and was, therefore, left unexamined.

That is not to say that the Czech side should have been surprised, after 17 November 1989, by the Slovak emphasis upon the national point of view. Nations, when they are materially and culturally wanting, usually do not demand autonomy, independence or the federalization of the country; indeed, quite on the contrary, it is when things are beginning to go well for them that they make such demands. It was no different for the Czech Lands, when one hundred years ago demands were made for autonomy from Austria. Czech society reacted to the painful process of modernization (the falling apart of the world of clear-cut relations), which it went through beginning in about the 1860s, with not only the creation of a national ideology, but also the creation of its own community which consisted of a dense network of clubs and various associations, parties, movements and mediation between individuals and the state; in short, the creation of a civil society.

In Slovakia, where the process of modernization began with the birth of the Czechoslovak state in 1918, gained speed in the Fifties and Sixties, and was completed in the next twenty years (in the period of normalization), civil society had been forming for only a few years prior to the end of communism. It could hardly get as far as civil society had done in the Czech Lands in the interwar period: 'civil society' and 'totalitarian regime' are clearly contradictory terms. Slovakia could not catch up quickly after so many centuries of being behind, which meant that in Slovakia the tension connected with modernization could not, unlike the Czech experience, be mitigated by civil society.

It is appropriate at this point to clarify some terminology: the completion of the Slovak nation's formation as a 'political nation' had most probably occurred in the years 1918 to 1938; a nation is completely formed if it contains all social strata and groups and has an awareness of its distinctness from other nations. The complete formation of a nation, however, does not automatically mean the complete formation of civil society. In the twenty years prior to November 1989, the self-confidence of the Slovak nation had dramatically increased; Slovaks had in massive numbers found positions at the highest level of authority. Federal posts were, however, considered to be 'un-Slovak', 'Czechoslovak', and those holding them were thought of as turncoats. In the Czech Lands, on the other hand, it was disrespectfully said that 'they have put another Slovak in just to keep things even'; in other words, the person does not hold the job because of merit but because of Slovak nationality. Slovakia, during this period, created practically all the organs which an independent state would need – with the exception of defence, foreign affairs and, to a certain extent, finance.

Only then did the homogenization of the Slovak nation occur. 'Homogenization of the nation' means the process of the gradual restratification of experiences of being members of individual Slovak regions (*kraje*) into the experience of being members of the Slovak nation as a whole. Up to that point in time, intensively experienced *krajanství* (regional solidarity, the regional Party lobby, nepotism) had the result that even standard Slovak had remained an artificial, bookish language which far from every Slovak had mastered. Indeed, the linguistic differences between the dialects of individual Slovak regions are still sometimes greater than the differences between standard Czech and standard Slovak.

The process of integration (linguistic homogenization), as well as the process of national self-realization, is the definite, positive creation of a national ideology, even if done implicitly rather than explicitly. That is all the more valid since the trauma of modernization could not be compensated for in Slovakia by the creation of civil society (as it had been in the Czech Lands, one hundred years ago), but rather only by its debased substitution with a system of nepotism and regional solidarity – in other words, corruption.

During the years 1969–89, the external face of the Slovak country changed more than ever before – the urbanization begun in the Fifties meant not only the further growth of towns (through state, cooperative and, last but not least, private construction) and the concomitant mobility of the population, but also the construction of family homes and the gradual disappearance of traditional Slovak villages. The standard of living was rising everywhere in Czechoslovakia at that time, but nowhere as strikingly as in Slovakia. It was important to the normalization regime that the beginning of the normalization period especially be economically successful – there is still no satisfactory explanation for how and why in the years 1969 to 1973 results were noted which not even Husák's boastful regime had expected (apparently, it has to do with the regularity of the industrialization cycles, which are at work regardless of changes in the political atmosphere). If the initially striking growth in the material level is seen in connection with the experience of national satisfaction (the external symbols of Slovak statehood, thousands of Slovaks in Prague in the offices of the federal government), it is no surprise that the Slovak population today perceives the last twenty years prior to the fall of the communist regime as a period of success. The Czechs at this time were clearly in a depression and, what is more, they were being ruled by Husák and Biľak, who were not too popular even in Slovakia. Certainly, in Slovakia it was possible to be sceptical about any sort of 'progress': the utterly ineffective investments were, in addition, frequently a catastrophe for the natural environment. And, together with the orientation towards heavy industry, which is demanding in terms of energy and raw materials, these large investments hurt rather than benefited Slovakia. The functionaries of individual regions made them mainly as confirmation of their own status in the Party hierarchy, similar to the way in which aristocrats once sought privileges and other emblems of the ruler's favour. And so this mania for the gigantic destroyed, for example, the historic centre of the capital city of Slovakia, Bratislava. In the Czech Republic, however, there is no one thing which should be mentioned more than any other: the decline was all-round and incontestable.

Despite the problematic character of the process of modernization, it can be said that the system of government in the declining phase of communism, which was based on the corrupt system of district and regional bosses, had been established much more easily and successfully in Slovakia than in the Czech Lands. Since modernization was something relatively new, and often accompanied by a traumatic experience, and since it was often still only external, this system of nepotism and corruption became the substitute for the clear system of relations which had once been typical in the just recently defunct rural community. In Slovakia, power continued to be something tangible and human rather than an impersonal institution: people now had an absolutely positive relationship with the various Party bosses, secretaries and chairmen, just like the relationship which had once existed between the peasants and the aristocrats in the old village.

The sources of modernization (industrialization and urbanization) in Slovakia were both domestic (at the expense of the countryside), and 'Czech': the redistribution mechanisms carried out by means of the state budget, but most probably by other means as well, reallocated for Slovakia finances which had been earned in the industrially more developed Czech Lands. While in Yugoslavia and the Soviet Union the differences between the individual republics were growing, in the Czechoslovak Socialist Republic, the differences were constantly getting smaller. Regardless of the political context, this was the incontestable civilized success of the Czechs and Slovaks, a success which in Europe, not just Communist Europe, was unique.

Redistribution, in the broadest sense of regional politics, is an attribute of not only the modern European state, but also of supranational groupings such as the European Community. The trouble with Czechoslovak redistribution was its opacity: in conditions of a non-market economy, no one was able to ascertain the true degree to which redistribution had actually occurred. This gave the impression that not only was the redistribution greater than had officially been declared, but it was in and of itself something illegitimate, which the state had to keep secret. From there it was only a short step to the hasty conclusion that the state keeps secret its redistribution process because it is a consequence of the unfair Czech-to-Slovak ratio of forces in the state leadership (and the governing Party). It is safe to assume that this fact contributed to the Czechs' growing distrust of the Slovaks and their animosity towards them. The Slovaks quickly repaid the Czechs in kind, and the net result was mutually reinforcing distrust and animosity.

The opacity of the redistribution mechanisms plus having Slovaks as the leaders of state and Party came to create, on the Czech side, the politically articulated will to change this state to the benefit of the Czechs. Even within the highest Party groupings, there were rumblings along these lines; ultimately a Czech (or rather anti-Slovak) lobby was formed within the highest Party organs, which tried to limit and then end the transfer of finances from the Czech Republic to the Slovak Republic.

Even though the greatest caution is in order when assessing these facts (the creation of Party cliques and lobbies was often a smoke screen, covering up completely different aims which, in the otherwise monolithic system, could not even be expressed), it is remarkable that at least these tendencies, which appeared in the Party and state establishment prior to November 1989, were in harmony with the mood which in the end – as far as the Czech side was concerned – dominated in the formulation of a negative point of view on coexistence in a common state. If this was, in fact, the case, then it was a matter of a more profound and, in the long run, extensive process of the moving apart and estrangement of the two nations. Consequently, even the incontestable mistakes made by the post-November 1989 political leaders of the two republics and the federation were not the decisive factor in the split.

Slovak self-confidence, as the self-confidence of a nation on the rise in the years of normalization, grew; Czech self-confidence decreased. With the rise in the standard of living in Slovakia, having a federation for the sake of appearances came increasingly to be perceived as unacceptable, while in the Czech Lands this problem was probably never even seen as one of the Czech national interests. Discreet public opinion (i.e. what was being whispered and muttered about) in the Czech Lands looked for the causes of the country's decline beyond the sphere of the ideologically taboo, and, therefore, in the wrong place. It saw it, paradoxically, precisely in what was basically tolerable for the regime: namely in the practice of redistribution, especially in so far as it was a matter of principle and not merely the debased (opaque) practice of redistribution.

Dissident circles, which after November 1989 became the source of political leaders, saw the situation completely differently, and were more critical of the local, Czech milieu, and for that very reason they gradually vanished from the political scene. First, their view was not and is not the least bit popular; secondly, this more severely critical position had the effect that the dissidents were generally incapable of the required radicalism, which stemmed from dashed hopes and from recognition of the fact that the transformation of society was far more difficult and protracted than anticipated by the very people who had endeavoured to put an end to the Slovaks' 'eating the Czechs out of house and home'. Czech dissidents had been contemplating the deeper causes of the decline, which were less connected with the Slovaks ('them') than with the Czechs ('us'), and were, therefore, connected with the historical development of the Czech Lands during the last two centuries. Czech dissidents, however, as an important part of Czech critical self-esteem, lacked a sufficient number of comparable partners on the Slovak side, who would have been willing and capable of similar critical self-examination; the politicians who had come out of dissident circles ultimately did not have them either.

Conclusion

A number of important indices showed that both nations were coming as close together as possible, without, however, managing to create one, single Czechoslovak society. Thus, no Czechoslovak political nation could come into being. Nevertheless, this was still a coming together by the civilized successes, something which in Europe could never be taken for granted. And when the time came, there was an absence of the subjective prerequisites needed to surmount the shock of meeting each other after twenty years of unauthentic communication under the supervision of the Party-state.

(Communication, mutual interest and even solidarity were at least manifested intensively among the intellectuals in the Sixties, but, in fact, they had never ceased to exist, not even in the 'independent' Slovak state and the German Protectorate of Bohemia and Moravia during the Second World War. Even during the twenty years of normalization the absence of communication, interest and solidarity was not as obvious as it has become since the division of the shared state.) The new political élites lacked political culture, noticeably more in Slovakia than in the Czech Lands.

In the post-communist world, the conditions for populism, including the kind which uses nationalist and nationalistic rhetoric, are exceptionally favourable everywhere. The unavoidable difficulties of the transformation, one of which is disappointment based on everything taking much longer than was initially anticipated, have tempted all post-communist countries to listen to populists, elect them and then depend on them. Czechs, and the Czech electorate, have so far resisted that temptation noticeably better than people and electorates elsewhere in the post-communist countries, and in cases where they have not resisted the temptation, they have been listening to populists of the right (whose nationalistic diction has so far been cautious and toned down) rather than to populists of the left. People in Slovakia have always been more surprised and disappointed than Czechs by developments after November 1989. They were not as well prepared for the difficulties of the transformation – as a result, also, of the way they experienced the twenty years prior to November 1989. This is why they have listened more to populists of the left, both to those for whom nationalism is second nature, and to those who only intentionally borrow nationalist rhetoric to get more votes. Public opinion polls show that today much of the electorate in Slovakia has sobered up from the intoxicating blend of socialist state paternalism and nationalism (or nationalist rhetoric), but the shared state has already been divided, and Czechs and Slovaks have been distancing themselves from each other with astonishing speed: contact with each other and being well-informed about each other is increasingly scarce.

Let us return to this essay's opening sentence, in an effort to capture the essence of the circumstances surrounding the split between the Czechs and the Slovaks, namely the different times: the objectively different one, and, in particular, the subjectively different one (the result of how time was experienced differently). The time of Czech modernization (once, long ago, during the Austro-Hungarian empire, pre-1918) and of Slovak modernization (1918 till the present) is the objective difference. Slovak modernization proceeded and culminated under completely non-standard conditions: Slovakia modernized under the protection of a paternalistic state, in this sense a social, not socialist, state, so that it did not become accustomed to the sacrifices which regularly accompany every modernization or, indeed, all progress. In the process of the transformation to a political democracy and market economy it understandably found itself without the necessary resistance and showed certain signs of a weakened immune system for facing the temptation of populism. In Slovakia, it was a nationalistic populism, combined with nostalgia for the certainties provided by the babysitter state. The populism which triumphed in the June 1992 elections in Slovakia was the embodiment of what people were used to: a run-of-the-mill system of clear-cut relations, in the spirit of those relations between people who accommodate each other, such as neighbours, relatives, locals and, ultimately, Slovaks. These were relations which made it possible to 'fix up' everything with an uncle or nephew, functionary or bureaucrat. What was the use of law and democracy with their formal character, and what good was the inhumane and unjust market, foisted on them by the alien federation and selfishly calculating Prague? Rather than nostalgia for socialism, it has been nostalgia for a golden age of authoritative, non-despotic democracy intermingled with national aspirations and national dreams.

Both were a common reaction to the transformation, especially the economic reform, which after November 1989 was clearly inconceivable without sacrifice, because the babysitter state was by then being rejected just as much as the oppressor state. The difficulty lay in the fact that it happened with a different intensity in the Czech Lands than in Slovakia. If further modernization is being refused today, it is in response to the stress of the new situation, by an individual choice which combines 'humane' authoritarianism with patriotism.

It was up to the political representatives to be able to confront that, because the divergent processes were probably irrevocable and fatal.

The twenty years in which Czechs and Slovaks lived in different times and experienced time differently began on 21 August 1968 and ended on 17 November 1989. Those days and the days which followed, full of excitement and euphoria, were in both cases, at least for a while, the source of the illusion which portrayed Czechs and Slovaks as not being divided by anything, or, in fact, being joined by everything. It took everyday life to show that not only do ordinary days outnumber the tragic and sacred days, but that the ordinary days are also much more important. For Czechs, with their dramatically fractured history, full of reverses, this is a discovery which is far from banal.

IV *The Process of Disintegration*

12 The Politics of Transition and the Break-Up of Czechoslovakia

SHARON L. WOLCHIK

The break-up of the Czechoslovak federation reflected the influence of many factors. The roots of the tensions between Czechs and Slovaks go back to the earlier history of the two groups and the differing nature of economic and national development that each experienced as part of separate, larger political units. They also reflect the different impact of communism on each region, particularly in the economic sphere, and the much harsher impact of the move to the market in Slovakia that resulted from the fact that most of Slovakia's industrialization occurred during the communist era. As the pages to follow illustrate, political factors also contributed. Important as the factors noted above were as conditioning factors, the end of the Czechoslovak state was a political decision that was shaped in critical ways by the structure of the political system and the decisions of political leaders and citizens. These in turn reflected the impact of the economic, social and psychological transitions that followed the end of communist rule, as well as the particular characteristics of a political system that was in transition. As others in this volume, as well as some of my earlier writings,[1] have discussed the impact of historical factors and of other aspects of the transition, this essay will focus on the role that transition politics played in increasing the political salience of ethnicity and bringing on the demise of the federation.

One of the more important aspects of political life in post-communist Czechoslovakia was the fact that the political system was very much in flux. Although Czechoslovakia had many of the preconditions necessary for establishing and maintaining a stable democratic system that were lacking in other post-communist states at the outset of the post-communist period, political life nonetheless shared, and continues to share in the Czech

226   *Sharon L. Wolchik*

and Slovak Republics, many of the same features as in other post-communist states.

There were a number of positive developments in Czechoslovakia's political life in the first three years after the end of communist rule. The end of the Communist Party's monopoly of power and the repluralization of the country's political life created new opportunities for citizens to be active in politics and new channels for relations between the masses and the élite. Free elections in June and November 1990 legitimized the government that had been formed immediately after the ouster of the communist system and resulted in the replacement of large numbers of political leaders at all levels. Led by Václav Havel, the country's new leaders also made a good deal of progress in revamping legal codes and revitalizing political institutions in the first two years after the collapse of the communist system. However, many serious political problems remain. As the results of the 1990 and 1992 elections and numerous public opinion polls indicate, the process of channelling the widespread desire for political change evident in late 1989 into coherent political directions and policy preferences has yet to be accomplished. As in other countries in transition from authoritarian rule, the political preferences of citizens are still volatile.[2] A stable party system is also still in the process of being re-created.

In both of these areas, the legacy of four decades of communist rule continues to be felt. Thus, in part as a reaction to the forced mobilization of the communist era, many citizens are reluctant to join political parties. Public opinion polls concerning partisan preferences in late 1991 found an increase in the numbers of citizens without attachments to any political party. Approximately 15 per cent of those questioned by the Institute for Public Opinion Research of the Slovak Statistical Office in September 1991, and 25 per cent in October 1991, for example, indicated that they did not sympathize with any political party.[3]

Citizens' reactions and allegiances to political parties have also been influenced by the multiplicity of political parties. As in many of the other post-communist states in the region, the repluralization of politics that followed the end of communist rule resulted in the resurrection of Czechoslovakia's multi-party tradition. Many of the parties that formed prior to the 1990 elections were winnowed out as viable political forces by threshold requirements preventing parties that do not gain a specified percentage of the vote from seating deputies in the republic and federal legislatures. However, in both the Czech Lands and Slovakia, there are numerous political parties that remain more or less credible political organizations.

Approximately 83 per cent of citizens actually voted in the June 1992 elections.[4] However, a sizeable portion of the electorate in both parts of the country were either undecided or did not plan to vote on the eve of the elections. Political preferences were somewhat more crystallized in Slovakia by 1991, where approximately 16 per cent of those surveyed were undecided in February 1992, and 12 per cent in April 1992.[5] Approximately a quarter of those surveyed in the Czech Lands in late 1991 and early 1992, and 31 per cent in April 1992 were undecided about which, if any, party to support in the elections. The apparent stability of support for various political parties during much of 1991 and the first half of 1992 suggested that political preferences were beginning to crystallize somewhat. However, the fact that one-half of all voters surveyed by the Centre for Social Analysis in Bratislava changed their minds at least once prior to the June 1992 elections indicates that partisan preferences were still volatile, despite the appearance of stability.[6]

The fluidity of the party system and the low levels of party identification in both the Czech Lands and Slovakia mean that citizens do not have the benefit of identification with a particular political party, which is used in more established democracies to simplify political decision-making and mediate political conflict. These features of transitional politics also mean that citizens are more readily available to be mobilized by political élites than those in political systems in which levels of party identification are higher and party alignments more stable. Political élites are also relatively unconstrained by mass preferences in such a situation.

The political implications of these factors are compounded by the psychological and social costs of the transition. This aspect of the current situation, which is well understood by all who live in post-communist societies, is often overlooked by outside commentators, in part because it is so difficult to quantify. However, living in times in which one must adapt to significant changes in all areas of life, ranging from the workplace to culture to the organization and availability of services, is clearly taking its toll on individuals and families. As Václav Havel noted in a November 1991 interview:

> We are living in a time of peculiar – I would say – social and psychological chaos. People are unsettled by the fact that they cannot see firm order, structure of values, or orderly community life anywhere. Everything has been thrown into uncertainty. The whole legal system and the constitutional set-up are uncertain. Political parties are quarrelling among themselves. They attack each other. Everybody says something different. Everybody proposes something different. It is not known what the reform will bring or what social shocks it will cause.[7]

Coupled with the decline in the standard of living and uncertainty about the future, this situation resulted in increasing levels of popular discontent and dissatisfaction with existing political institutions and political leaders.

Public opinion polls document a steady decline in optimism and satisfaction among the population between early 1990 and mid-1992. Thus, 86 per cent of a sample of 2,400 respondents surveyed in January 1990 were satisfied with recent political developments, and most (83 per cent) believed that the political changes underway would result in a major transformation of the political system rather than only a change of leaders.[8] By May 1990, 66 per cent of those surveyed indicated that they were satisfied or very satisfied with the political situation. However, the fading of the euphoria of the first months after the revolution was reflected in the fact that nearly half of those surveyed felt that the velvet revolution had gone well in the beginning but had 'somehow turned sour'.[9] Popular dissatisfaction with the results of the transformation continued to grow during 1991 and 1992, particularly in Slovakia. By September 1991, for example, 61 per cent of respondents in the Czech Republic but 78 per cent in Slovakia were rather or very dissatisfied. Equally telling, only 3 per cent of the population in each republic was very satisfied.[10]

Levels of dissatisfaction continued to increase in 1991 and 1992. In January 1992, from 64 to 79 per cent of citizens surveyed in the country as a whole were dissatisfied with social welfare provisions, domestic politics, the economy, and the standard of living. As in previous surveys, levels of dissatisfaction were higher in Slovakia than in the Czech Republic. These differences were particularly marked with regard to levels of dissatisfaction with the economy (84 per cent of Slovaks, compared to 68 per cent of Czechs), and the living standard (78 per cent of Slovaks and 74 per cent of Czechs).[11] By May 1992, 73 per cent of those surveyed in the Czech Lands, and 86 per cent in Slovakia, were either rather or very dissatisfied with the overall political situation.[12] Expectations regarding further developments, particularly in the standard of living and the economy, were also much less positive in Slovakia.[13]

Public trust in political institutions and political leaders decreased significantly in 1991 and 1992 in both republics. This trend was particularly notable with respect to the federal government and the Federal Assembly. As Table 12.1 illustrates, by late 1991 less than half of respondents in the Czech Lands and less than a third in Slovakia trusted the federal government. Trust in the Federal Assembly was slightly greater in Slovakia, but substantially lower in the Czech Lands. Trust in the republic governments and parliaments also fell, particularly in Slovakia. Levels of trust in these institutions continued to decline in 1992. A January 1992 survey by the Institute for Public Opinion Research, which found that 52 per cent of respondents in Slovakia felt that the federal government worked to the advantage of the Czech nation, while 41 per cent of Czechs felt that it benefited Slovaks disproportionately, provides some insight into the low

Table 12.1   Trust in public leaders and institutions: January 1991, December 1991, February 1992, May 1992 (in %)

	Jan 1991		Dec 1991		Feb 1992		May 1992	
	CR	SR	CR	SR	CR	SR	CR	SR
President Havel	90	60	82	50	86	52	78	52
Federal government	78	46	46	30	50	28	46	26
Federal parliament	65	51	27	33	25	29	25	26
Republic government	79	85	55	35	52	29	51	28
Republic parliament	71	69	49	33	47	26	46	24

Source: Information from the Institute for Public Opinion Research, 'Postoje čs. veřejnosti k základním politickým institucím' ('Attitudes of the Czechoslovak public to political institutions'), Prague, May 1992.

regard in which the federal government was held in both parts of the country.[14]

Support for former President Havel, who served as a symbol of the country's hopes for the future immediately after the revolution, also decreased, particularly in Slovakia. As Table 12.1 shows, by January 1991 the proportion of those who trusted the President in Slovakia (60 per cent), was substantially lower than levels of trust in the Slovak government (85 per cent), the Slovak National Council (69 per cent) and several Slovak politicians, including the Prime Minister of Slovakia Vladimír Mečiar. By August 1991, less than half of respondents in Slovakia, compared to 84 per cent in the Czech Republic, trusted Havel.[15] Support for the President increased somewhat in Slovakia in late 1991 and 1992 but remained far lower than in the Czech Lands.

The political situation in the first two years after the collapse of communism, then, created fertile ground for the growth of ethnic tensions and extreme nationalism. Coupled with the hardship and dislocations that accompany large-scale economic change, growing popular dissatisfaction and increasing distrust of most political leaders and institutions also provided incentives for those leaders to use nationalism as a tool to gain or to keep influence and power in the new system. Finally, although the tensions between Czechs and Slovaks may be traced largely to factors within the country, developments in the larger international community also heightened the political salience of ethnicity in Czechoslovakia. These included the break-up of other multi-ethnic former communist states and, paradoxically, the movement towards greater unity in the rest of Europe. In support of their claims, advocates of independence for Slovakia often pointed, for example, to the independence of the Baltic countries and to international recognition of Slovenia and Croatia as independent states. Slovak leaders, such as former Minister of International Relations, Pavol Demeš, who wished to see the federation maintained argued that a break-up of the federation would decrease the likelihood of Czechoslovakia or its successor states being admitted to the EC. For many others, however, the prospect of eventually entering the European Community fuelled their desire to see Slovakia enter Europe on its own. As former Prime Minister Ján Čarnogurský commented in October 1991, with reference to a pre-1989 discussion in which he had argued that the countries of Central and Eastern Europe would be 'beggars' should they enter Europe: 'Now, paradoxically, it seems to me that we are still coming to Europe as beggars, but our great contribution to the treasure of European culture is the revival of the national idea. Under the influence of events in Central and Eastern Europe, its revival can be seen in Western Europe, too.'[16] Although he supported the maintenance of a common state with the Czechs for the near future, Čarnogurský also called for Slovakia to enter Europe on its own chair.

Leadership and Popular Attitudes

The continued inability of Czech and Slovak leaders to agree on the division of powers between the federal and republic governments prior to the June 1992 elections, despite the fact that most citizens did not want to see the state break up, led many outside commentators to see the ongoing political crisis as largely an affair of political élites. As an article in the *Economist* in November 1991 put it, Czechoslovakia appeared to be headed towards a 'divorce that was occurring by accident.'[17] A similar view of the situation was reflected in President Havel's call for a referendum to resolve the issue of the future of the state and in the effort he made to mobilize the public to pressure members of the federal legislature and republic governments to reach a compromise in November 1991.[18] Numerous public opinion polls concerning relations between the two groups and the form of state at first glance also support this view. Nonetheless, the situation in fact was more complicated. For while citizens in both parts of the country continued to oppose a break-up of the state even as it was being negotiated, the political values and preferences of Czechs and Slovaks differed in many respects.

As noted earlier, in contrast to the situation in what was Yugoslavia and in many areas of the former Soviet Union, disagreements between Czechs and Slovaks over political and economic issues were not conditioned by either a history of armed conflict against each other or atrocities by one or both sides. Nor were they reflected in a marked deterioration in personal relationships between the two groups. Although rates of intermarriage and the number of members of each ethnic group who resided in the other republic remained at low levels throughout the communist period,[19]many Czechs and Slovaks had a fair degree of contact with members of the other ethnic group. A 1991 study conducted by the Institute for Social Analysis at Comenius University in Bratislava, for example, found that 31 per cent of Slovaks had relatives and 57 per cent friends in the Czech Lands.[20] Nonetheless, sizeable portions of each nation held the other responsible for the country's ills, and substantial numbers felt that the other group benefited more from the federation. Thus, 1 per cent of those surveyed in the Czech Republic in January 1992 felt that the federation benefited Czechs at the expense of Slovaks; 41 per cent felt that it benefited Slovaks at the expense of Czechs. Three per cent of Slovaks agreed, but a majority (52 per cent) felt that the federation benefited Czechs at Slovak expense.[21] A survey conducted by the Association for Independent Social Analysis (AISA) in April 1992 found that 73 per cent of respondents in Slovakia, and 16 per cent in the Czech Lands, felt that the federal system favoured the Czech Republic.[22]

Survey results also document a substantial degree of misunderstanding between the two groups, as well as different perspectives on how each group is treated by the other. Sixty-eight per cent of respondents in Slovakia surveyed by AISA in April 1992, for example, felt that Czechs often treated Slovaks as an underdeveloped nation. Eighty-four per cent of Czechs, on the other hand, disagreed.[23]

Sizeable portions of both Czechs and Slovaks also ascribe negative traits to members of the other group. Forty-one per cent of Czechs surveyed by the Centre for Social Analysis in Bratislava in October 1990 attributed only negative characteristics to Slovaks. Slovaks were somewhat less likely to see Czechs in a negative light, but nearly a third (31 per cent) did so. As the authors of this study note, 'in the background of these reproaches there is ... a feeling of having been underestimated and wronged; distrust and suspicion of the Czechs; excessive self-confidence or even self-admiration; a negative attitude towards the communist past and future, and stressing the independent actions of the Slovak nation regardless of the value message.'[24] The authors note that the Slovak stereotype of the Czechs includes the view that a Czech is 'a self-interested and sly egoist who prefers useless sophistry to an honest piece of work, and who feels ... superior to the Slovak'. The negative Czech stereotype, on the other hand, is of a 'nationally excitable Slovak suffering from an inferiority complex; combined with a rather sceptical interpretation of the behaviour of the Slovak nation in history'.[25] Slovak perceptions of being treated unfairly increased between October 1990 and May 1991 as did levels of distrust between the two peoples.[26] However, as late as May 1992, the majority (64 per cent) of respondents in the Czech Lands characterized their relationships with Slovaks as good. Slightly higher proportions (72 per cent) of Slovaks felt they had good relationships with Czechs. These proportions were higher than those obtained in October 1991.[27]

Surveys conducted after the June 1992 elections also found a fair degree of dissent from the positions articulated by the dominant political leaders in both parts of the country. Thus, although a quarter of those surveyed in the Czech Republic agreed strongly with the viewpoint of Václav Klaus regarding the form of the state and another 40 per cent more or less supported his position, approximately 27 per cent did not agree or strongly disagreed. Approximately equal proportions of those surveyed in Slovakia either agreed (31 per cent) or strongly agreed (37 per cent) with the positions articulated by Vladimír Mečiar; but 27 per cent either disagreed (16 per cent), or strongly disagreed (11 per cent).[28]

Many citizens in Czechoslovakia shared the view that their political leaders were primarily responsible for the growth of ethnic tensions and the difficulties that arose over the form of the state. Over three-quarters of respondents in the Czech Lands, and 40 per cent in Slovakia, for example, identified the person of Vladimír Mečiar as a reason for the difficulties of the federation after the 1992 elections. Thirty-nine per cent of those in the Czech Lands and 48 per cent of those in Slovakia traced these difficulties to Václav Klaus, and 33 per cent in the Czech Lands and 40 per cent in Slovakia, to Václav Havel. Seventy-one per cent of respondents in the Czech Lands and 65 per cent in Slovakia surveyed in late 1991 for Radio Free Europe agreed or strongly agreed that politicians were using nationalism for their own purposes. Far smaller numbers (13 per cent in the Czech Lands and 10 per cent in Slovakia) disagreed or strongly disagreed with this statement.[29] An April 1992 survey carried out by AISA found somewhat higher levels of support for the view that politicians were using national differences for their own aims in both the Czech Lands (81 per cent) and Slovakia (87 per cent).[30]

There is thus ample support for the view that political leaders, particularly in Slovakia, played a key role in mobilizing the population around ethnic issues in order to increase their own support prior to the June 1992 elections. Similar criticism was levelled against Václav Klaus and other Czech leaders for their refusal to consider Slovak proposals for a confederation of two independent states and their role in pushing for a rapid dissolution of the common state after the June 1992 elections. However, the situation is considerably more complex than it appears at first glance. As Table 12.2 illustrates, most citizens continued to prefer a common state even as political leaders negotiated the end of the federation. But, as the numerous public opinion polls conducted since the end of communist rule

Table 12.2 Position if a referendum were held on state arrangements (in %)

Would vote to:	October 1991		December 1991			July 1992	
	CR	SR	CSFR	CR	SR	CR	SR
Maintain a common state	70	52	68	73	58	53	42
Divide the state	9	18	13	12	16	24	32
Don't know		31	12	9	6	20	23
Would abstain			7	6	20	–	–

Note: Percentages do not all add up to 100 per cent because those who indicated they would not participate in a referendum are excluded.
Source: Information from the Institute for Public Opinion Research, 'Názory čs. veřejnosti' ('Opinons
of the Czechoslovak public'), Prague, 31 January 1992, pp. 12–13.

document, there were important and growing differences in the attitudes and
political preferences of Czechs and Slovaks in many areas prior to the split.

Attitudes towards the holding of a referendum to determine the country's
future are illustrative of these differences. Most citizens of the country
supported the holding of a referendum, as called for by President Havel in
1991. For example, 74 per cent of the total population, including 80 per
cent in the Czech Lands and 69 per cent in Slovakia, favoured such a
referendum in November 1991. Eighty-nine per cent indicated that they
would participate in a referendum, and 64 per cent that they would vote to
preserve a common state.[31] Somewhat higher proportions of respondents
in the Czech Lands (90 per cent) and in Slovakia (80 per cent), surveyed
in October 1991 by the Centre for Empirical Research of the Sociological
Institute of the Czechoslovak Academy of Sciences (STEM), indicated that
they would participate in a referendum. Of these, only approximately 8 per
cent in the Czech Lands and 23.8 per cent in Slovakia indicated that they
would vote to divide the state.[32]

Popular support for preserving a common state remained high
throughout 1991 and early 1992 (see Table 12.2). However, these figures
mask significant differences in the attitudes of Czechs and Slovaks. Thus,
while 70 per cent of the inhabitants of the Czech Lands surveyed in October
1991 indicated that they would vote to remain in a common state, this
proportion dropped to 52 per cent in Slovakia. Only 18 per cent of
Slovakia's inhabitants (and 9 per cent of those of the Czech Lands) favoured
separation of the two parts of the country at that time. But nearly a third of
the inhabitants of Slovakia indicated that they would abstain or were
undecided about how they would vote on such an issue.[33] A similarly large

proportion of citizens in Slovakia were undecided or planned to abstain in December 1991.

Most citizens in both the Czech Lands and Slovakia continued to support the holding of a referendum to decide the future of the state even after the June 1992 elections. In July 1992, when the Institute for Public Opinion Research next asked citizens the same questions about holding a referendum, similarly high proportions (85 and 83 per cent) of citizens in both the Czech Lands and Slovakia indicated that they would participate in such a referendum. Eighty-two per cent of respondents in the Czech Lands and 84 per cent in Slovakia agreed that the further existence of the state should be determined not by politicians but only by citizens in a referendum. As Table 12.2 illustrates, support for dividing the state doubled in both parts of the country between December 1991 and July 1992. However, in neither case was the proportion of citizens who supported this option sufficient under the terms of the existing law concerning the referendum to bring about a change in the composition of the state.[34]

At the same time, inhabitants of the Czech Lands and Slovakia clearly had different preferences in regard to the form of the state. These became evident early in the post-communist period. Almost half (42 per cent) of those surveyed in the Czech Lands in June 1990, for example, preferred a common state with a strong central or unitary government; an additional 30 per cent supported a common state with strong republic governments. Inhabitants of Slovakia, on the other hand, were far more supportive of a common state with considerable powers for republic-level governments (41 per cent) and also favoured confederation in substantial numbers (30 per cent). Support for two independent states was also slightly higher in Slovakia (8 per cent) than in the Czech Republic (5 per cent) at this time.[35]

Differences in the views of inhabitants of the Czech Republic and Slovakia on this issue increased in the course of 1991 and 1992. As is shown in Table 12.3, most of the inhabitants of Bohemia and Moravia favoured either a unitary state or a federation in late 1991 and the first half of 1992. A sizeable portion, particularly in Moravia, favoured a regionally based republic that would recognize Moravia as a distinct entity. In Slovakia, on the other hand, approximately equal numbers of citizens preferred either a confederation or a federation. One of the most significant differences in the results of polls conducted in 1990 and 1991–2 is the decrease in support for a federal arrangement in Slovakia. Thus, while approximately 40 per cent of those surveyed in Slovakia in June 1990 and January 1991 preferred this type of state arrangement,[36] by November 1991 this proportion had decreased to 26 per cent. More striking evidence of the degree of dissatisfaction with the federal system in Slovakia prior to the June 1992 elections is reflected in the result of a study conducted in October 1991 by the

Table 12.3   Preferred state arrangements, 1991 and 1992 (in %)

Type of state arrangement:	Nov 1991		Dec 1991		Jan 1992		Mar 1992		May 1992		June 1992		July 1992	
	CR	SR	CR	SR	CR	SR	CR	SR	CR	SR	CR	SR	CR	SR
Unitary state	39	20	36	17	38	17	34	13	34	12	29	11	38	14
Federation	30	26	27	31	32	33	27	24	28	33	28	26	19	27
Lands-based republic	20	6	24	4	15	5	18	9	22	6	21	6	18	8
Confederation	4	27	4	30	4	30	6	32	6	31	5	31	3	30
Independent states	5	14	6	11	5	12	11	17	6	11	13	18	16	16
Don't know	2	7	3	7	6	3	4	5	4	7	4	8	6	5

Sources: Institute for Public Opinion Research, 'Názory čs. veřejnosti na státoprávní uspořádání a na konání referenda' ('Opinions of the Czechoslovak public on constitutional arrangements and on carrying out the referendum'), 15 November 1991; information from a survey of 1,006 people conducted by the Institute for Public Opinion Research, 4–11 December 1991; and 'Názory čs. veřejnosti na státoprávní uspořádání a na konání referenda', July 1992.

Institute for Public Opinion Research in Bratislava, which found that only 8 per cent of respondents were satisfied with the nature of the federation at that time.[37]

It can be seen from Table 12.3 that support for a common state also declined significantly among citizens in the Czech Lands in the course of 1991. While the proportion of respondents in Slovakia who saw two independent states as preferable remained at approximately the same level between November 1991 and July 1992, the proportion of respondents in the Czech Republic who supported this option increased threefold during this period (see Table 12.3).

Citizens in both parts of the country agreed in mid-1992 that separation would have negative economic consequences. Although, when surveyed by AISA in April 1992, more respondents in Slovakia (34 per cent) than in the Czech Lands (21 per cent) thought that they would be better off if a split occurred, a sizeable majority of respondents in both the Czech Lands and Slovakia (75 per cent and 61 per cent) felt that the standard of living would not be better if the country separated.[38] Of those surveyed in early July 1992, almost the majority of citizens in the Czech Republic (49 per cent) and 40 per cent of those in Slovakia felt that the break-up of the federation would lead to a temporary worsening of the situation in the Czech Republic. Twenty-three per cent of respondents in the Czech Lands and 15 per cent of those in Slovakia felt that it would make rapid economic and political progress easier to attain. Views concerning the consequences for Slovakia were more differentiated by republic, as 17 per cent of respondents in Slovakia but only 1 per cent in the Czech Lands felt that a split would make rapid economic and political progress easier in Slovakia. Forty per cent of those in Slovakia and 19 per cent in the Czech Lands expected a temporary worsening of the economic situation. Fifty per cent of respondents in the Czech Lands and 26 per cent in Slovakia anticipated a long-term worsening of the situation. Nearly 20 per cent of respondents in the Czech Lands, but only 7 per cent in Slovakia, thought that separation would lead to the complete loss of the opportunity to continue to move toward democracy and economic prosperity in Slovakia.[39]

Czechs and Slovaks also differed considerably in their evaluations of the pace and worth of the economic and political changes that occurred after the end of communist rule, and in their expectations of the state and their political preferences. These differences, which became evident very early after the fall of the communist system,[40] increased in the course of 1991 and 1992. In the economic realm, citizens' perceptions concerning the desirability of the shift to the market have been coloured by the different impact of the economic reform in the Czech Lands and Slovakia. Surveys conducted in 1990, for example, found that a much larger proportion of respondents in Slovakia (47 per cent) than in the Czech Lands (32 per cent) wanted the state to retain responsibility for ensuring employment for all citizens. Inhabitants of Slovakia were also less supportive of a radical and rapid move to the market (51 per cent compared to 60 per cent in the Czech Lands), and far more likely to agree that unemployment should be avoided, even at the cost of significantly hindering or suspending the economic reform (34 per cent, compared to 9 per cent in the Czech Lands). Respondents in Slovakia were less willing to accept the loss of their current jobs, more fearful about a decline in the standard of living, and more likely than those in the Czech Lands to indicate that they would strike if there were major increases in the costs of essential goods. Relatively small differences existed between respondents in the two republics in levels of interest in becoming independent entrepreneurs or working for private enterprises.[41]

Support for the re-creation of a market economy continued to be lower in Slovakia in 1992. In April 1992 fewer respondents in Slovakia (39 per cent) than in the Czech Republic (52 per cent) favoured a market economy. Respondents in Slovakia favoured a mixed market and socialist economy to a greater extent than those in the Czech Lands (43 per cent, compared to 33 per cent). Opinions regarding the impact of the move to the market on the standard of living were also more negative in Slovakia, where 40 per cent of respondents held negative opinions and an additional 14 per cent strongly negative opinions. In the Czech Lands, by way of contrast, the majority of respondents either agreed (48 per cent) or strongly agreed (17 per cent) that developments were moving in a positive direction. Those surveyed in Slovakia were also considerably less optimistic about the long-term effects of the shift to the market. Seventy-four per cent of those surveyed in Slovakia, compared to 58 per cent of those in the Czech Republic, for example, felt that the move to the market would in the long run benefit only a small number of people financially.[42] An October 1991 survey conducted by the Centre for Empirical Research (STEM) found similar differences in the attitudes of respondents in the Czech Republic and Slovakia on a range of questions related to economic changes, including privatization, restitution, the influx of foreign capital, and greater wage differentiation.[43]

A study conducted by the Centre for Social Analysis in Bratislava in January 1992 further documents the generally negative attitude towards privatization that prevailed in Slovakia prior to the split. Slovaks were more favourable towards small privatization than large-scale privatization. However, even in this area, expectations were more positive among respondents in the Czech Lands. Whereas 43 per cent of those questioned in the Czech Lands wanted to see privatization extended, compared to 17 per cent who wanted to see less privatization, in Slovakia 25 per cent supported more privatization, while 35 per cent wanted to see less.[44]

These results are paralleled by those of surveys conducted by the Institute for Public Opinion Research in Prague in the first five months of 1992. Thus, 50 per cent of respondents in the Czech Lands felt either that the economic reform should be implemented more quickly, or that it was going well. Twenty-three per cent of Slovaks shared these views, but a large majority of Slovaks (77 per cent) felt that the reform should either be changed or stopped. Differences between the two regions remained substantial throughout the spring of 1992. In May, 28 per cent of respondents in Slovakia, compared to 49 per cent of those in the Czech Lands, held positive attitudes towards the economic reform. Seventy-two per cent of those surveyed in Slovakia, compared to 51 per cent in the Czech Lands, held negative views. Support for ending the reform was much stronger among those who had reservations about it in Slovakia than in the Czech Lands, where most of those who did not support the reform wanted to see it modified rather than ended. Citizens in Slovakia were also more concerned than those in the Czech Republic with problems related to unemployment and the decrease in the living standard in the first six months of 1992.[45]

These differences in attitudes were reflected in the results of the June 1992 parliamentary elections. The level of support for the left-of-centre successors to the Communist Party in Slovakia (the Party of the Democratic Left) and the Communist Party of Bohemia and Moravia in the Czech Lands was approximately the same. However, the most popular party in the Czech Lands and the victor in the June 1992 elections, the Civic Democratic Party led by Václav Klaus, has a centre-right orientation and advocated a continuation of the move to a free market economy and a limited role for the state. The right-of-centre Christian Democratic Union led by the People's Party, and the extreme-right party, the Republicans, also won enough votes to seat deputies in the federal as well as republic legislature in the Czech Lands. Neither of the two other parties that emerged from the former Civic Forum, the Civic Democratic Alliance and the Civic Movement, won enough votes to enter the Federal Assembly, although the right-of-centre Civic Democratic Alliance, with 5.9 per cent of the vote, won representation in the Czech National Council. The left-of-centre Liberal Social Union and regionally based Movement for Self-Governing Democracy and Association for Moravia and Silesia were also represented in the Czech National Council (see Table 12.4).

In Slovakia, by way of contrast, the left-of-centre Movement for a Democratic Slovakia (MDS) led by Vladimír Mečiar emerged as the strongest party. Support for Mečiar's party, which challenged the government's economic programme and also advocated greater autonomy for Slovakia during 1991 and prior to the June 1992 elections, fluctuated somewhat in 1991 and 1992, but the MDS was consistently the most popular party in Slovakia. Mečiar himself was consistently one of the two most popular and trusted politicians in Slovakia prior to the split.[46]

Support for the Slovak National Party, which pushed the discussion of Slovakia's future in a more radical direction, ranged from 12 to 15 per cent in the last half of 1991 and the first half of 1992. This party, whose leaders also called for radical change in the economic reforms, won approximately 9 per cent of the vote in both houses of the federal parliament and 8 per cent of the vote for the Slovak National Council in June 1992.[47] The parties that formed the coalition which governed Slovakia from the June 1990 to the June 1992 elections did poorly in those elections. The Christian Democratic Movement led by Ján Čarnogurský, the incumbent Prime Minister at the time of the June 1992 elections, received only 9 per cent of the vote to both the federal and republic legislatures. The Civic Democratic Union, which was formed by members of the former Public against Violence who opposed Mečiar, did not receive enough votes to seat deputies in either legislature (see Table 12.4).

Conclusion

As the discussion above has illustrated, the values and orientations of citizens of the Czech and Slovak republics differed in many important ways

Table 12.4 Results of the 1992 parliamentary elections in Czechoslovakia

Czech Lands	House of the People % (seats)	House of Nations % (seats)	National Council % (seats)
Civic Democratic Party, Christian Democratic Party	33.9 (48)	33.4 (37)	29.7 (76)
Left Bloc (Communist Party of Bohemia and Moravia)	14.3 (19)	14.5 (15)	14.1 (35)
Czechoslovak Social Democratic Party	7.7 (10)	6.8 (6)	6.5 (16)
Republican Party	6.5 (8)	6.4 (6)	6.3 (15)
Christian Democratic Union/People's Party	5.8 (7)	6.1 (5)	6.3 (16)
Liberal Social Union	5.9 (7)	6.1 (5)	6.5 (16)
Civic Democratic Alliance	4.9 (–)	4.8 (–)	5.9 (14)
Association for Moravia and Silesia	4.9 (–)	4.2 (–)	5.9 (14)
Civic Movement	4.4 (–)	4.7 (–)	4.6 (–)

Slovakia	House of the People	House of Nations	National Council
Movement for a Democratic Slovakia	33.5 (24)	33.9 (33)	37.3 (74)
Party of the Democratic Left	14.4 (10)	14.0 (13)	14.7 (39)
Slovak National Party	9.4 (6)	9.4 (6)	7.9 (15)
Christian Democratic Movement	9.0 (6)	8.8 (8)	8.9 (18)
Coexistence/Hungarian Christian Democratic Movement	–	–	7.42 (14)
Coexistence/Hungarian Christian Democratic Movement/Hungarian People's Party	7.4 (5)	7.4 (7)	–
Social Democratic Party	–	6.1 (5)	–
Civic Democratic Party	4.0 (–)	4.0 (–)	4.0 (–)
Hungarian Civic Party	2.3 (–)	2.4 (–)	2.3 (–)
Democratic Party/Civic Democratic Union	3.7 (–)	3.4 (–)	2.3 (–)

Source: Jiří Pehe, 'Czechoslovakia's Political Balance Sheet, 1990–1992', *RFE/RL Research Reports*, vol. 1, no. 25, 19 June 1992, p. 29; and 'Volby 1992' ('Elections 1992'), *Respekt*, 8–14 June 1992.

prior to the creation of two independent states. These differences, which were not limited to views concerning the organization of the state, reflect the influence of each people's history and levels of economic development, as well as the legacy of the communist period. They also reflect the different impact of the transition to the market in the two regions.

The threat to the continued existence of a common state was also heightened by the features of transitional politics discussed earlier. As a result of the June 1992 elections, Václav Klaus and Vladimír Mečiar, neither of whose parties won a majority of the popular vote in their region, negotiated the end of the federation. Popular opinion in both the Czech Lands and Slovakia continued to be against the break-up of the state even as their leaders negotiated it, but the main political forces supporting the continuation of a common state did very poorly in the June elections in both regions. As the difference in the number of citizens in Slovakia who supported separation of the country into two states and who voted for Mečiar indicates, voting preferences in the June elections depended on other factors, such as attitudes towards the economic reforms, in addition to voters' preferences in regard to the future form of the state. But although the majority of Slovaks wanted to see some form of common state preserved, the most popular political parties in Slovakia supported Slovak independence.

The momentum towards separation created by the impasses and the failed negotiations during the first two years after the end of communist rule also contributed to the demise of the federation. Although most citizens in 1991 and the first half of 1992 did not support the break-up of the state, the situation had reached the stage in which most political actors saw this as, if not a desirable, at least a possible outcome of the current political and economic situation. This sentiment was well captured by a headline in a Prague tabloid in late November 1991: 'It's time for a divorce!'[48] As most marriage counsellors know, the very act of seriously considering divorce can imperil a shaky marriage and is frequently a sign that the marriage is already over. Relations between the Czechs and Slovaks clearly had reached that point by mid-1992.

The increase in the political salience of ethnicity that occurred after the ouster of the communist system in Czechoslovakia resulted in part from the ability of political leaders to channel the dissatisfaction and uncertainty that inevitably accompany large-scale economic and political changes into support for ethnic aims. The still relatively uninstitutionalized party system and the degree of flux evident in many other elements of the political system facilitated such actions. However, as is the case in many other situations in which ethnic issues have come to dominate political life, the ability of ethnic leaders to use such circumstances to their own advantage derived in part from the fact that there were important differences in the objectives and perspectives of the two groups involved. The demise of the Czechoslovak federation, then, illustrates the complexity of the factors that operate to increase the significance of ethnic divisions in the post-communist world. It also highlights the interplay of historical influences and more recent economic and political developments in creating support for nationalist movements and conditions in which political decision-making becomes differentiated along ethnic lines. As the Czechoslovak case demonstrates, differences between ethnic groups do not have to result in violent conflicts to be significant, or be based on great differences in language, culture or religion.

Notes

An earlier version of the argument presented in this chapter was delivered at a workshop on nationality and ethnicity in Eastern Europe at the Center for European Studies, Harvard University, on 6 December 1991, and at a conference on Europe and the Disintegration of Empires at Cornell University in April 1993, and was published as 'The Politics of Ethnicity in Post-Communist Czechoslovakia', in *East European Politics and Societies*, vol. 8, no. 1 (Winter 1994). The author is grateful to the publishers for their kind permission to reproduce it in this volume.

The author would like to thank Valerie Bunce, Michael Hechter and Milada Polišenská for their useful comments on an earlier version of this article. She is also indebted to Naomi Warbasse, Kevin Jernegan, Waldek Wajszczuk and Nancy L. Meyers for their assistance.

1   Sharon L. Wolchik, 'The Politics of Ethnicity in Post-Communist Czecho-slovakia', in *East European Politics and Societies*, vol. 8, no. 1 (Winter 1994).

2   See Samuel H. Barnes, Peter McDonough and Antonio Lopez Pina, 'The Development of Partisanship in New Democracies: The Case of Spain', in *American Journal of Political Science*, vol. 29, no. 4 (November 1985), pp. 695–720.

3   'Občan pomaly chladne' ('Citizens are slowly cooling off'), in *Nový čas*, 23 October 1991, p. 30.

4   Jan Obrman, 'The Czechoslovak Elections', in *RFE/RL Research Report*, vol. 1, no. 26, 26 June 1992, pp. 12–19.

5   From information from the Institute for Public Opinion Research, Prague (Institut pro vyzkum veřejného mínění), 24 April 1992, Tables I and II.

6   Centre for Social Analysis, 'Current Problems in Slovakia after the Split', Bratislava: Centre for Social Analysis, March 1993, p. 9.

7   Stanislava Dufková, 'Conversations at Lány', Interview with President Václav Havel recorded at the President's cottage in Hrádeček on 2 November 1991. Broadcast on Prague's Československy Rozhlas Radio Network in Czech at

242   *Sharon L. Wolchik*

13:15 GMT on 3 November 1991; as reported in 'Havel on Bratislava Events, 3 November Hrádeček Talks', Foreign Broadcast Information Service – East European Report (91-213, LD031184491), 4 November 1991, pp. 9–11.

8   Wolchik, *Czechoslovakia in Transition: Politics, Economics and Society*, London: Pinter, 1991, pp. 116–7.

9   ibid., p. 119.

10 Ivan Gabal, director of the Presidential Office for Political Analysis, as reported in 'Poll Views Czech, Slovak Attitudes on Issues', Foreign Broadcast Information Service – East European Report (91–185), 24 September 1991, pp. 13ţ14.

11 Information from a representative sample of 1,320 persons surveyed by the Institute for Public Opinion Research, Prague, 2–9 January 1992.

12 Information from the Institute for Public Opinion Research, Prague, May 1992.

13 See note 11.

14 Institute for Public Opinion Research, 'K pocitům národnostní nevraživosti v. r. 1991' ('Feelings of national animosity in 1991'), Prague: 1992.

15 Gabal, p. 14.

16 Karel Kříž and Petr Husák, 'Two Hundred Years with Lucifer', in *Lidové noviny*, 23 October 1991, p. 11, as reported in 'Čarnogurský Discusses Liberalism, Slovak Issues', FBIS-EER (91–211), 31 October 1991, p. 15.

17 'Ready for a Divorce', the *Economist*, 2–8 November 1991, vol. 321, no. 7731, p. 46.

18 See 'Prezident žádá občany o pomoc' ('The President asks citizens for help'), *Mladá fronta dnes*, 18 November 1991, pp. 1–2; 'Ofenzíva Hradu' ('The Castle's offensive'), *Lidové noviny*, 18 November 1991, pp. 1, 8; jlk, nel, 'Prezident v parlamentu' ('The President in parliament'), *Lidové noviny*, 22 November 1991, pp. 1, 16.

19 See Wolchik, *Czechoslovakia in Transition*, pp. 161–4, 180–205.

20 'Dnešná tvár Slovenska' ('Slovakia's current face'), *Lidové noviny*, 19 September 1991, p. 3.

21 'Vztahy ČR–SR' ('Czech Republic–Slovak Republic Ties'), *Hospodářské noviny*, no. 34, 18 February 1992, p. 1.

22 Jindřich Beránek, 'Jako bychom se míjeli' ('As though they were fighting'), in *Právo lidu*, 12 June 1992. An AISA poll conducted in late 1992 found similar results. Sixty-seven per cent of respondents in Slovakia and 12 per cent in the Czech Lands thought the federation benefited the Czechs. For earlier studies see Michael J. Dees, 'A Study of Nationalism in Czechoslovakia', in *RFE/RL Research Report*, 31 January 1992, p. 11.

23 Beránek, 'Jako bychom se míjeli'.

24 Pavol Frič, Zora Bútorová and Tatiana Rosová, 'Relations Between Czechs and Slovaks in the Mirror of Research' (manuscript, Bratislava: 1991). See also Marian Timoracký, 'Verejná mienka o česko-slovenských vzťahoch' ('Public opinion on Czech-Slovak relations'), in F. Gál et al. (eds.), *Dnešní krize česko-slovenských vztahů* ('Today's crisis in Czech-Slovak relations'),

Prague: Slon, 1992, pp. 68†90.

25 Frič, Bútorová and Rosová, p. 6.

26 ibid., p. 8.

27 Česi a Slováci' ('Czechs and Slovaks'), in *Hospodářské noviny*, 5 June 1992.

28 See Institute for Public Opinion Research, 'Názory čs. veřejnosti na státoprávní uspořádání a na referendum' ('The attitudes of the Czechoslovak public concerning state arrangements and the referendum'), 28 July 1992, p. 5.

29 Dees, p. 12.

30 Beránek, 'Jako bychom se míjeli'.

31 'Nespokojeno 69 procent' ('Sixty-nine per cent are dissatisfied'), in *Lidové noviny*, 1 November 1991, p. 2.

32 Milan Tuček, 'Jaké by byly vysledky referenda ke státoprávnímu uspořádání?' ('What would the results of a referendum concerning state arrangements have been?') in *Data & Fakta*, February 1992, p. 3.

33 See 'Poll: Sixty-four Per Cent Support Federation', in FBIS-EER (91–212, LD 0111044191) Prague ČSTK in English at 19:11 GMT on 31 October 1991, 1 November 1991, p. 5.

34 Institute for Public Opinion Research, 'Názory čs. veřejnosti' ('The attitudes of the Czechoslovak public'), p. 13. A poll conducted in January 1991 found similar results. See L. Beneš, 'Daňová reforma – ale kdy?' ('Tax reform – but when?')in *Hospodářské noviny*, 29 August 1990, p. 1; and Wolchik, *Czechoslovakia in Transition*, pp. 124–5 for further details.

35 Wolchik, *Czechoslovakia in Transition*, pp. 124–5.

36 ibid.

37 'Federace a dvě ústavy' ('A federation and two constitutions'), in *Lidové noviny*, 24 October 1991, p. 2.

38 Beránek, 'Jako bychom se míjeli'.

39 Institute for Public Opinion Research, 'Názory čs. veřejnosti', p. 11.

40 See Wolchik, *Czechoslovakia in Transition*, chapters 2 and 4 for a discussion of these differences in the early post-communist period.

41 Marek Boguszak and Vladimír Rak, 'Czechoslovakia – May 1990 Survey Report', Prague: AISA, 1990, Table 1; see also Wolchik, *Czechoslovakia in Transition*, pp. 122–4.

42 ibid.

43 See Jan Hartl, 'Nad výsledký našich výzkumů' ('On the results of our research'), Prague: STEM, 1991.

44 V. Krivy and I. Radičová, 'Atmosféra dôvery a atmosféra nedôvery?' ('An atmosphere of trust and distrust?' in *Sociologické aktuality*, no. 2, 1992, pp. 12–13.

45 Institute for Public Opinion Research, 'Jaké problémy dnes lidé považují za naléhavé?' ('What problems do people think are important today?') Prague, 30 June 1992.

46 Trust in Mečiar decreased somewhat to 64 per cent of respondents in Slovakia in March 1992 and 73 per cent, compared to 69 per cent for Alexander Dubček,

in May and July 1992. See Institute for Public Opinion Research, 'Popularita politiků' ('The popularity of politicians'), Prague, March 1992; 'Žebříček popularity politiků' ('Thermometer of the popularity of politicians'), Prague, May 1992; and 'Žebříček popularity politiků' ('Thermometer of the popularity of politicians'), July 1992. Other politicians, including President Havel and Slovak Premier Ján Čarnogurský received far less support (17.1 and 9 per cent respectively). See 'Komu věří Slováci' ('Whom the Slovaks trust'), in *Lidové noviny*, 25 October 1991, p. 2.

47 From information from the Institute for Public Opinion Research, Prague, January, March, May and June 1992.

48 'Je čas pro rozvod!' ('It's time for a divorce!') *Večerní Praha*, November 1991.

13 The Velvet Divorce – Institutional Foundations

VÁCLAV ŽÁK

Institutional Foundations for the Break-Up

The Organization of Legislative Bodies in the Federation

In November 1989 Czechoslovakia was a unique, two-member federation. The two-chamber federal parliament had a special structure, consisting of the House of the People, whose members were elected in proportion to the population of the country as a whole (and which therefore had a greater number of deputies from the Czech Republic than from Slovakia); and the House of Nations, which had an equal number of deputies from the Czech and Slovak Republics. The Federal Assembly's rules demanded that important laws were passed by a majority of all deputies in the House of the People and a majority in each of the Czech and Slovak sections of the House of Nations (a three-fifths majority was, moreover, required for constitutional bills).

Given that the House of the People had 150 members and the House of Nations 75 deputies in each of the Czech and Slovak sections,[1] 30 deputies from one section of the House of Nations were enough to block a constitutional law – that is one-tenth of the total number of deputies! Why did the procedural regulations contain such a provision? From its inception in the occupied Czechoslovakia of 1968, the federation included several confederative elements. The right of veto accorded to deputies representing each of the republics in the House of Nations was one of these. Another even more important constitutional provision was the right to secession that the law on Czechoslovak federation of 1968 guaranteed to both republics.[2] It gave a mandate in the Federal Assembly to deputies from the Slovak National Party, whose campaign platform in the elections was division of the state!

Government Organization

In the absence of separate constitutions for the republics, the positions of the governments were set by several articles of the 1968 law on Czechoslovak federation. The original version of this law gave the republics a relatively broad range of authority. During negotiations in 1968, however, the Slovak side already took as its premise the intuitive model of a dual federation (see below). The Slovak side consistently requested that Czechoslovakia be considered a state that was composed of two national states and that the federation serve to perform certain functions. And to a certain extent this conception was asserted in the law: the preamble makes an outright reference to the right of self-determination up to the point of secession. Article 2 states that 'the basis of the Czechoslovak Socialist Republic is the voluntary union of equal nations, the Czech nation and the Slovak nation, based on the right of self-determination for each'.

In 1970, as part of the normalization process, many powers were returned to the central state authorities. The republics, however, maintained important roles.

The law on Czechoslovak federation based itself on the principle that powers that were not given outright to the federation belonged to the republics. Powers entrusted solely to the federation were relatively few: foreign policy, defence, currency and federal legislation. There were many shared powers, however. The republics had sole authority in healthcare and cultural and educational policy. All other areas (agriculture, industry, foreign economic relations, transportation, postal service and telecommunications, social policy, state security, and others) were shared between the federation and the republics. This was a relatively standard method of division of powers in a federation.

The Scheme of the Conflict

In the years 1989–92, the constitutional question was perceived quite differently in the Czech Lands and in Slovakia. While the primary issues in Czech politics were economic reform and coming to terms with forty years of communism, in Slovakia it was undoubtedly the question of future constitutional arrangements that was uppermost. The basic difference was one of self-identification, which was a key factor in the development of the conflict. In the first elections in 1990, while leaders of Czech parties saw election to the federal parliament as more desirable than a place in the Czech Republic's National Council, the more important legislature in the eyes of many Slovak politicians, including the chairs of Public Against

Violence (PAV) and the Communist Party of Slovakia, who stood for it, was the Slovak National Council.

Right from the beginning, the political scene in Slovakia was much more structured than in the Czech Lands. The Slovak side imagined the model of mutual relations to be something along the lines of a monetary union with a common president and army. We can call this model, which appeared in its rough outlines as early as 1968, the *dual federation*: both constituent units saw themselves as sovereign states. The federation was an integration of these sovereign states and performed only certain service functions for both of them: defence, partially foreign policy, and a common currency. The Czech side rejected a dual federation at that time and asserted a *tripartite* model – the federation too was sovereign, together with the two sovereign national states. The tripartite model assumed that the national states were subordinate to the federation in certain matters. This subordination,[3] however, did not succeed in being explicitly set forth in the law on Czechoslovak federation.

In 1989 Slovak politicians – with a considerably higher self-confidence stemming from twenty years of experience of national government, and in an entirely different international situation – returned to the dual federation model. The federation was to change into a state built 'from the bottom up'; that is the integration of two national states was to be the consistent idea. The campaign programme for PAV, entitled 'A Chance for Slovakia', stated that: 'We support the viewpoint that *original sovereignty is the sovereignty of everyone from both national republics – while the sovereignty of the federation is derived, delegated.*'[4] It continued: 'Both national republics must resolve their matters themselves, while leaving foreign policy, defence, financial policy and in a transitional period even some other unavoidable, clearly defined functions to the federation. The goal of our federative model is strong republics, and competent republic governments and parliaments'. It is clear that even the 'most pro-federalist' Slovak political party did not see the federal republic as *its* state. This thesis became the acid test of the entire negotiation process: the Czech right wing refused to agree to it.

Even in constitutional issues money was at the forefront of the discussion. In the twilight of the communist era the governments held talks on limiting the transfer of resources from the Czech Lands to Slovakia. These transfers were carried out on the basis of the principle of eradicating differences between the republics, contained in the constitution.[5] They were made through the federal budget: the amount which the two republics deposited into this budget bore no connection with what they withdrew. From the early 1980s it was clear that investments in modern technology in Slovakia had brought smaller results than investments in the Czech

Lands. Limiting investments in the Czech Lands, however, led to technological obsolescence there. The Czech public saw investments in Slovakia
as 'paying for Slovakia'.

One of the basic motives for changes in the constitutional arrangements
was 'making Slovakia visible'. In Slovakia there was an overwhelming
feeling (and, it is necessary to say, in many ways it was justified) that Prague
monopolized foreign relations. This feeling grew even stronger after
November 1989. The issue was offers of foreign aid and cooperation, which
in many cases the Slovak ministries did not find out about because of the
inability of the administration to process the offers. For investments,
however, there was another problem: the real market evaluation of investment opportunities. Investors did not ignore Slovakia because of bias in
Prague, but because they placed priority on investing in the Czech Lands.
In Slovakia the majority felt, however, that foreign capital preferred the
Czech Republic because Slovakia did not have direct foreign contacts and
was therefore unable to press its own case.

The constitutional relationship between the Czechs and Slovaks was to
have a new appearance. This 'gesture of a new beginning' was to demonstrate
the will of both nations to live together in a common state. Slovak politicians placed priority on National Councils, and in Slovakia, even though
their interests were protected by their over-representation in the House of
Nations, the Federal Assembly was seen as something alien. From a constitutional standpoint, however, only the Federal Assembly had the right to make
legal changes in Czech-Slovak relations! Slovak politicians nevertheless
asserted the idea of a contract that would express the will of both nations
to live in a common state and that would establish the principles of a federal
constitution. This agreement was to be signed by the National Councils.
Negotiations on the constitutions included constant conflict about the
character of the contract, and this conflict could not be resolved.

President Havel had a concept of an 'authentic federation', by which he
wanted to indicate how different it was from the way the Communist Party
of Czechoslovakia had managed the state. Some Slovak politicians began
to interpret this concept as a dual federation, even though – paradoxically
– it was not entirely clear to some of them what this implied. In practice
the latter would have meant seeing the federation as a common, not unified
area with parallel instruments in each republic for conducting independent
economic policies:[6] the existence of two federal reserve banks in the
republics, the possibility of setting different taxes, the collection of taxes
'from the bottom up', the possibility of price and customs regulation, etc.
It also meant a separation of the railways, postal services, telecommunications, energy, oil and gas supply networks, etc., as well as the elimination
of federal radio and television. In foreign policy it meant the republics were

separate, and later completely independent international entities. Only the army remained clearly shared.

An 'authentic federation' for most Czech politicians meant an improvement of the tripartite model in which sovereignty would have rested clearly with the federation. They were not overly enthusiastic about a transfer of authority to the republics, but they saw it as an opportunity to guarantee the transition to a market economy in a multinational state (i.e. so that the economic consequences of reforms could not be interpreted as injustices to nationalities).

Almost from the beginning, then, the maximum visions of one side about the changes lay quite far below the minimum visions of the other side. To prevent a development that would accelerate a break-up, the policy of the centre and of both republics would have to be almost clinically precise and error-free. It is almost pointless to add that in the post-revolution period this was an unachievable request.

The different evaluation of the communist era in the Czech Lands and in Slovakia was another important difference between them. For Czech political representatives, the communist era represented a period of one of the deepest crises in modern Czech history, with a decline in almost all areas. Slovakia, on the other hand, experienced a period of its greatest economic – and in a certain sense even cultural – growth. In contrast to the First Republic, the communists included in the constitution a programme for bringing the level of development in Slovakia up to that of the Czech Lands. A blanket condemnation of the entire communist era aroused distrust in Slovakia, which was strengthened by the ill-considered steps of certain Czech politicians, especially the decision to stop arms manufacturing.

One must not ignore the important role of institutions in post-revolution Czechoslovakia. The coordination and pre-negotiation of political decisions that normally take place in political parties was weakened, and sometimes eliminated entirely. Thus coordination between institutions suffered as well. The people who managed the revolution took government posts, and real power went with them. Few of them understood the necessity of pre-negotiating decisions, vital for formal relations between institutional representatives; for most of them the impersonalization of politics was a problem. Some of them saw their functions as a personal responsibility, with which collective decision-making would interfere. They considered consultations with advisers, who were usually friends without expertise, to be sufficient.[7] Amateurism, i.e. decision-making without considering the consequences which those decisions would bring, significantly marked agreements between political representatives which then could not be implemented. This led to political frustration and the growth of distrust between politicians.

Negotiations Between Czech and Slovak Political Representatives

From the Revolution to the Elections in 1990: Authentic Federation

From the very beginning, the political representatives of the Civic Forum (CF) realized the sensitive nature of the Slovak question. As became clear later, however, they did not recognize this sufficiently. Thus the development of federal political forces that would be identified with the revolution and with the programme of change was not considered the top priority. From November, the CF began appearing in Slovakia, much earlier than PAV began functioning in Bratislava. After PAV became the mouthpiece of the revolution in Slovakia, the CF recommended to its Slovak organizations that they become part of PAV. In this way the chance (it is hard to judge how great a chance this was) for unified political management of the reform process in the entire country disappeared.

Before the first elections in 1990, some Czech politicians tried to change the overall parliamentary structure. They were not successful, however: Slovakia viewed any changes to its protected status with suspicion. Thus the only change that occurred in the Federal Assembly before the elections was a reduction in the number of deputies in that body.

The Hyphen War

On 23 January 1990 President Havel, led by 'a responsibility to negotiate in accordance with the awakened will of the public', gave a speech in the Federal Assembly in which he presented 'proposals for mutually implemented changes' to the surprised deputies. These changes were 'expected by most people; and the public, to whom I feel my primary responsibility, calls for them'. The President then presented a proposal for changing the name and symbols of the country, leaving out the word 'socialist'. The new name was to be the 'Czechoslovak Republic', practically the same as the one used during the First Republic.

The President assumed that the deputies would pass his proposals on the spot. His reasoning was precise: he felt responsible to the public and wanted results. It was exactly this approach that led to his greatest successes at the head of the CF: as one of the few who managed to keep up with the demands of the public and raise goals, so that the revolution proceeded for those miraculous ten days. Unfortunately, he had not changed his conceptions about the leadership of an institution that is joined with other institutions by a range of procedural rules. The Federal Assembly, to the great disillusionment of the President, did not approve his proposals immediately, and instead began to discuss them publicly. This apparently so took the President aback that he attacked the Federal Assembly rather strongly in a public speech on 25 February 1990. This aroused doubt among the deputies as to whether the President really wanted to develop a parliamentary democracy.

The issue of the country's new name immediately brought up the problem of the 'visibility of Slovakia'. Slovak deputies wanted the name to show that Slovakia was also a republic. For this reason they insisted on a hyphen in the name – thus indirectly invoking the post-Munich discussion, this being the period when the hyphen first appeared in the country's name. In the Czech Lands this evoked an angry reaction – and brought on the ridiculous proposal for the country's name to be written in Slovakia with a hyphen and in the Czech Lands without. The Federal Assembly actually passed a law that allowed the country to have two names! The decision then led to demonstrations in Bratislava, on 30 March 1990. In the end, the name Czech and Slovak Federative Republic (ČSFR) was passed, which fulfilled the requirements of 'making Slovakia visible'. Czech-Slovak relations, however, were needlessly burdened with their first conflict.

National Governments Versus their Federal Mother-In-Law

After the revolution, when the demands on the operative management of the country rose steeply, the national governments began to stumble over federal authority at every step – and vice versa. At the same time, 'federalists' regarded representatives at the republic level somewhat from above – they suffered from 'federal arrogance'. This feeling was felt intensively in the relationship between Czech and federal representatives but was not interpreted as a national issue.

In January 1990, the Czech Minister of Finance hurried to the Czech National Council and let the Presidium approve a resolution that recommended going over to the principle of 'each on his own' in budget management. In this way the Czechs stopped paying for Slovakia. (Slovakia, on the other hand, believed it was paying for the Czechs.)

During negotiations between the national governments – without the participation of the federal government – in Lnáře, on 11 April 1990,[8] the national governments agreed that the easiest way to stop all arguments over who paid for whom was for each republic to live off the taxes collected on its own territory; the federation would get only a set amount for necessary expenses. In the Slovak National Council, Slovak premier Číč called this agreement a significant success of his government.

The agreement between the national governments is confirmation of the thesis that gross errors were caused by uncoordinated policy. In the given

tax system, it was not at all possible to allocate budget revenues regionally! Moreover, it was difficult to imagine a federation that did not have
its own revenues and did not further divide them. What purpose would the
federation then have? It was not surprising, then, that right after the
elections the issue of finances became one of the first points of conflict
between Václav Klaus, then Federal Minister of Finance, and the premiers
of the national governments. Klaus announced in the Federal Assembly:
'The national governments are working toward the dissolution of the
federation, because without an economic centre and autonomy of revenues
in all three budgets, it is impossible to imagine a unified economy.'

The Delusion of Czech Statehood

At the beginning of their independent operations, the Czech and Slovak
governments did not have an equivalent status. The Slovak government
had a clear priority: to achieve the rectification of Slovakia's status. The
extent of this 'rectification', however, ranged from achieving a status of
'equals' to the complete independence of Slovakia. In this situation, the
Czech government in its programme presented a plan to achieve 'Czech
statehood'. It consisted basically of an appeal to the national consciousness of the Czechs – specifically, to 'complete the national revival'. The
Czech government tried to imbue the Czechs with a similar relationship to
the state that the Slovaks had in their nature.

The Czech public, which had been awakened by the conflict over the
name of the country, saw their statehood differently: the federation is 'ours'.
If they do not want it, let them go. On 3 May 1990, Ludvík Vaculík, a
prominent Czech novelist and journalist, published an article in *Lidové
noviny* in which he compared the argument over the new constitutional
arrangements to the constant efforts of his younger brother to move the bed
in his apartment. He called on him to have his own little house. In this way
he broke a taboo in the Czech Lands and the break-up of the state became
a theme for public discussion. The insulted Czech pride made an appearance, seeing the Slovaks as ungrateful, and unable to differentiate between
the excesses of Slovak separatists and politicians with national feeling. The
newly emergent Czech right wing absolutely refused to understand how
vitally important the 'Slovak theme' was to Slovak politicians. They
considered them nationalists who were falsely evoking 100-year-old
national spirits when they should have been building a liberal civil society.
The Czech right wing repeated, without realizing it, the arguments that the
Hungarians had used before the First World War to assert the strong
Magyarization of Slovakia.

Before the Elections of 1990

The effort to 'reform the federation' brought few results before the first elections. Except for the change in the number of seats in the Federal Assembly, institutions were not altered. There were no significant changes in the constitution, if we ignore the elimination of the article on the leading role of the communist party. Legislative bodies, whose main task was to be the approval of a new constitution, received instead a hyphen war and demonstrations in Slovakia with open separatist demands, as well as Slovak National Party separatist deputies in the Federal Assembly and the Slovak National Council.

The Constituent Parliament 1990–92: Looking for an Agreement

Government Declaration

After the elections, all three governments presented their programmes in Parliament. The Czech government's programme was similar to that declared in Lnáře: hail to the federal mother-in-law. It contained a passage which stated that 'the federation will have such authority as granted to it by the republics ... after mutual agreement'.[9] It went on to say that 'the Czech National Council will decide about the use of resources collected in its republic with the exception of those resources allocated for the needs of the federation'.[10] In other words, the regional parliament would determine the financial revenues of a sovereign state! The premier of the federal government commented on this in the newspapers: 'The republics have revolted'.[11]

The federal government resolved problems dialectically: in its programme we read that 'strong republics mean a strong federation'. In other words: if we weaken the federation wherever possible, we will strengthen the republics, and if the republics resolve their own problems, there will be no room for conflict with the federation. The federation will be reinforced in this way.

The declaration of the federal government, however, went even further. The Christian Democratic Movement (CDM) refused to participate in the coalition if the declarations of the Slovak and federal governments did not include a formulation from its election platform: 'The Czech and Slovak Republics will become members of the European integration process as two independent entities.' Translated into comprehensible language, this meant that Czechoslovakia should break up before its acceptance into the European Community. Surprisingly, the deputies did not discuss this passage of the federal government's announcement at all!

The governments' programmes are proof that the initial Slovak and Czech ideas about the constitutional arrangements had very little common ground. While the Czech government declared a willingness to recognize the Slovak request to create a federation 'from below', i.e. a federation consisting of republics that gave it authority (a conception which in reality did not have political support from the Czech public), the Slovak government declaration saw in this request the absolute minimum of what it wanted to achieve.

A Wasted Opportunity

In July 1990 the federation transferred authority for a number of policy areas to the republics, especially in the field of practical management of the economy. Agriculture, the machine-tool industry, and ore-mining were transferred to a republic level.

The changes had already tentatively been agreed upon before the elections. After the elections, the CF leadership made an offer to the leadership of PAV (Gál, Langoš and others) to compose a whole package of changes.[12] The post-election atmosphere encouraged change; the PAV leadership of that time, however, composed mostly of liberal intellectuals, did not place the highest priority on dividing authority.

With the election of Vladimír Mečiar as Slovak premier on 27 June 1990 came a new political direction. Mečiar was not an intellectual, and he did not belong to the small group of Slovak politicians that held the principle of establishing citizenship according to place of residence. At that time he was one of the most common group of Slovak politicians: those who were not separatists, but were nationally oriented. For them it was important to satisfy the national ambitions of Slovakia – and of course even their own ambitions for power. In their thinking, these two aspects were inseparably connected (that was also true of politicians in the Czech government).

The Struggle for Authority

The representatives of the federal, Czech and Slovak governments agreed that a change in authority implemented right after the elections would not mean a definite division of power, but only the beginnings of change. The governments began to negotiate autonomously, and political movements began to lose control over their negotiations. There appeared a desire to allow individual conscience to govern policy rather than to submit to collective decision-making. Later even President Havel promised the three prime ministers that further changes in authority would take place even before the constitution was approved.

With hindsight, this was the first in a significant series of mistakes. A whole package of changes was to be prepared as part of accepting the constitution. A second change in authority, which the Federal Assembly began to discuss less than three weeks after an earlier change had passed without problems, led to a very irritated reaction from some of the Czech press. In the campaign against the changes the Czech press stopped differentiating between separatist and nationally oriented politics, labelling every effort to make new arrangements as hidden separatism. The competition for authority brought Mečiar enormous popularity in Slovakia. Reactions on the Czech side moved him closer to separatism.

At the beginning of August 1990, representatives of all three governments, at the invitation of the federal government, met to discuss the programme of changes in authority in the Slovak spa town of Trenčianské Teplice. With the support of the Czech premier, Premier Mečiar presented to astonished federal government representatives a plan of extensive transfer of power from the federation to the republics. This now represented a really fundamental change in the country's constitution! Mečiar, however, proceeded in accordance with the declaration of his government and with PAV's election programme. What was the nature of the basic requests presented in Trenčianské Teplice? The Slovak side proposed the dual model, to be supplemented with 'visibility' – the recognition of both the Czech and the Slovak Republics in international law. The federation was to keep defence, currency, foreign policy, the legislative framework and overall economic decision-making, i.e. basic taxation.

Federal government representatives could hardly agree to such requests. This was not a case of ill-will – the federation was recognized in international law and if it was to be considered a sovereign state, it had to be capable of guaranteeing certain functions without mediation.

No conclusions were reached in Trenčianské Teplice. No party had a mandate for such negotiations (not even Mečiar!), either from government or from a political party. The representatives of federal government therefore refused to sign any communiqué. It was agreed only that negotiations would continue. As has already been mentioned, however, the public reacted with irritation. Almost immediately people criticized the negotiations of the ultranationalist party (among whom were members of the Slovak National Party, and even some representatives of the ruling CDM!), and they demanded the independence of Slovakia. This provoked a crisis in the Slovak government, and CDM withdrew from the negotiations. Some journalists in the Czech Lands interpreted the plan in Trenčianské Teplice almost as a betrayal. At a meeting with President Havel on 17 August 1990, Jan Urban, a journalist and leading representative of the CF, read a letter from the prominent dissident Petr Uhl, who threw into the Slovak premier's face the fact that he was promoting not a free civic society but nationalism.

At that time President Havel prevented open conflict, yet the tension in the Czech-Slovak relationship began to grow.

The Second Czech-Slovak Crisis

Mečiar's proposal met with criticism in both the Czech and Slovak National Councils – but on different points.

The negotiation process significantly affected the polarization of the political arena in the Czech Republic. A fragile consensus of general support for reform, on the basis of which even the communists were to share in the transformation, began right after the elections to give way to the population's anti-communist sentiments. Deputies of the CF club in the Federal Assembly, who did not agree with parliamentary offices being shared among all parties which had been successful in the elections (this gave a particularly large representation to the communists, who formed the members of the strongest opposition party!) established a 'right-wing club'. They also agreed that the federation already existed in law, and so it was not possible to build 'from below' as if anew. They rejected the national character of the two-member federation and they considered any reference to 'nation' an expression of Slovak nationalism. They claimed that 'it is only possible to speak of the federative nature of the state if the authority of both national republics is based on the authority of the federation'.[13] Their motive was clear: to reject the conception of building the federation 'from below' and to block Slovak demands with legal arguments.

The Slovak National Council, on the other hand, criticized backing away from the original proposed amendments at Trenčianské Teplice.

Premier Mečiar intervened on both sides – in the Czech Lands as well as in Slovakia. The non-discriminating means that he chose for this had serious consequences for further developments. In Prague he refused to negotiate with the federal government. He warned the Czech government that if the proposals for constitutional changes were dropped, the next few days would see the declaration of federal laws being subordinated to those of the Slovak National Council – and so the break-up of the state. As became clear later, this was purely a bluff that Mečiar played before the completely dismayed members of his government. Unfortunately, none of his ministers said that this threat was not a possibility!

Czech Premier Pithart pointlessly informed the Czech National Council about it, and the Council reacted with a request to prepare for a worst-case scenario in case of the sudden break-up of the country. The Czech government's move, however, evoked a feeling in Slovakia that the Czechs wanted to break the federation. A vicious circle began.

Slovak separatists criticized Premier Mečiar, because they said the proposal for constitutional changes presented to the Federal Assembly was not as significant as the proposal in Trenčianské Teplice. In the Slovak National Council, Premier Mečiar defended himself against this criticism by indicating that the words he used during the negotiations were not his own.

For this Czech newspapers made him out to be a blackmailer who had fooled the Czech premier. The public's reaction was predictable: Mečiar stopped being an acceptable politician, and Pithart got the label of one who backs down. In a difficult situation, the Czech premier began to change course. His pro-Slovak position and willingness to meet Slovak demands halfway began to lose not only the support of the public but also the support of the deputies.

In the end the Federal Assembly, after long debate, accepted the constitutional amendments with which it was presented (on 12 December 1990). The approved model was a tripartite federation in which most state administration functions were transferred to the republics. Shared authority disappeared from this law. The federation maintained sole authority over defence, currency, transportation networks, the postal service and legal amendments in many areas. Both republics were recognized in international law and given some degree of freedom of action in certain areas of international relations.

Mečiar gave an impassioned speech in the Slovak National Council about the results, ending it with a paraphrase of Comenius's declaration: 'Your government, oh Slovak people, has returned to your hands.' Ludvík Vaculík commented on the results of the constitutional negotiations in a slightly different way: 'If today we are offended by Slovak politics, then we are offended as humans and not as a nation! In some respects we do not care about Czech statehood. Rather than feeling something for that question we are more tired of it, annoyed, and wish to have peace from it … After Slovakia breaks away, no one will prevent us from calling our state Czechoslovakia.'[14] Vaculík expressed a very widespread feeling. Parties betting on the break-up of the state had good prospects.

Constitutions

The debate in the Federal Assembly about the constitutional changes was agitated, but there was an overwhelming willingness on the part of the Czech deputies to meet the Slovak demands halfway; on the condition, however, that that was the last time the Federal Assembly addressed the question until an overall, lasting constitutional settlement could be reached. Slovak representatives (from the Slovak National Council), however, agreed to the amendment to the law only as an interim step to a definitive constitutional division of authority. A conflict was imminent.

At the end of September 1990, the Presidia of the National Councils had met to discuss the constitutions of the two republics.[15] The result of the negotiations was a commitment that the constitutional changes would be implemented within the constitutional framework and that the federal constitution would be drafted by a commission of ten deputies from the Czech National Council, ten deputies from the Slovak National Council, and fourteen deputies from the Federal Assembly.

In addition to the problems over the division of authority, some purely constitutional problems arose during the negotiations. The first concerned the symbolic expression of a new beginning, which the state agreement was to make.[16] Others included the number of parliamentary chambers, the implementation of rule by the majority, the necessity of ratifying constitutional changes in the National Councils, the relationship between the federal constitution and the agreement, the order of passing the constitutions, and the issue of the so-called 'pure' constitution, i.e. the constitution of the supreme state. Slovak demands wanted first to approve the republic constitutions, which would contain the empowerment and the explicit transfer of authority to the federation. Some of the Czech politicians thought that the federal constitution should be approved first and that the republic constitutions should be within the framework of the federal constitution.

It was not long before it became clear that the commission, made up of ten members of the Czech National Council, ten members of the Slovak National Council and fourteen members of the Federal Assembly, was not capable of giving a group of experts the political task of writing a constitution. For that reason President Havel ordered a constitution to be drafted and then presented it to the commission for discussion. Not even during a discussion on the text, however, was the commission able to agree on anything.

The Federal Assembly reacted to the failure of the commission by beginning to change the constitution piecemeal. Ultimately, a fundamental change to the constitution was also an amendment to the constitutional law on Czechoslovak federation. One important change was the passing of the Bill on Basic Rights and Liberties on 9 January 1991. In this way the ČSFR – at least formally – became a liberal, law-based state. The Federal Assembly then reformed the judicial system, including the constitutional court, and established the instrument of referendum. The only three chapters of the constitution that still had to be passed to make it complete were those reforming the position of the president, the federal government and the Federal Assembly.

The President's Initiative – Castles and Palaces

The President reacted to the delay in preparing the constitution by beginning to call political parties to negotiations on the document. At the first of these negotiations, on 17 February 1991, the CDM chair, Ján

Čarnogurský, put forward his party's request that the constitution be passed before the agreement between the Czech and Slovak Republics. The CDM evidently got its inspiration from the state agreement that was to transform the Union of Soviet Socialist Republics into the Commonwealth of Independent States. The Czech political representatives, the majority of whom were right-wing, totally rejected Čarnogurský's not very well-formulated request. Čarnogurský, however, wanted the negotiation to be about an interstate agreement between the republics in which only the federation was recognized in international law.

During further negotiations, which ultimately began to be ridiculed as 'touring castles and palaces', the situation in Slovakia changed fundamentally. The conflict between the leadership of PAV and the government, especially Premier Mečiar, became acute: Slovakia's Minister of Foreign Affairs, M. Kňažko (a former actor), accused the leadership of PAV of an attempt to censor Premier Mečiar's television speeches. He described those changes which had so far been made to the constitution as 'a gnawed bone thrown by the Czechs to the Slovaks'. The Presidium of the Slovak National Council – at the same time as demonstrations in support of Mečiar were being held – recalled the Premier from his post and elected Čarnogurský in his place. That move led to the splintering of PAV and to the birth of PAV's platform, Towards a Democratic Slovakia, later the Movement for a Democratic Slovakia (MDS). Mečiar – with the confidence of 80 per cent of the public – quickly became involved in a game of 'Wait, I'll show you who is a better Slovak'. He shortened the timescale for 'making Slovakia visible' – Slovakia would establish its presence not in ten years, but after the elections. The federational model he proposed was very convenient: to the voters he pretended that it meant the break-up of the state but, on the other hand, it allowed him to pretend that it would enable them to achieve the advantages of an independent state as well as to remain in the federation. In contrast to the CDM, which now found itself responsible for the economic consequences of the reforms in Slovakia, he could stand at the head of even the socially dissatisfied Slovaks. The popularity of Mečiar's MDS began to grow rapidly.

In the end, the negotiations between the President and the political parties ended in a compromise (Kroměřiž, 17 June 1991). During the negotiations, President Havel distributed to the representatives of the parliamentary political parties a questionnaire with basic questions on the future constitutional arrangements. In the meantime all Slovak parties had registered their support for the CDM's suggestion. The Slovak National Party was against the federation, while the MDS was for a confederation. The participants at the negotiations agreed that the federal constitution would be approved before the agreement on the principles of state arrangements was approved by the National Councils. The Councils would then ratify the federal constitution. This agreement, however, was to be a kind of legislative initiative for the Federal Assembly; in other words, it was not to have any legal validity and would not bind the Federal Assembly in any way. The Czech political parties rejected the method that would meet Slovak requests – passing a constitutional law on the approval of a constitution by which the Federal Assembly would entrust the National Councils with developing an agreement and committing themselves to acting in accordance with this agreement while the constitution was being drafted.

Negotiations Between the Presidia of the National Councils

The points of contention that had appeared during negotiations on the law on authority and on the constitution again appeared on the bargaining table. In the interim, however, the situation had polarized in both republics. In Slovakia speeches by separatists, including insults directed at the President of the Republic, multiplied,[17] and in the Czech Lands threats were made that the budget would no longer be so generous to Slovakia.

The negotiations between the Presidia of the two National Councils included two spheres of issues: the first dealt with the distribution of power and the second with the nature of the agreement between the two republics. The familiar requests for the dual model again appeared in the negotiation about the distribution of power (i.e. the demand for two federal reserve banks).

A more serious conflict, however, was the issue of the agreement's character. The Slovak side insisted that it must be an agreement between the two republics, which would express the original division of power between them. The Czech right wing asserted the conception of the contract as being an agreement on giving legislative initiative to the Federal Assembly. This was a fundamental question: Is the federation sovereign? A national agreement would indicate that it was not. In the CDM's logic – and CDM politicians made no secret of it – it was a step on the road to Slovakia's complete independence. For other Slovak parties, PAV and the Party of the Democratic Left Wing, however, the agreement represented the beginning of Slovakia's voluntary membership of the federation. The Czech right wing (especially the Civic Democratic Alliance) decided to provoke a conflict on this point. This strategy was perfect: the Czech public regarded the uncompromising stance toward the Slovaks with gratitude, whereas in Slovakia it evoked a reaction which in the Czech Lands only proved that 'it was impossible with the Slovaks'.

Preparation of the Worst-Case Scenario – the President Versus the Parliament

The President reacted to the growing tension provoked by the unsuccessful constitutional negotiations by trying to put pressure on the Federal Assembly through the public. He gave a speech on television for the second anniversary of the velvet revolution (in November 1990), in which he announced that he was presenting the Federal Assembly with a proposal for laws that should enable a resolution of the potential constitutional crisis. The most significant proposal was for a referendum which the President could call for in order to find out the public's opinion on important questions. The referendum law was meant to scare the republics away from an attempt to gain independence. If one of the republics decided to leave the federation, the recognition that the federation had had in international law would transfer to the republic that had not left the federation.

The President used public opinion to pressure the parliament. Demonstrations erupted once again on city squares, and great efforts were made to petition in favour of the referendum. However, one major difference was evident: Slovakia was calm. Of the almost 2.5 million signatures, fewer than 400,000 were collected in Slovakia.

The Parliament shuffled and dodged but did not succumb to this pressure. The referendum was not declared. The deputies could not agree on the question.

Negotiations in Milovy – Failed Efforts at a Constitution

The experience of the Presidia's negotiations showed that it was necessary to pre-negotiate the agreement. Thus, in February 1992, after Slovak deputies in the Federal Assembly had blocked the passage of three chapters of the constitution, commissions of the Presidia of the National Councils were established. Their task was to draft an agreement on the basis of which it would be possible to ratify the federal constitution.

The week-long negotiations, in which members of the federal government and relevant experts participated, ended in a balanced compromise on the issues of distribution of power and the structure of the new federal bodies. The Slovak side, however, did not assert its most important request – for a new expression of the composition of the federation 'from below'. The Czech right wing rejected the original proposal that the agreement be signed by the Czech and Slovak Republics, because it pointed to the alleged loss of the ČSFR's recognition in international law.

The Presidium of the Slovak National Council rejected the agreement by a narrow margin. A close result in the Presidium, however, did not mean that the agreement would have a chance of being passed in the general assembly. On the contrary, a vote in the general assembly would probably have rejected the agreement even more vehemently. One can assume that even the Presidium of the Czech National Council would have rejected it. With this the negotiation process on the constitutions stopped. Without the agreement, the Federal Assembly was not able to pass the remaining three chapters of the constitution.

After the 1992 Elections – The Agreement to Disagree

The 1992 elections were won by parties that were 'clear' on constitutional issues. On the Czech side, the Civic Democratic Party (CDP) supported a 'functional federation'. Long before the elections, in November 1991, Václav Klaus had proclaimed that he 'must give a warning that today's maimed federation was not capable of guaranteeing a continuation of economic reform'. He avoided, however, any invectives against Vladimír Mečiar. It was apparent that it would be Mečiar who would be his partner in Slovakia.

The President of the Republic entrusted Václav Klaus with setting up the federal government. Two intentions came into conflict at the negotiations between the CDP and the MDS. They were already so pre-set that there was minimal room for agreement. Of the three options – a functional federation, separation and confederation – the first was unacceptable to the MDS and the last to the CDP. Václav Klaus was apparently counting on the pragmatism of the Slovak political representatives and assuming that it was impossible to take speeches made by the MDS during the election campaign too seriously, but he encountered the firm intention of his partners to assert Slovakia as an internationally recognized state. This was an absolutely unacceptable demand for the CDP. Thus the only point on which the delegation managed to agree was to agree to disagree: the Czech and Slovak Federative Republic would divide.

Rejection of the Referendum

Klaus and Mečiar, the leaders of the most successful Czech and Slovak parties respectively, became the premiers of the national governments. This was clearly a signal that the days of the federation were numbered. The political agreement between the CDP and the MDS, concluded in Bratislava on 20 June 1992, enabled the setting up of a federal 'liquidation' government. Part of the agreement was this government's programme, and it took into account the differences in views on the future constitutional arrangements and decreed that the National Councils would agree on a resolution by 30

September 1993. It even took care of the federal deputies: in the case of the federation ceasing to exist, they were to go into the National Councils.

President Havel immediately pointed out that the constitutional division of the state was possible only through a referendum.[18] The CDP and the MDS, however, announced that the constitutional division of the state which the National Councils were to agree on by 30 September should not be implemented merely by means of a referendum. The law on the referendum was meant to harm the republic that would leave the federation. Moreover, the referendum would be very risky, especially for the MDS in Slovakia. It was not at all certain that the proposal to break up the ČSFR would gain the necessary majority.

It was apparent that neither the CDP nor the MDS wanted the referendum. Thus they searched until they found a method by means of which it would be possible to divide the state without holding a referendum.

Division of the State

Even after the agreement with the CDP, the MDS did not give up its plan for a confederation. This plan was not unrealistic: it wanted the ČSFR to be transformed into a form similar to that of the European Union after Maastricht, i.e. the same authorities would remain at the federal level as Brussels would have after Maastricht. After their own membership in the European Union, the Brussels administration would take the place of the federal government. Given that the Maastricht Treaty contained a range of strict elements, especially in fiscal policy, and that it contained federative elements, there was a chance to give the federation a looser form. In this way the federation could continue to have an influence on the potentially explosive relations with the Hungarian minority, which was seen as the greatest risk of instability in Central Europe in the future.

For the CDP, however, this opportunity was unacceptable. They did not trust the MDS as a dependable partner, and they did not want to assume a broader responsibility. The MDS had a different economic programme, in which it rejected 'Klaus's reform'. Premier Mečiar was the least acceptable Slovak politician in the Czech Lands. From that point a schizophrenic situation began to develop: some of the right-wing politicians and journalists began to paint a Slovakia under the MDS as being infected with a post-communist plague. The sooner they separated from it, the better for them. On the other hand, the leadership of the CDP, primarily Václav Klaus, took on a positive tone – the division of the state was not a tragedy but the culmination of the emancipation process of the Slovak nation.

The last nail in the coffin for the idea of possibly transforming the federation, however, was hammered in by Premier Mečiar himself. On 3 July 1992, in the Federal Assembly, the MDS blocked the election of Václav Havel as president. Mečiar was settling accounts for his recall as premier. There was also opposition to Václav Havel's candidacy within the CDP, but the Czech Republic held the MDS responsible for Havel's not being elected. Without Václav Havel in the post of president (his term was due to expire in October), the division of the state without a referendum was much more realistic.

It was then simple for the CDP to reject all the MDS's attempts at asserting some form of a common state – no longer a federation, but a limited economic and defence union. The opposition seized on the idea of a union, and the MDS flirted for some time with the possibility of agreeing with the opposition on this point. The CDP, which had enough deputies in the Federal Assembly to block any constitutional change, forced the MDS to return to the original agreement: the federation would split.

A Declaration of Sovereignty and the Slovak Republic's Constitution

Developments were rapid in Slovakia. On 17 July 1992 the Slovak National Council passed the Declaration of Sovereignty of the Slovak Nation, a declaration that before the elections it had consistently refused to pass.[19] The same day, President Havel announced his resignation. The end of a country that had lasted for more than seventy years drew palpably closer.

In August the script for the break-up of the state was written during the negotiations of the MDS and the CDP. Three laws were to guarantee its constitutionality: the law on the end of the federation, the law on the division of property, and the law on the successor rights of the republics. In addition, it was agreed that the republics would form a monetary and customs union that would be secured by a whole array of individual agreements. There would not be one 'contract', which would have been too reminiscent of the MDS's original plan.

In resolving this situation, Václav Klaus proceeded just as he had in many other respects: behind forceful rhetoric hid a policy that had little in common with that rhetoric. The MDS achieved many of its original demands, yet almost no one noticed. For the complete satisfaction of the MDS, the union lacked only a joint army leadership and some coordinating bodies. Otherwise it was tight, as a monetary union must be. It was reformed by dozens of partial agreements. This union was very risky, especially for the foreign-currency reserves of the central bank, and in fact it did not last longer than a month. Using this approach, which had been very convenient for Slovakia, the government was able to make the dissolution smooth; the degree of the union's latitude determined the real economic policy of both governments.

The ratification of the Slovak constitution on 1 September 1992 practically meant the end of the common state. This was the constitution of an independent state, even though several articles did not become valid until after 1 January 1993, which was the agreed term for the ending of the Czech and Slovak Federative Republic. It was almost symbolic that on that very day Alexander Dubček was fatally injured in an automobile accident on the way to the Federal Assembly.

After the August negotiations with the MDS, the opposition understood that the MDS took seriously its demand for Slovakia's recognition in international law. The question of the further existence of the country thus changed to a question of the legitimacy of the break-up. Some politicians pointed out that the break-up of the state without a referendum would place a constant question mark over its legitimacy in the future. The question, the gravity of which would still be felt, was whether the deputies, who had received a mandate by promising fidelity to this very state, could divide it.

On 1 September 1992 the Federal Assembly rejected the government proposal for a law on ways to end the federation. The opposition requested a referendum. The work on dissolution, however, continued. The Federal Assembly approved a further transfer of power from the federation to the republics. A range of federal institutions began to undergo liquidation. The Federal Assembly passed a law on dividing federal property between the two republics, in a ratio of 2:1 (according to population) and on historical principles. Generosity in dividing property, especially military property, in a ratio of 2:1 was one of the reasons that the break-up of the federation proceeded smoothly.

The Law on the End of the Federation

The government then presented the Federal Assembly with a proposal for the law on the end of the federation. On 14 November 1992 representatives of the parliamentary parties agreed in Bratislava that the Federal Assembly would pass this law, to which both National Councils would adopt a recommending resolution. Three days later both National Councils did so. On 25 November 1992 the law on the break-up of the federation was approved at the second reading. On 1 January 1993 the break-up of the state became a reality.

Conclusion

The negotiation process on the constitutional arrangements proceeded against a backdrop of the break-up of the Soviet empire. The achievement of independence by the Soviet states and the states of the Yugoslav Federation, some of them considerably smaller than Slovakia, substantially encouraged the national aspirations of Slovak politicians. Many of them saw the current situation as a starry opportunity for the Slovak nation that might not ever present itself again. The country's fate was decided by the fact that the primary issues concerning Czech and Slovak societies were different, and thus political success demanded an entirely different theme in the Czech Lands than in Slovakia. While in the Czech Lands the premise of success was anti-communism, in Slovakia it was national and social issues. In a republic with three times as much unemployment as its Czech neighbour, which the ill-considered decision to convert arms production affected considerably, this was not too surprising. The burden of mistakes made when living together in the past and the resulting suspicion turned out to be greater than it had appeared during the post-revolution euphoria. Maintaining the country in this situation would apparently have been a difficult task even for much more experienced political representatives than those that the velvet revolution had lifted into leading posts.

The success of the negotiations depended to a great extent on the foresight of the political élite, their ability to differentiate the common good from their own assertion of power, their ability to judge the intentions of partners who lacked foresight, and a certain generosity. The federation's existence depended upon their willingness to share power. Once that willingness is absent, a federation is threatened. In Czechoslovakia there were few politicians on the federal and republic level who were willing (and able) to share power.

The opportunity to prevent an escalation of the conflict by the Czech side's offering the Slovak side a new 'proposal of marriage', one that would have dulled the edges of a national break-up and prevented the development of Slovak demands, remained unused. Federal representatives were unable to present the Slovak public with an attractive plan for a common future which would hold advantages for them. Federal Premier Čalfa, a Slovak, held a weakened position in the Czech Lands because of his communist past and in Slovakia because he was 'federal'. The ideologized Czech right wing, which stirred up the anti-communist wave in the Czech Lands, artificially set itself national and civic principles and reproached the Slovaks because the Czechs were paying for them. This right wing in fact encouraged nationally oriented politicians in Slovakia to move towards separatism and reinforced their conviction that Czech politicians were not interested in resolving Slovak problems. In Slovakia itself few political representatives could imagine any solution to the current Slovak problems other than having the Bratislava government take them in hand. Meanwhile, negotiations were being held in a rapidly changing post-revolution period when the public had little patience. In that situation, the quickest solution was – naturally – the break-up of the state.

It is certainly possible to give the political élite credit for not considering the use of force. The positively formulated dissolution programme – ending the federation in order to fulfil efforts for the emancipation of the Slovak nation – despite a somewhat purpose-built character, prevented a conflict and allowed relations between the Czechs and the Slovaks to remain free of resentment after the break-up of the state. Compared to some other post-communist countries, this is not a negligible result.

Notes

1 The reduction of the number of deputies from the previous 200 to 150 in the House of the People and the House of Nations was the only change in the structure of the Federal Assembly to which the Slovak partners from Public Against Violence agreed before the elections in 1990.
2 Law No. 143/1968.
3 This was equivalent to Article 31 of the Basic Law of West Germany: the constitutional law of the federation was subordinate to the constitutional law of the country.
4 On this they could base their argument on the constitutional law on Czechoslovak federation. Article 1, Paragraph 3 stated that 'the Czechoslovak Federation is an expression of the free will of two independent, sovereign nations, the Czech and the Slovak, to live together in a common federative state'.
5 Article 4, Paragraph 4 of the law on Czechoslovak federation stated: 'An important task of the Czechoslovak Socialist Republic is the eradication of the economic and social differences between the two republics, especially by creating the same conditions and opportunities for the creation and utilization of national revenues.'
6 Given the rapid differentiated development in the Czech and Slovak Republics, these requests took on greater significance. Shortly after liberalization, unemployment in the Slovak Republic was three times that in the Czech Republic. The decision of President Havel and Minister of Foreign Affairs Dienstbier to stop the export of arms caused considerable problems in Slovakia, where much of the arms industry was based.
7 President Havel, for example, did not have working relations with the chair of the Federal Assembly, Alexander Dubček, nor with the chair of the House of Nations, Šutovec. Dubček had almost no part in important decisions.
8 It was at this meeting that the national governments proposed the change of the country's name to the Czech and Slovak Federative Republic.
9 Shorthand report on the second meeting of the Czech National Council, July 2–3 1990, p. 36.
10 ibid., p. 37.

11   *Mladá fronta dnes*, 159/90.
12   According to information given verbally by Petr Kučera of the Civic Forum.
13   Viewpoint of the democratic right wing, on the ninth meeting of the Czech National Council, 28–29 November 1990.
14   *Literární noviny*, 27 December 1990.
15   *Svratka*, 25–26 September 1990.
16   At that time the state agreement for the Commonwealth of Independent States was being prepared, and this was apparently an inspiration for the Christian Democratic Movement, which ultimately asserted this agreement uncompromisingly.
17   Such as those made on 14 March 1991, during a celebration of the establishment of the Slovak state in 1939, and on 28 October 1991, during a celebration of the establishment of Czechoslovakia.
18   Talks in Lány, 21 June 1992.
19   In a vote by acclamation, out of 147 deputies, 113 voted for, 24 against, and 10 abstained. Against the declaration were deputies from the Hungarian parties and – long live the irony of history – the CDM.

V The International Aspects

14 *The International Context*

JACQUES RUPNIK

Since its inception in 1918 the main turning points in the history of the Czechoslovak state have coincided or been, to a large extent, shaped by external factors. However, the break-up of the Czechoslovak federation in 1992 was brought about from within, although it was influenced by the international environment and has serious regional and international implications.

All the famous 'eights' which punctuate the history of Czechoslovakia were directly brought about by major shifts in the international environment. The foundation of the Czechoslovak state in 1918 was a result of the collapse of the Habsburg empire and the spread of Western influence in Central and Eastern Europe. The collapse of that state in 1938 occurred under the combined effects of the failure of the Western security guarantee and of Germany's *Drang nach Osten*. The 1948 communist takeover was the by-product of the country's insertion into the Soviet bloc. The crushing of the Prague Spring of 1968 was the clearest and most brutal confirmation of the postwar status quo and of the partition of Europe. The fall of communism (the so-called 'velvet revolution') was to a large extent part of the break-up of the Soviet empire and the tail-end of a chain reaction which swept Central and Eastern Europe in the autumn of 1989.

The external weakness of the Czechoslovak state was an important stress factor in the relationship between Czechs and Slovaks. It strengthened Czech tendencies to centralize, thus exacerbating the dissatisfaction of the Slovaks who, in the words of Skalnik Leff, 'compensated for an unequal balance of power within the state by alignment with foreign allies ... Slovak nationalism has thus appeared to Czech opinion, successively, as the cat's paw of Magyar irredentism, German imperialism, and Soviet hegemony; the perception of Slovak opportunism in such cases has put additional stress on Czech-Slovak relations.'[1]

Although it has been argued *post-factum* that the division of Czechoslovakia came about as a result of the shaping of a new Central European system under German influence,[2] there is little evidence to substantiate the argument. One should certainly be cautious in distinguishing the consequences of the separation, which might well benefit Germany, from its causes, which were primarily internal: different perceptions of a common history, different attitudes towards modernity and particularly the transition to a market economy, different political orientation and strategies of the post-communist élites.

In contrast to this seventy-year-old pattern it could be argued that the process of Czech-Slovak separation in the early 1990s took place without outside interference and without foreign policy playing a major part in it. The international environment (regional and pan-European) provided a favourable context in which divergent internal trends could be expressed and carried through to their conclusion. This weakness of the external constraint on the behaviours of the protagonists of the divorce was due essentially to the transitory nature of the current European realignments: the retreat of Russia, the self-absorption of Germany, the disintegration of the Soviet empire not yet compensated by a process of integration in the (West) European Community.

An important element in assessing the role of the international environment is the question to what extent the Czech-Slovak divorce is part of a more general pattern of national fragmentation in the post-communist world. This was the prevailing thesis in the early Western interpretations and it is indeed tempting to see the partition of Czechoslovakia as the failure of the third federal state inherited from communism (after Yugoslavia and the Soviet Union) under the combined effects of the collapse of the communist system and of the Soviet bloc. To be sure, there are certain common features, namely that the word 'federation' (much like the word 'socialism') has been largely discredited by the experience of the communist monopoly and centralism which Havel described as 'federalized totalitarianism'. Secondly, in all three cases the word 'sovereignty' has been used and abused by (old and new) political élites for their own political strategies. Indeed in the Slovak case, much like in the republics of the former Soviet Union or of Yugoslavia, the key ingredient of sovereignty has been presented as the recognition of the republic's status as a subject of international law with its own representation abroad. The insistence on this demand made the separation inevitable even for such committed federalists as the former foreign minister of Czechoslovakia. It also rendered impossible the suggestion favoured by some in the autumn of 1992, both inside the country and in the West, of a 'Czecho-Slovak Maastricht', i.e. a monetary and security union. But can you have a common currency and two economic policies? And how plausible is a common defence system combined with two separate foreign policies?

Beyond the similarities, however, important differences were at work. It has been argued (by J. Linz and A. Stepan)[3] that the electoral sequence in the transition to democracy is of crucial importance for the survival of a multinational state: the fact that the first free elections took place on the level of the republics (Slovenia and Croatia in ex-Yugoslavia, or the Baltic countries in ex-USSR) instantly delegitimized the federal state. In Czechoslovakia the break-up cannot be directly ascribed to such a pattern of introduction of democracy from the periphery to the centre. Free elections took place twice simultaneously on the whole territory of the state. Despite dubious parallels made by the press between Slovenia (*Slovinsko*) and Slovakia (*Slovensko*) there was a major difference: unlike in the former Yugoslavia or USSR the process of separation was not initiated by the more democratic, more Western and more prosperous member of the federation.[4] Though the division of Yugoslavia might, in its early stages (until June 1991), have inspired some advocates of Slovak independence, the violence and war which followed have if anything been a deterrent or a moderating influence on the protagonists of the Czech-Slovak divorce. The Yugoslav counter-example has no doubt made them aware of the risks involved and thus contributed to its peaceful and negotiated outcome.

This was made possible not only because in their commitment to the preservation of the federal state the Czechs are no Serbs and Havel is no Milosevic,[5] but also because (unlike in ex-Yugoslavia and ex-USSR) there were no conflicts or controversies concerning borders and national minorities.

Neither Yugoslav-style break-up nor Maastricht-type compromise, the Czech-Slovak separation has important implications both for the Central European region and for the relations of both nations with the European Community. Czechoslovakia presented itself after 1990 as a pillar of democratic stability in Central Europe. One of the consequences of the separation has been not only to dispel that image but also to foster elements of instability in the region. Although there is no immediate danger of regional destabilization (as in the Balkans, through the possible extension of the Yugoslav conflict to neighbouring countries), there are serious repercussions for the cooperation of the Visegrad group (Poland, Hungary, Czechoslovakia) launched in the spring of 1990.

This is first of all due to the fact that both new states have somewhat different geopolitical constraints and foreign policy priorities. The Czechs have rediscovered the primacy of their relationship with Germany, the Slovaks that with Hungary. Both are trying to establish their place in the new European landscape. For the Czechs that means new answers to their old dilemma concerning their position between East and West.[6] Until 1918 part of Czech politics sought in the East a counterweight to German influence (Kramář) while others (social democrats and Catholics) preferred the Central European k.u.k. solution (i.e. to remain in a federalized Austro-Hungarian monarchy). At the end of the First World War Masaryk imposed an explicitly Western orientation which lasted twenty years. Between 1935 and 1945 Czech foreign policy sought a new balance (a 'bridge') between East and West, while in 1948 a complete shift eastwards was imposed for forty years. Since 1990 the pendulum has shifted heavily to the West while the Czech-Slovak partition has sometimes been presented as an acceleration of that process. 'Alone to Europe or together to the Balkans', read the headline of the influential Prague weekly, *Respekt*, giving an over-simplified (if not misleading) version of the argument (the corrolary of which could read: 'Czech democracy or communist legacy in the common state' or 'rapid market reform or common state').

This radically Western orientation seemed however to be combined with two new trends:

(1) A British Conservative-style criticism of the EC.[7] There seemed to be a special political –one is almost tempted to say 'ideological' – relationship with Britain, not one of the most influential actors in the shaping of EC policies.

(2) A clear distancing from the Central European cooperation scheme known as the Visegrad group. This indeed was the very first foreign policy signal of the new Czech state. Prime Minister Klaus described it (in *Le Figaro*) as 'a totally articifially created process by the West'.[8] According to the Czechs, regional cooperation with the Poles and Hungarians smacked of a Comecon legacy and, above all, should not be used as a substitute for early integration into the European Community. Rather than being an instrument of political or economic cooperation the Visegrad group should, in their opinion, at the very best become a free trade zone.

Both these features of the new foreign policy of the Czech state brought to the fore the primacy of its relationship with Germany. Germany is the Czech Republic's most important neighbour and its prime Western economic partner (providing half of its foreign investments). The difficult negotiation of the German-Czechoslovak treaty, signed in 1992, left unresolved some of the issues concerning the legacy of Munich and of the expulsion of the Sudeten Germans in 1945. President Havel's daring moral stance has not been repaid by a willingness in Bonn to settle the issue 'once and for all'. Unlike Poland's uncompromising stance on the Oder-Neisse border issue in 1992 which, in the context of the 'four plus two' negotiations on German reunification, obtained Bonn's recognition of the border, Czechoslovak diplomacy missed the opportunity to reach a similar settlement while there was goodwill on both sides and a feeling that the new Europe should not be burdened by unsettled scores from the past.[9]

While the Czechs rediscovered the primacy of their relationship with

Germany, the Slovaks rediscovered that with Hungary. Whereas the Czechs have been looking resolutely to the West, Slovakia has also cultivated the Eastern connection (Mečiar's meeting with Chernomyrdin within days of his nomination as Russian Prime Minister, and his close contacts with Kravchuk's Ukraine). Kiev and Vienna are Slovakia's possible counterweight to its difficult relations with Budapest.

Slovakia's independence has also brought into the open two issues which had been hitherto contained by the Czech balancing factor in the relations between Hungarians and Slovaks: one is the Gabčíkovo-Nagymáros dam on the Danube; the other is the status of the Hungarian minority in Slovakia. The former started as a contentious legacy of the communist era and subsequently turned into a symbolic confrontation of national pride. Prague's withdrawal from the negotiating process has given all the more importance to the mediating efforts of the European Community. While Slovakia became more assertive in the controversy after the separation, the new development in the Hungarian position was a shift from an ecological argument to one questioning the modification of the border as a result of the dam.

The second contentious issue concerned the Hungarian minority in Slovakia. The more than 600,000-strong minority (in a country of five million) had been loyal to Czechoslovakia, but its spokespersons expressed serious reservations about the new Slovak state, defined in the Constitution of 1 September 1992 as the 'state of the Slovak people' (rather than that of the citizens living in Slovakia) and in which Slovak was proclaimed as the 'state language'. The problem was made all the more difficult because the situation of the Hungarian minorities was deteriorating simultaneously in three countries: in Serbia (Vojvodina), where 'ethnic cleansing' was under way; in Romania (Transylvania, where two million Hungarians have been subjected to worsening conditions), and in Slovakia.[10] The danger lay in the possibility that a flare-up would occur in one of them (Serbia being the most likely), with repercussions in the other two. A Hungarian government (so far fairly moderate) would probably not stand idle in the case of an open conflict in which its minority was involved, and a nationalist shift in Budapest would have obvious repercussions for relations with Bratislava.

The danger is there but it should also be pointed out that serious reasons exist on the Hungarian side for maintaining a moderate course. One is that public opinion is even more cautious than the political élite (two-thirds oppose border changes and 77 per cent of the remaining third would oppose them if violence was entailed). The Czech-Slovak break-up has confirmed Hungary's image as the model pupil of democratic transition and of European integration. The country would stand to lose a lot in embarking on a nationalist course. Finally, Hungary's strategic position is weak: defence spending has been neglected for more than a decade and the ill- equipped 100,000-strong army is hardly a match for that of Serbia or Romania (one is not too sure about Slovakia yet). Above all: a conflict with one of its three neighbours would be likely to consolidate an unholy alliance of Belgrade-Bucharest-Bratislava: a nightmare for any Hungarian government.

Slovakia's renewed tensions with Hungary and the Czechs' overtly expressed scepticism towards the Visegrad group thus imply that the Czech-Slovak divorce was a major setback for Central European cooperation which, literally, came to resemble an effort to 'square a triangle'. However, it could also be argued that the existence of the Visegrad group could help contain some of the Czech-Slovak differences of views or interests.

The break-up of Czechoslovakia also had consequences for the two successor nations' relations with the European Community. Both protagonists tried to make a virtue out of necessity: the Czechs were convinced that on their own they stood a better chance of speeding up their application for membership of the EC; for the Slovaks (Čarnogurský was the first to make the point) more than the speed what seemed to matter was that they should enter the European Community as a separate, independent subject.

As for the Community's attitude, it could be described as non-interference mixed with disappointment. Unlike in Yugoslavia (or perhaps because of the poor performance of crisis-management in Yugoslavia) the EC kept a low profile in the Czech-Slovak divorce. M. Pinheiro, then EC spokesman, said as soon as the separation became likely (on 22 June 1992) that it was an 'internal decision' for Czechoslovakia, but also expressed disappointment 'because the aim should be integration rather than disintegration'. This was indeed the most widespread attitude in Western Europe. At the EC conference on Central and Eastern Europe in Copenhagen in April 1993, the French Minister for European Affairs summed it up as follows: 'It is paradoxical that commercial barriers are being erected between Bohemia and Slovakia, or between Slovenia and Croatia, at the very moment when we are considering doing away with them between the EC and these countries.'[11]

Beyond such paradoxes two issues came about as the result of the separation:

(1) The re-negotiation of the association agreement with the EC which was signed in December 1991. Simultaneously a new process of application to the Council of Europe was necessary for both republics, with emphasis on democracy and the observance of human rights provisions. Its successful conclusion came in June 1993.

(2) The EC attaches great importance to the capacity of Central European nations for cooperation. It is seen as a test of their future capacity for integration into the Community itself. The negotiations and the association agreement of December 1991 were therefore signed simultaneously with Czecho-

slovakia, Poland and Hungary. The repercussions of the divorce for the Visegrad group therefore also affected the two states' relations with the EC.

The disappearance of Czechoslovakia (after that of Yugoslavia) highlights the fact that what is withering away is not only the legacy of Yalta and of the partition of Europe but also that of Versailles. As a consequence borders are being delegitimized in the whole of Central and Eastern Europe and greater instability is affecting the environment of the transition to democracy. The break-up also raises the question of who, in the long run, will be the beneficiary of the divorce. Will it speed up Czech integration into Europe or will it enhance instability in Central Europe, which would affect all the countries of the area? Are concerns over the emergence, following the break-up of Czechoslovakia and Yugoslavia, of a new 'Mitteleuropa' as a German sphere of influence justified? Or is nation-state building in Central Europe a precondition for future integration in the European Union?

The fact that the divorce was a 'velvet' one de-dramatized these questions but did not make them obsolete. Especially as divorce Czechoslovak-style has an echo in the West. Quebec is considering breaking away from Canada, and in Western Europe Belgium and Italy have their own concerns. In Belgium explicit references are being made, on the Flemish side, to the feasibility of a peaceful separation. In Italy some of the economic arguments of the Lombardian League are reminiscent of those heard earlier in Prague ('get rid of the economic burden of the south and make them believe it is they who wanted independence').

All these developments point to the fact that the 'national question' today is by no means just a by-product of post-communism and the disintegration of the Soviet empire. It also highlights the East-West interaction of today's Europe: if integration does not spread from West to East, the opposite might happen instead.

Notes

1 Carol Skalnik Leff, *National Conflict in Czechoslovakia*, Princeton: Princeton University Press, 1988, p. 275.
2 K. Zavacka, 'Rekviem za europské siroty' ('Requiem for European orphans'), *Slobodný piatok*, Bratislava, 5 November 1993. See also Gen. P. Gallois, 'Vers une prédominance allemande', *Le Monde*, 16 August 1993.
3 J. Linz and A. Stepan, 'Electoral Sequence in the Transition to Democracy', *Daedalus*, Spring 1992.
4 See J. Rupnik (ed.), *De Sarajevo à Sarajevo*, Brussels: Complexe, 1992.
5 V. Havel, interview with J. Rupnik in *Politique Internationale*, Winter 1992–3.

6 See the introductory chapter of Gordon Skilling's *Czechoslovakia's Interrupted Revolution*, Princeton: Princeton University Press, 1976.
7 V. Klaus, interview in *Český deník*, 9 June 1993.
8 V. Klaus, interview in *Le Figaro*, 7 January 1993.
9 J. Rupnik, 'Mít Němce za sousedy' ('To have Germans as neighbours'), *Lidové noviny*, 18 August 1993.
10 G. Schöpflin, *La Hongrie et ses voisins*, Paris: Institute for Security Studies, WEU, 1993.
11 A. Lamassoure in *Le Monde*, 15 April 1993.

Index

Agrarians 187
Andrássy, Gyula 110–11
Association for Independent Social
	Analysis (AISA) 231, 232, 235
Association for Moravia and Silesia 238,
	239
Austro-Hungarian Compromise (1867)
	100, 110, 117, 159–60
'awakeners' 107, 109, 111

Bacílek, Karol 200n.34
Bálek, A. 70
Banská Bystrica 162, 188–9
Barnovský, M. 70–1
Baťa conglomerate 53
Belgrade Declaration (1918) 168
Beneš, Edvard
	and establishment of Czechoslovakia
		100, 113, 163, 168
	planned reforms 48–9, 59, 176
	resignation 180
	in wartime 185–6, 187, 188–9, 190,
		199n.26
Biľak, Vasil 206, 211, 218
Bill on Basic Rights and Liberties (1991)
	258
Board of Commissioners, Slovak National
	Council 120, 189, 190, 192, 194
Boguszak, J. 196
Bohemia and Moravia, Protectorate of 28,
	54–5, 57, 119, 183, 184
Bohemian Historical Right 99–100,
	102–3, 161
Bratislava 15, 33, 169, 190
	demonstrations 251

development and modernization 72, 84,
	218
Brno 23, 214
Brož, Václav 88
Budapest 163, 164
Buzuluk 186

Čalfa, M. 266
Čarnogurský, Ján 132, 147–8, 230, 238,
	258–9, 276
Catholic Church 26, 115, 193, 215
	privileges and land owning of 40–1, 42,
		50, 57, 60
	strength in Slovakia 131, 134, 135,
		147–9
CDM see Christian Democratic
	Movement
CDP see Civic Democratic Party
Centre for Empirical Research (STEM)
	233, 237
Centre for Social Analysis, Bratislava 227,
	231, 237
Černík, Oldřich 196
CF see Civic Forum
Charles IV of Luxembourg 117
Charter 77 movement 142, 214–15
Chernomyrdin, V. 275
Christian Democratic Movement 147–9,
	253, 255, 258–9, 260
	in elections 148–9, 238, 239
Christian Democratic Party 239
Christian Democratic Union 238, 239
Christmas Agreement 187
Číč, Milan 76n.8, 251
Civic Bloc 187, 191

Civic Democratic Alliance 238, 239, 260
Civic Democratic Party 238, 239, 262–4
Civic Democratic Union 238, 239
Civic Forum 238, 250, 254, 255, 256
Civic Movement 238, 239
Clementis, Vlado 193
CNC *see* Czech National Council
Coexistence 239
COMECON 66, 67, 72, 73
Comenius 257
Communist party 49, 61, 65–6, 70
  in 1946 elections 60, 120–1, 149, 192,
    201
  loss of power 226
  seizure of power 6, 63, 64, 134
Communist Party of Bohemia and
    Moravia 237, 239
Communist Party of Czechoslovakia 61,
    63, 70, 248
  and Prague Agreements 191–2
  and Prague Spring 203, 210–11
  seizure of power 64, 134, 192
Communist Party of Slovakia 61, 70,
    210–11
  1938 prohibition 181
  and Slovak nationalism 187, 191–2,
    246–7
Council for Mutual Economic Assistance
    see COMECON
CPC *see* Communist Party of
    Czechoslovakia
CPS *see* Communist Party of Slovakia
Croatia 230, 273
Cyril, Saint 142, 153
Czech National Council 190, 196, 208,
    246
  and breakup of Czechoslovakia 257–8,
    259–60, 261–3, 265
Czecho-Slovak National Council 185–6
Czecho-Slovak Social Democratic
    Workers Party 111
Czechoslovak Church 26
Czechoslovak Intelligence Service 186,
    187
Czechoslovak National Council 167, 170
Czechoslovak Social Democratic Party
    239
Czechoslovak-Soviet Treaty (1943) 186

Daladier, Edouard 185

Declaration of the Slovak Nation 166,
    169, 264
Delegation of the SNC for the Liberated
    Territory 189
Demands of the Slovak Nation (1848) 100
Demeš, Pavol 230
Democratic Party (Slovakia) *see* Slovak
    Democratic Party
Dérer, I. 165, 166
Detva 81
Deutschnationalen 110
Dubček, Alexander 195, 197, 203, 265
Ďurčanský, Ferdinand 181, 182, 184

European Community 122, 230, 253, 274,
    276–7
Evangelical Church 26

Federation Law (1969) 196–7
Fourastié, J. 91
Franz Ferdinand, Prince 164
Friedrichs, J. 79

Gabčíkovo-Nagymáros hydroelectric
    project 72, 275
Gál, F. 254
Gellner, Ernest 1, 6
German-Czechoslovak treaty (1992) 274
Golian, Ján 187
Gottwald, Klement 192–3, 194–5,
    199–200n.29
Grospič, J. 196

Hácha, Emil 182, 190
Hajnal, J. 83
Harminc, Milan 185
Havel, Václav 118, 150–1, 248, 272, 273,
    274
  call for referendum 230, 233, 261, 263
  changing support for 229, 232, 263–4
  and constitutional change 226, 227,
    254–6, 258–9, 261, 262
  hopes for Charter 77 214–15
Hechter, M. 91
Herder, Johann Gottfried 131, 153
Hitler, Adolf 52–3, 110, 113, 126n.4, 134,
    182
Hlinka, Andrej 103, 137, 141
Hlinka's Guard 181
Hlinka's Slovak People's Party

between the wars 27, 86, 103, 141
Christian nationalism of 27, 141, 148
loss of support 186–7, 192
renamed Party of Slovak National Unity
   181
totalitarian autonomy as aim 54, 144,
   180–4
Hodža, Milan 162, 164–6, 167, 173, 174,
   185–6
Hohenwart, Karl 110
HSPP *see* Hlinka's Slovak People's Party
Hungarian Christian Democratic
   Movement 239
Hungarian Civic Party 239
Hungarian People's Party 239
Hurban, Vladimír 184
Husák, Gustáv 126n.4, 137, 187, 188,
   199–200n.29, 218
   and federalization 195, 196, 197,
      204–5, 206, 208
   normalization 4, 197, 209, 211
   sentence and rehabilitation 193, 194,
      195, 203

Ilava concentration camp 184
Institute for National Economic
   Infrastructure 175
Institute for Public Opinion Research,
   Prague 237
Institute for Public Opinion Research,
   Slovak Statistical Office 226, 228–9,
   234–5
Institute for Social Analysis, Bratislava
   231

Jánošík 139–40
Jičínský, Z. 196
Josko, Matej 187
Juriga, F. 164, 166
Jurovský, Anton 139–40

Károlyi, Baron 167, 168
Khrushchev, Nikita 194
Klaus, Václav 252, 274
   and 1992 elections 147, 237–8, 240,
      262
   and break-up of Czechoslovakia 232,
      263, 264
Kňažko, M. 259
Kollár, Jan 109

Košice 23, 33, 69, 189
Košice Government Programme 65, 73,
   190–1
Kravchuk, Leonid 275
Krofta, Kamil 117
Kühnl, K. 89

Ladislas the Posthumous 116
Langoš, J. 148, 254
Left Bloc 239
Lenárt, Jozef 195
Lettrich, Jozef 144, 187
Ležák-Borin, V. 185
Liberal Social Union 238, 239
Lidové noviny 128, 129, 252
Linz, J. 273
Lipták, L'. 43, 141–2
Liptovský Mikuláš 163
'L'udáks' *see* Hlinka's Slovak People's
   Party

Mach, Alexander 181, 182, 184
Machonin, P. 86
McKay, J. 91
Markus, Jozef 152
Marshall Plan 63
Martin 163–4, 166
   Declaration of the Slovak Nation 166,
      169
Marx, Karl 125n.1
Marxism 6
Masaryk, T.G. 10, 42, 274
   and birth of Czechoslovakia 100, 102,
      109, 113, 163, 176
   concepts of nationhood 107–8, 109, 115
Matica Slovenská 142, 152
MDS *see* Movement for a Democratic
   Slovakia
Mečiar, Vladimír 257, 263–4, 275
   in 1992 elections 147, 238, 240, 262
   and devolution of power to Slovakia
      147, 208–9, 255, 256–7
   and Movement for a Democratic
      Slovakia 151, 238, 259, 262, 263–4
   as Slovak premier 208–9, 229, 254,
      262, 263–4
   support for 229, 232, 238, 255, 259
Memorandum of the Slovak Nation (1861)
   100
Methodius, Saint 142, 153

Mihailovič, K. 81
Mikloško, F. 148
Movement for a Democratic Slovakia 143, 151, 238, 239, 259, 262–5
Movement for Self-Governing Democracy 238
Munich agreement 54, 110, 180, 181, 274

National Bank of Slovakia 55
National Committee (Beneš's) 185–6
National Front 196
National Socialist Party 61–3
Nazi-Soviet Pact (1939) 186
Němec, František 189
Novomeský, Ladislav 187, 189, 193, 199–200n.29
Novotný, Antonín 194–5, 203
Orthodox Church 26

Ostrava 31, 81
Osuský, Štefan 184, 185

Palacký, František 109–10, 125n.1
Pantůček, F. 164, 165, 166, 167
Party of the Democratic Left 237, 239, 260
Party of Slovak National Unity 181
PAV *see* Public Against Violence
People's Party 238, 239
Pinheiro, M. 276
Pithart, Petr 256, 257
Pittsburgh Agreement (1918) 113, 134
Polakovič, Stefan 141
Potsdam Conference 29, 59
Prague 75, 114, 163, 164, 169, 214
Prague Agreements (1945–6) 191–2
Prague Spring 71, 72, 135, 142, 203–4, 271
Prchala, General 185
Preiss, J. 164
Prídavok, Peter 185
Protestantism 107, 109, 115, 117, 131
Public Against Violence 143, 148, 213, 246–7, 250
  breakaway movements from 143, 148, 238
  and break-up of Czechoslovakia 254, 255, 259, 260

Rašín, A. 166

Reichsbank 55
Republican Party 238, 239
Revolutionary National Council 188
Roško, R. 87
Rupnik, Jacques 135–6
Ruthenia 15, 23, 44–6, 48, 120
  annexed to Hungary 54, 183
  and creation of Czechoslovakia 102–3, 181–2
Ružomberok 163

Šáfařík, Pavel Josef 109
Saint-Germain-en-Laye, Treaty of 173–4
Schönerer, Georg 110
Schwarz, F. 185
Senica 81
Sidor, Karol 182–3
Široký, Viliam 194–5, 199–200n.29
Sivák, Jozef 182
Skalica 163
Skalnik Leff, Carol 271
Slavík, Juraj 166, 184
Slovak Christian Democratic Movement 143, 149
Slovak Democratic Party 61–3, 148, 191, 192
  in 1946 elections 60, 121, 149, 150, 192
  in 1992 elections 239
Slovak National Council 120, 190, 196, 246–7
  before 1919 162, 164, 166–7, 170
  Board of Commissioners 120, 189, 190, 192, 194
  dissolution in 1919 171
  from 1939–48 185, 187, 188–90, 191–3, 194, 198n.12
  from 1948–89 195–6, 206–7, 208
  from 1989–93 229, 246–7, 256–8, 259–60, 261–3, 265
Slovak National Party
  before 1938 85, 86, 162
  since 1989 143, 145, 238, 239, 259
Slovak National Uprising (1944) 58, 120, 141–2, 184, 188, 195
Slovak People's Party 144
Slovenia 230, 273
Šmidke, Karol 187, 188
SNC *see* Slovak National Council
Šnejdárek, General 185
Social Democrat Party 181, 201, 239

Šrobár, Vavro 170–1, 187, 188, 189
Stacey, M. 87
Stalin, Joseph 126n.4
Standpoint and Requirements of the
    Slovak Nation 189
Staněk, F. 165
'State Party' 206
Štefánek, A. 85–6
Štefánik, Milan Rastislav 100, 112, 142,
    163, 176
Stepan, A. 273
Stodola, E. 164, 166, 172–3, 174
Štrougal, L. 73
Štúr 142
Šusta, Josef 126–7n.5
Svoboda, General Ludvík 195, 196
Syrový, Jan 180
Szálasi, Ferenc 189
Szatmáry, Ladislav 185
Szelenyi, Ivan 81–2, 89

Tiso, Jozef 134, 135, 137, 192
    as leader of HSPP moderates 180–1,
        182–3
    as President 184, 186
Tolerance Edict 109

Transcarpathia 173–4
Trebišov 189
Trenčianské Teplice 208, 255, 256
Trianon, Treaty of (1920) 15, 168
Trnava 163
Tuka, Vojtech 137, 181, 182, 184, 186
Turzovka 81

Uhl, Petr 255
Urban, Jan 255
Ursíny, Ján 187, 189

Vaculík, Ludvík 252, 257
Váh (River) hydroelectric works 175
Versailles, Treaty of 277
Vesel, Mirko 189
Visegrad group 5, 273, 274, 276–7
Vnuk, F. 142

Warsaw Pact 71, 72, 151, 197, 205
White Mountain, Battle of (1620) 99, 109
World Congress of Slovaks 145

Yalta 277

Zápotocký, Antonín 194